Voices in Flight:
The Royal Naval Air Service
During The Great War

Voices in Flight:
The Royal Naval Air Service
During The Great War

by
Malcolm Smith

Pen & Sword
AVIATION

First published in Great Britain in 2014 by
Pen & Sword Aviation
an imprint of
Pen & Sword Books Ltd
47 Church Street
Barnsley
South Yorkshire
S70 2AS

Copyright © Malcolm Smith, 2014

ISBN 978 1 78346 383 1

Printed and bound by CPI Group (UK) Ltd, Croydon, CR0 4YY

Pen & Sword Books Ltd incorporates the Imprints of Pen & Sword Aviation, Pen
& Sword Maritime, Pen & Sword Military, Wharncliffe Local History, Pen and
Sword Select, Pen and Sword Military Classics and Leo Cooper.

For a complete list of Pen & Sword titles please contact:
PEN & SWORD BOOKS LIMITED
47 Church Street, Barnsley, South Yorkshire, S70 2AS, England
E-mail: enquiries@pen-and-sword.co.uk

Website: www.pen-and-sword.co.uk

In Association with the Society of Friends of the Fleet Air Arm Museum

The object of the Society is:

The education of the public by promotion, support, assistance and improvement of the Fleet Air Arm Museum through the activities of a group of Members.

To find out more about the Society, go to our website at www.fleetairarmfriends.org.uk.

Contents

Acknowledgements

I must first of all acknowledge my great debt of gratitude to Barbara Gilbert, the Archivist of the Fleet Air Arm Museum, whose unrivalled knowledge of the extensive resources of the Museum's archive has made this book possible. Both in helping me to select the written material and also in sifting through thousands of photographs, Barbara's patience and help has been invaluable.

I must also acknowledge the, mostly anonymous, people who have, at various times over the past century, transcribed many written diaries and records into legible typescript. One of the entries in this work is also anonymous, or at least I have been unable to identify its author. This is the 'Contemporary History', which was probably written before the end of the war, as it includes a copy of a report in the *Daily Sketch* of 5 December 1917, entitled 'Saving Britain from Starvation'. The somewhat triumphalist and jingoistic style of writing in this History would have fallen out of favour soon after the Armistice in 1918.

George Bentley Dacre left copious, well-written diaries. He was awarded the Distinguished Service Cross for his exploits over the Dardanelles and retired as an air commodore. In a short foreword to his prisoner of war experiences, he said 'It is because I have to kill time that I have written this little book ... the penalty for keeping a diary is Jail, but should I ... bring this back to old England with me, it may prove of interest to those who wish to know how I fared as a prisoner of war in Turkey'.

R. S. W. Dickinson also left lengthy diaries, very revealing in their impressions of a sensitive young man, who had only recently left Eton.

The lower deck is well represented. Petty Officers Watson and Martin both served in the Armoured Car Division, the former in harrowing conditions at Gallipoli, the latter on the Russian front. Their entries appear to have been transcribed from hand-written diaries. Air Mechanic Stammers gives a most detailed description of the lengthy journey to his posting in Malta, at a time when very few young men of his background would have travelled through France and Italy.

Another Air Mechanic, H. Gamble, provides a most detailed description, originally entitled 'Life in Blimps'. The memoirs of C. Hibberd are drawn from photocopies of his hand-written diary – a most neatly-written and legible document. I was fortunate to be able to study the small pocket diary of William Edward Bryan, who enlisted as a driver in 1916. He kept up his diary for many months, writing in black ink in immaculate, minuscule copperplate. The vivid anecdotes of early flying by E. L. Ford were kindly presented to the Museum by Mrs K. M. Hamel-Jones.

The undated letter, signed by A. Soresby-Gissel and purporting to describe the first flight from a warship, is a curiosity. The original appears to be genuine, although it ascribes a different, earlier, date from the usually agreed one. The photograph of the occasion included in this book is generally credited as 'photographer unknown' (although is generally thought to have been taken by an employee of Shorts) so if the author of the letter genuinely did take the photograph, it adds a minor footnote to the history of naval aviation. However, I have found no trace of a Soresby-Gissel in naval records.

The description of the destruction of Zeppelin L-53, although written partly in the third person, seems to have been all the work of S. D. Culley, who took off from a towed lighter and climbed to great altitude to achieve this feat. It is drawn from a typescript dated 'Milan, Italy, May 1959'. The detailed descriptions of the early days of flying by one of the 'first four' naval aviators, E. L. Gerrard, also seems to have been written some time after the events described, as the copy carries the by-line 'Air Commodore Gerrard'.

Commander Locker-Lampson, CMG, DSO, whose report on Armoured Car operations in Russia is included here, was both politician and naval officer. It has been alleged that, while he was serving in Russia, he became involved in the plot to assassinate Rasputin.

All these authors deserve to be acknowledged, both for their various exploits and for recording them so clearly. Finally, I must acknowledge the forbearance of my dear wife, Dorothy, who once again has put up with my almost total absorption for many months in the early days of naval aviation.

Foreword

By Graham Mottram,
Director of Collections, Research and Learning, National Museum of the
Royal Navy; Museum Director, Fleet Air Arm Museum.

Although it existed for little more than four years under the title of Royal Naval Air Service, the RNAS had its first seed planted in May 1909, when the Admiralty placed the contract for the first naval aircraft, the rigid airship *Mayfly*. It has been said that the Royal Navy had experienced, for Victorian times, a long period of extremely rapid technological change. In little more than fifty years the Navy had seen its ships change from wood to iron and steel, their mode of propulsion change from sail to steam and screw, their guns change from smoothbore cannon on wooden carriages to rifled guns in motorised turrets. Totally new technologies such as the torpedo, wireless telegraphy and the submarine had also forced themselves into the Navy's operations. The advent of aviation in the first years of the twentieth century was almost one new tool too many.

In many ways the Royal Navy of 1910 was still a hidebound Victorian institution whose track record of building and then controlling the British Empire had given it a unique place in British society, and its senior officers held high social status. Aviation was seen by many as the plaything of the rich sportsman or the eccentric inventor, and the light and unreliable aircraft of 1908 would never develop into a worthwhile capability for a fleet at sea. An offer by the Wright Brothers to the Admiralty in that year was declined for such a reason. Other countries were not so casual in adopting aviation for military uses and the British Government gradually accepted that the country could not be left behind. The Navy was voted funds to build the airship, and the Army Balloon Factory moved from Andover to Farnborough so that it had more space for experiments.

Unfortunately, *Mayfly* suffered a catastrophic structural failure in September 1911 but, by then, the wealthy aviator and patriot Francis K. McClean had offered the Navy the facilities so that four naval officers could learn to fly at Eastchurch. The Committee of Imperial Defence examined Britain's position in early 1912 and recommended that military aviation must be formalised and properly organised. In April of that year the Royal Flying Corps was formed, whose major elements were a Military Wing, a Naval Wing, and a Central Flying School. Over the next two years it was obvious that the Army's demands over a land battlefield were significantly different to those of the Navy over a massive ocean. The Admiralty declared independence in July 1914 and the Naval Wing became the Royal Naval Air Service.

It was less than four years later that the RFC and RNAS were combined again, to form the Royal Air Force. By that time, the RNAS had achieved an enormous amount, its crowning glory being the creation of the aircraft carrier. The often buccaneering spirit of the RNAS led it down some unusual roads, not least the creation of armoured cars, which had a major influence on the development of the tank. It had fought in all the major theatres of war and some fairly minor ones as well. Malcolm Smith has harvested a wide range of material, which demonstrates just how much the men of the RNAS attempted, and often suffered. Much of the book's content is personal reminiscence, in the words of the individuals themselves. If nothing else, being published as it is during the centenary of the First World War, it will show its readers that the Great War was not just about the dreadful slaughter on the Western Front. It was also fought all over the world by men in dark blue.

Author's Preface

In its relatively short life, the Royal Naval Air Service (RNAS) saw the birth of naval aviation and the most extraordinarily rapid increase in the operational capability of this new military arm, before it was absorbed into the newly-formed Royal Air Force in April 1918. This book provides an insight into many of the elements that contributed to this capability; an insight drawn from the diaries, journals, letters and reports of the very people who made it happen. We hear about the decision of the Admiralty in March 1911 to form a nucleus of trained pilots and how from these small beginnings, naval aviation expanded enormously, both in the numbers of trained airmen and in the quantity (and variety) of naval aircraft. Some of the articles in the book have been published previously in *Jabberwock*, the Journal of the Society of Friends of the Fleet Air Arm Museum (SOFFAAM) of which I have been the Editor for several years. As far as I can establish, very few have been published elsewhere. All the material is drawn from the extensive archives of the Museum, which provides a treasure trove of fascinating and irreplaceable documentation.

For reasons of balance, I have had to abridge some of the longer documents. I have also corrected obvious anomalies and standardised some spellings of place names. These editorial interventions apart, I have taken care to preserve the authentic voices of the contributors, who speak to us from a century ago. The authors are a varied crowd, almost all of them very young and from differing backgrounds. Voices of young public-school-educated officers are heard alongside those of the lower deck, with dramatic descriptions of airborne combat and peril, but also including many caustic comments on discipline, living conditions and food. Some of the original material is in the form of diaries, and I was impressed by the impeccable copperplate handwriting in several of these.

The articles are placed in a broadly chronological context but the book has no pretensions to providing a complete historical record. The early days of flying training are well described by those who took to the air in remarkably unstable and flimsy machines. Alongside the well-known exploits of the RNAS in support of the Royal Flying Corps in France, the book provides lengthy eye-witness accounts of naval aviation involvement in the ill-fated operations against the Turks at Gallipoli. It was for this campaign that the RN developed a significant capability in the operational deployment, maintenance and support of its air arm, far from home. The important contribution made by dirigible airships to anti-submarine warfare is well described, although the sheer monotony of these patrols comes across very clearly. We also see the preliminary steps towards the launch of wheeled fighters from ships that culminated, just too late to be involved in hostilities, in the first true aircraft-carrier, HMS *Argus*.

Two interesting anecdotes stand alone: one a rather highly-coloured description of spy-catching that reflects the contemporary belief that there were swarms of

German spies on the mainland of England; the other an altogether more sober account by an RNAS pilot captured by the Turks.

The book finishes on a completely different note. The Royal Naval Armoured Car Division was part of the RNAS and, after somewhat losing its *raison d'être* in the static conditions on the Western Front, elements of it were deployed in Gallipoli and in Russia. Although fighting in very different conditions from their airborne brothers in the RNAS, the men of the armoured cars were naval officers and ratings, complying with naval disciplines and procedures. Their participation in fighting in various campaigns is perhaps not as well known as others described in this book, but their bravery deserves to be recognised.

Researching into the RNAS has opened for me a window into a different era. The participants were all born in the nineteenth century and the tone of their diaries and reminiscences is resolutely Edwardian. They are boyish, reckless, occasionally xenophobic, often sentimental; yet always recognisable as the founders of naval aviation. If by some miracle of time travel, they could see modern aircraft rising from warships, they would probably be astonished at the technology. However, they would have no difficulty in recognising the high morale, dedication and proficiency of their descendants, the people of the modern Fleet Air Arm.

Part One

Pre-War

THE ROYAL NAVAL AIR SERVICE

A Contemporary History

In the days to come the year 1912 will be memorable for the establishment of a sure foundation of a British naval aeronautical corps. Some four or five years earlier, it had been decided arbitrarily by the authorities to divide the application of aeronautics between the land and sea services by giving to the former the aeroplane and to the latter the airship. The decision was accepted by the seamen and the construction of the lighter-than-air machine was in hand at the Barrow for the purpose of carrying out trials. Meanwhile, however, the belief that sea flying was bound to become an important asset for the Royal Navy led to developments. On 1 March 1911, four officers of the Royal Navy and Royal Marines were granted permission to undergo training in aeroplane work at Eastchurch while others, at their own expense, started experimental work with hydroplanes (seaplanes) on Lake Windermere and similar places. At this time the Government had not awakened to the necessity for creating air fleets and training airmen to navigate and handle them. The destruction of the first naval airship before she could make a trial trip acted as a deterrent to progress and the experience gained by its construction was wasted. It was the patriotism and public spirit displayed by the *Daily Mail* for offering prizes for long flights which gave impetus to the development of the air services and did much to make the importance of the new arm recognised in high quarters and its value to the Navy appreciated. Until towards the end of 1911, the only machines which the Navy possessed were gifts from private donors and no proper organisation for their employment existed. In the following year, under the inspiration of Winston Churchill, who had become first Lord of the Admiralty, the Navy took up the practice of aviation with enthusiasm and rapid development followed. The first four months of 1912 showed far more progress towards the provision of an adequate and qualified core of flying men with efficient machines than that made in the four preceding years. The First Lord himself qualified as an air pilot and when King George V visited his fleet at Weymouth in May the naval flyers were able to provide an exhibition of the advances made. In March 1912 a School of Naval Aviation was established at Upavon and in July the First Lord announced that a new department had been formed to coordinate the various branches of aerial navigation and develop the training and material to the best advantage. The Central Flying School on Salisbury Plain, the aerodrome of the Naval Wing in the Isle of Sheppey and the Air Department at the Admiralty were all instituted at this time. It is astonishing now to reflect that only two and a half years before the Great War none of these departments were in existence.

In fact the Royal Naval Air Service under its present name was not formed until within six weeks of the outbreak of hostilities. Today its personnel is numbered in thousands and it has aerodromes, air stations, training centres, repair depots and experimental depots in large numbers, not only in the British Isles but in many places abroad. With its organisation in such an underdeveloped state, it is little short of marvellous that the RNAS did what it did in the early days of the war. One advantage was that those who had been responsible for its establishment in peace were still in office when the war came and so had the handling of the machine they had brought into being.

EARLY DAYS OF FLYING

By Air Commodore E. L. Gerrard

In England little attention was paid to flying until Blériot flew the Channel, violating our inviolate moat. The Army had a Balloon Battalion, and it began to take an interest in heavier-than-air craft. In 1909 they enlisted the services of an American showman, Colonel Cody. Captain J. Fulton, Royal Artillery, bought the machine on which Blériot flew the Channel and taught himself to fly on it; later he became an instructor at the Central Flying School. The Navy first turned its attention to airships and laid down a most ambitious venture at Barrow in Furness, embodying many untried experiments, and bigger than anything previously attempted anywhere.

In 1910 I was appointed to HMS *Hermione*, which was commissioning at Portsmouth as tender to the Airship No. 1 under construction at Barrow. *Hermione*'s crew consisted almost entirely of Marines, the handling party for the airship. A Captain and the navigating officer were the only deck officers for the short trip to Barrow. Soon after we sailed the weather began to get sick; the captain sent for me and told me we might have to anchor and I would be in charge of the operation on the forecastle. I had never even seen a ship anchored, my job had always been aft on the quarterdeck. I saw visions of mangled Marines being pulled through the hawse pipe by the cable. I got a book on seamanship from the ship's library and sweated at it. Of course, like a cookery book, it omitted all the things you really wanted to know; cat davits and capstans were mysteries to me. But Zeus was on my side: the weather cleared!

Many private individuals had been experimenting with aeroplanes: Maxim (of the machine gun) built a machine on very sound lines but its steam engine was too heavy. A. V. Roe was perhaps the most successful of the very early experimenters in England, and it is good to think that he remained at the forefront for many years. It is the common lot of inventors to fade away and see others exploit their ideas, but aviation furnishes a notable exception: in addition to Roe there are Short, Sopwith, de Havilland, Handley Page and Fairey. The Honourable Charles Rolls did not survive to see the engine he helped produce encircle the world; the tailplane of his aircraft broke off as he came in to land in a competition in 1910.

My personal connection with aviation began with Airship No. 1. One of my duties was that of meteorologist to the airship; of course I knew nothing of meteorology, nor did anybody else, so at least they had no solid grounds for criticism. The only book I could find on the subject was one by a naval officer. Considering the period at which it was written, it was extraordinarily good. The cyclone and the anticyclone were well described but, of course, much remained unexplained. For example, if you pointed out it was raining and the barometer had not fallen, you were told, 'Oh that is non-isobaric rain'! It was my horrible responsibility to name the date and time for the launch. If quite a mild gust of wind struck her when partly out of her shed, she would break in two. I had to issue a weather forecast every night (the local green keeper was useful). She did, in fact, break her back at the second launching but, fortunately for me, by then I'd gone off to learn to fly heavier-than-air craft. This airship took so long to build that the press called her the *Mayfly*. Vickers personnel, of course, had no experience of airship building and things often had to be done over again. We were all highly amused one afternoon when a very worried young man from Vickers came into the mess carrying a paper which notified the despatch by rail of 500,000 cubic feet of hydrogen. He had calculated that that amount of hydrogen would lift the railway truck into the air! He had forgotten that it was highly compressed into heavy steel cylinders.

I never had any confidence in airships; what I knew of meteorology convinced me that their life was ephemeral, and when the Navy called for volunteers for aeroplanes my name was easily first in. The knowledge of aeronautics it was thought I possessed accounted for my being among the four officers selected from over 300 applicants. The first choice to be the senior in charge of us was Ramsay, an excellent choice (many years later he commanded the Navy at the invasion of Normandy) but it was found he was married! So, Lieutenant Commander C. R. Sampson was appointed. He came to us from the Persian Gulf where he had been hunting pirates; doubtless his fierce pointed beard helped to inspire terror in the wrongdoer.

In mid-Victorian times the thwarted swain went lion hunting in Africa; Gregory's modern version was to go up in one of those crazy things called aeroplanes. He was very superstitious: one day he was starting a flight, and had just left the ground, when he switched off and the aircraft came to rest at the far extremity of the aerodrome. He got out and strode over to our hut; I followed to enquire the trouble, he was looking worried with a very large whiskey and soda in his hand. He said 'My God, I nearly left the ground and it is Friday!'

Longmore says he was selected because he was regarded as expendable and would leave no widow to claim a pension. I think his good looks and tactful bonhomie must have helped. Cockburn was flying instructor, unpaid of course. He had studied with Henri Farman in France; he took infinite care and none of us so much as broke a wire up to the time of taking our 'tickets', though afterwards we had some adventures. Horace Short, underpaid again, taught us theory. Horace was very serious over anything to do with flying but gave full rein to humour between whiles. His favourite quip was the invention of ridiculous words, some of which passed into the language and are now found in the dictionary, e.g. *Blimp* for a non-rigid airship. He pretended the words were invented by his son. An expression of Henri Farman is also in the dictionary: 'joystick'. He told us an incident at his school; a pupil got out a machine on a Sunday and put his sweetie in the backseat. Seeing a joystick between her legs she instinctively pulled it towards her and stalled the machine.

We four – Lieutenant Commander C. R. Sampson, Lieutenant Gregory, Lieutenant A. M. Longmore, and myself, Lieutenant E. L. Gerrard, RM, assembled at Eastchurch, Isle of Sheppey, in January 1911 to start the difficult process of getting the Navy into the air. The Admiralty was very disinclined to start, but their hand was forced by Frank McLean who gave a gift of two Short aeroplanes and offered the aerodrome as well. For some reason the gift was not accepted and their Lordships insisted on paying him one shilling a year rent! We were fortunate in finding a tin-roofed bungalow available, practically on the aerodrome. By now I was becoming accustomed to taking on jobs of which I was completely ignorant, so raised no demur when voted in charge of domestic arrangements. Two Marine batmen had been allotted us. I fell the men in, the two-badge man to the right, the one-badge man to the left. I said to the right-hand man, 'Can you cook?' He said 'yes'. I said, 'There is the kitchen' and, to the other, 'You take charge of the rest of the house'. It turned out afterwards that the one-badge man was much the better cook, but he got his opportunity later when we taught the two-badge man to fly. Often, when the dinner hour approached, cook was a mere dot above the distant horizon. I fed them chiefly on mutton chops, though later got more ambitious. We were lunching a Royal party, the weather was very hot so I determined on consommé glacé. I designed and built an ice chest, and put the soup in it in plenty of time in ginger beer bottles. When the great moment arrived I began to pour it out, but nothing happened, it was frozen solid. I thawed it out and then found it was lukewarm. Once more into the ice chest! The party exhibited Royal tact during the long wait and great appreciation when, eventually, lunch started.

THE FIRST ROYAL MARINE PRIVATE TO FLY

By Captain Roy Swales BSc RN
The first naval officers to qualify as pilots were granted their certificates by the Royal Aero Club in late April and early May 1911. Major Eugene L. Gerrard, Royal Marine Light Infantry (RMLI), was one of the pioneering four who were trained at Eastchurch. Other RM officers would follow his example over the next three years. By the time that the 500th Royal Aero Club Certificate was issued in May 1913, nine members of the Corps were qualified as pilots. Eight of these were officers, but one man – the third member of the Corps to learn to fly – did not hold a commission.

John Edmonds was born in Walworth, London, on 4 December 1881 and by the age of eighteen he was earning a living as a slater's labourer. In 1912, at the age of thirty, he became the first non-commissioned pilot of the Royal Navy, the twentieth qualified naval pilot, and one of the earliest pioneers of manned flight. He achieved this singular distinction as a private in the RMLI. Edmonds enlisted on 29 June 1900, at the age of eighteen and a half. He followed the usual recruit training at Deal until February 1901 and for the next ten years had a typical career. His first draft was what must have been a pleasant three years (1902-05) in HMS *Terror,* the base ship on the island of Bermuda, for duty at the 'Commissioner's House'. His sea time was spent mainly in cruisers, including two years on the China Station in HMS *Astraea* and twenty-one months in the scout cruisers *Attentive* and *Foresight.* Throughout this time he remained a private RMLI, consistently assessed as 'VG' and being awarded two Good Conduct badges, with no time forfeited. His 'crime sheets' show a couple of minor offences: one charge of 'Parading with his rifle in a filthy condition' shortly after leaving Deal and a charge of 'Idling on the works' one (probably sunny) afternoon in Bermuda. A run ashore in 1908 resulted in one more serious charge: 'did return from leave drunk and remained unfit for duty 9 hours'. In April 1911 he was drafted to HMS *Wildfire*, the shore base at Sheerness.

In September 1911, his career took a major change of direction. He was drafted to HMS *Actaeon*, also at Sheerness. *Actaeon* was the depot ship for torpedo training, but she was also the pay and administration base for the Naval Flying School, which had just been established on the Isle of Sheppey at Eastchurch, the cradle of Royal Navy aviation. John Edmonds was formally drafted into the Royal Naval Air Service from this date (he was, presumably, a volunteer for this exciting new trade), retaining his RMLI register number and rank of private. Strictly speaking, the RNAS did not yet exist. The Naval Flying School, Eastchurch, and the Air Battalion of the Royal Engineers were the aviation units in 1911. The Royal Flying Corps was formed on 13 April 1912 and absorbed these two units, but the staunchly independent Eastchurch organisation was soon known as the Naval Wing. On 1 July 1914 the Naval Wing became the Royal Naval Air Service under direct RN control.

From September 1911 until May 1913, Edmonds served at Eastchurch as a private, but was undoubtedly employed as an aircraft mechanic. His record of service gives no indication as to where a former slater's labourer acquired any technical skills. Presumably, like most early aviation experience, it was gained on the job. The Commanding Officer at Eastchurch was Lieutenant Charles Rumney Samson RN, the first qualified naval pilot. It must have been under Samson's patronage that John Edmonds was taught to fly. Why an RMLI private should have been the first man selected for this training is unclear, because the Eastchurch school had many more senior and more experienced technical ratings than Edmonds. One of Edmonds' flying instructors was Captain Robert Gordon RM, who was noted as having flown with him in the 'School biplane' on 13 July at Eastchurch. *Flight* magazine recorded that on Friday 26 July John Edmonds went for his *brevet*, but was unable to land within the specified distance of the landing spot. He again tried on Saturday, but had to come down owing to engine trouble, which was apparently due to castor oil having found its way into the petrol feed through a leak in the tank. This was rectified, and on Monday he successfully accomplished the test.

FROM CANADA TO THE RNAS

By James Steel Maitland

In 1907 I emigrated to Montreal, Canada. I was twenty years of age, a trained and qualified architect, who had found that the old country did not want more architects. In Scotland I was offered £45 per annum. In Canada I found full scope, working ultimately on the University of Saskatchewan which was in the course of erection at Saskatoon. There I earned £250 per annum. The work, of course, ceased at the outbreak of the Great War.

I had made friends with fellow Scots who had gone out before me, colonials now, yet all of us bound by strong ties to the Mother Country. The threat of war had been already in the air and we all wanted 'to do our bit'. My particular friend was keen to join the local Air Training Corps, and I was soon talked into taking an interest in flying. We found they were full up with recruits at Montreal and short of machines and instructors. At Toronto the situation was similar. Then we learned that the 'flying ticket', which was essential, could be gained at the Thomas School of Aviation at Ithaca, NY State, and I joined that private company which offered lessons and training on their 'hydro-planes'. The advertised course proved to be a scandal; only one plane was in use, and it crashed the day I joined. As they seemed in no hurry to supply another, we students, all Canadians, combined, and with the Company, built one for ourselves! The Company supplied the engine and the float, and from drawings we made the wings which balanced the plane. We learned that the Company at that time was busy supplying planes for the British Army and Navy, and, after our arrival in Britain, we found that all those machines had been scrapped. They burned easily as they were made of thin wood.

There lay our plane on the water of Lake Cayuga. But our instructor would not go up in it, nor would he allow his pupils to face the risk. Such was his faith in the craft we had constructed that he made constant excuses as to the weather and the like, and the hydro-plane remained quietly at its moorings. Near the end of the course I asked permission to run it over the twenty miles length of the lake. On condition that I did not take it into the air, permission was granted. After taxiing around the lake for a bit, I thought I might venture a little more. I increased the rpm from 800 to the full 1,500, and, before I fully realised what had happened, I was airborne! In that early type of plane there was no cabin. One sat on a spar, with the water or the land visible under one's feet, while the engine spluttered away at the back of one's neck. It was an exhilarating experience and an alarming one to a tyro and, from the lack of knowledge and practice, I found difficulty in controlling the machine. How to return and land were real problems. But I managed, somehow, to get it safely back on the water, and taxied back to base, where a stern reprimand awaited me. They were quite right. I had disobeyed orders and broken my word, but I did want to fly! I got their certificate, which was essential before applying for a Probationary Commission in the Royal Naval Air Service. I still have it, dated 1915. The Company issuing it must have been French, for it is made out entirely in the French language. Why, I do not know.

We wanted to help Britain, yet we felt frustrated. So I wrote to the British Navy Officer in Ottawa, Lieutenant Commander Pinsent RN, who came to inspect the situation, and agreed that we had our grievances. He made it clear that three choices were before us.

1. To remain at Ithaca till the Company supplied another plane, and then to continue our training.

2. To join the Royal Navy in Canada and await developments.

3. To return to our bases, and await further instructions regarding a draft to Britain.

For me the first was impossible. I had no money left. There were no grants from any source, and the training had already cost me £200 – almost a year's salary. We all chose the last option. Commander Pinsent worked nobly on our behalf; within a fortnight we had returned to our homes in Canada, and in due course were drafted to Britain for full instructions in flying. I have never met any of those friends again.

AN UNDATED LETTER

Lawford
Paignton
Devon

First Flight from the Deck of a Warship

On 5 May 1912, HMS *Hibernia* left Sheerness for Portland Harbour, Dorset. From the fore bridge to the bows had been erected a wooden structure designed to be a runway for the first attempt of an aeroplane to fly from the deck of a warship. A varied assortment of planes was carried on the quarterdeck. (Deperdussin was the make of at least one machine.)

The machine in which the attempt was to be made was a Short 'pusher' biplane and this was in readiness at the aft end of the 'scenic railway'. Embarked from Eastchurch aerodrome we carried as passengers the brothers Short, Captain E. L. Gerrard, Royal Marines, and Lieutenant Charles Rumney Samson, Royal Navy. I remember being greatly impressed by the latter with his golden beard and brilliant blue eyes – he did not seem to consider that the attempt could be anything but successful. At a lamentably early hour on 5 May, I found my way on to the forecastle armed with a large box camera, which even at that date was old and which is even now in my possession.

The ship was steaming into a fairly stiff breeze and Portland Bill was in sight right ahead, though it was somewhat hazy. The attempt was timed for 6.00am and, after what seemed to be a long wait while the engine of the machine was being warmed up, mechanics were making a last minute examination to see that all was well. At last Lieutenant Samson was satisfied and climbed into the pilot's seat, raced the engine a bit and then after a word he started his run. As will be seen from the photograph, the machine made a perfect take-off and left the slip-way about ten feet forward of the muzzles of our forward 12-inch guns.

He was soon lost to sight, but as soon as we entered harbour and secured to our buoy, he came alongside in a picket boat and shortly after8 o'clock he was sitting amongst us in the wardroom making a hearty breakfast. He treated the whole matter with complete unconcern, rather as if he had engaged in a rather foolhardy boyish escapade and had got away with it.

He made his second attempt a day or so later, but this time the ship was moored in Portland Harbour and it was a flat calm evening. He ran right off the end of the slip-way and the machine seemed about to fall into the water, but at the very last second it recovered and slowly gained height to soar away and land in a meadow on the outskirts of Weymouth where a temporary aerodrome had been established.

It is doubtful whether, even in those days, a similar attempt would meet with success – only a Samson could have pulled a machine up in that masterly fashion.

(Signed) A. Soresby-Gissel

A Contemporary History

Captain Murray Sueter, as he then was, had been Director of the Air Department at the Admiralty since July 1912 and Captain Godfrey Paine had served as Commandant of the Central Flying School since May 1912. These and other pioneer officers of the RNAS, who managed to crowd the work of several years into the months immediately preceding the war, had been appointed during Mr Churchill's regime at the Admiralty. Much has been heard of the celerity which the Navy itself passed from peace to a war footing; well, the same applies to the air branch. The air stations, a string of which had been disposed around the coast, were quickly mobilised and very soon in a position to undertake their war work. Very fittingly, the first occasion on which the branch was first mentioned officially as having been represented in action was in connection with the Army in France. On 16 September 1914, Commander Samson, with a small armoured car force acting in support of a flight of aeroplanes, encountered a patrol of five *uhlans* near Doullens on the River Authie about seventeen miles north of Amiens. The force killed four of the *uhlans* and wounded and captured the fifth. They themselves suffered no casualties.

On 27 August 1914 an aeroplane squadron was sent to Ostend; at the time the town was occupied by the British Marines. The aeroplanes flew across via Dover and Calais. Later this aviation camp was moved to Dunkirk, which was destined to be the centre and headquarters of a vast amount of aerial activity over land and sea. The first business of Commander Samson was to establish advanced bases some distance inland and, with the help of the armoured cars, much valuable work was done in conjunction with the artillery and infantry. Out of these early experiences grew the RNAS Armoured Car Brigade, the doings of which in France, Gallipoli, Russia and many other theatres of war would make a long chapter in themselves. While the aeroplanes in France and Belgium were thus performing good service, the air stations along the eastern seaboard were supplying machines to keep their watch and ward off the coast. Another section was assisting in guarding the transport across the English Channel. An announcement by the Admiralty described briefly how this was done:

> While the expeditionary force was being moved abroad a strong patrol to the eastwards of the Straits of Dover was undertaken by both airships and seaplanes of the RNAS. The airships remain steadily patrolling the sea between the French and English coast, sometimes for twelve hours on end. Whilst further to the east a steady patrol was maintained between Ostend and the English coast, it was impossible for the enemy to approach the streets without being seen for many miles. The naval airships were used more and more as the war proceeded but thanks to the skill and efficiency of their crews, only one is recorded unofficially as lost. This vessel left an east coast station on patrol duty on 21 April 1917 and failed to return. It was apparently set on fire and destroyed in the straits by an enemy plane.

AN EARLY SEAPLANE STATION

By David S. Simpson.

On 18 September 1913 the seaplane depot ship HMS *Hermes* arrived in the River Tay. Meetings were held between Captain Vivian and Commander Scarlet with Dundee Harbour Board and agreement reached for a seven-year lease of eight acres of ground at Carolina Port for the establishment of a seaplane station. Tentsmuir Point south and Buddon Ness, north of the river's mouth, with sandbanks in between, protected the estuary from North Sea gales.(Not always, the storm in 1879 blew down the first rail bridge, but generally the water is seldom as rough as the River Forth.) This, in part, was the reason for the station being moved from Port Lang, North Queensferry. The town was also the base for a submarine flotilla whose co-operation could be sought in training.

There was little further activity until early January 1914, when Short seaplane No.42 piloted by Major Gordon RMLI with Captain Barnaby RMLI landed by the West Sands, Saint Andrews, damaging a float in the process. Despite the attentions of a crowd of well wishers, mostly very young, the aircraft survived to be repaired, fitted with a wheeled undercarriage and flown to Montrose. Upper Dysart, close to that town, was the original home of No.2 Squadron RFC, the first air station in Scotland set up in 1913 and sited on a suitably windswept hillside above bleak Lunan Bay.

In early February the hangars were dismantled at Port Lang and transferred to be erected at Dundee. On the 9th, to the excitement of spectators, most of whom had never seen a flying machine, a spindly Borel monoplane appeared over the estuary, flew upriver, turned and landed downstream, nearly hitting a barge on the way. The machine, piloted by Major Gordon, OC of the new station, with Chief Air Mechanic Shaw as passenger had flown the coastal route from North Queensferry in under an hour.

Work now commenced under Gordon with Barnaby, Chief Air Mechanic Shaw,

Leading Seamen Walker and Hamilton and nine air mechanics. A Maurice Farman arrived by rail and was left in its crate, the wheeled Short and Borel were flyable, and with the arrival of the rescue launch *Mylesnie* the establishment was complete.

Rough weather and the lack of a slipway prevented the use of the Borel, except for the odd occasion when it could be launched down an outfall sewer. Short 42 was flown from an unsafe sloping grassy area bounded by houses, assorted buildings, telegraph wires and the river. One landing was made under the wires, presumably unintentionally. Its forays ended temporarily when engine failure forced Gordon down near Leuchars village. The repair squad then made the journey by land and water to discover they could not repair the broken inlet valve, leaving the only useable aircraft stuck in Fife. This was unfortunately several years before the well-known Leuchars Air Station was established.

In early March, the station was officially opened, and most of the personnel promptly left to prepare a temporary base at Leven on the Forth, where, with the arrival of three new wireless-equipped Shorts they would participate in the 1914 fleet manoeuvres. The weather was unhelpful. On the 17th a gale sank the *Mylensie* in the fish dock. Hooked out, she was taken to Leven aboard the submarine depot ship HMS *Vulcan*. Work started on the slipway, but in mid-month it was washed away plank by plank by another gale. Even the football match against the cast of 'Halloo Ragtime' from a local theatre had to be cancelled due to torrential rain.

REMINISCENCES

By Flight Lieutenant E. L. Ford, RNAS

Few of us who learnt to fly during the early days of the 1914/1918 War fully appreciated that we were indulging in a dangerous bout with the elements. Although at that time it really wasn't natural to fly at all, we budding airmen thought otherwise and blithely undertook risks which, even today when I think of them, send shivers rippling down my spine to tickle up my third lumbar vertebra which fractured during my last crash. As a Sub-Lieutenant, probationary, Royal Naval Air Service, I was taught the preliminaries of flight at the Grahame White Flying School, Hendon. Here our civilian instructors, Mr Marcus Manton and Mr Winter, took us aloft in Bristol Boxkites. Flying these machines of wood, wire and canvas was allowed only in practically still air conditions which usually ushered in the dawn, hence the necessity for waking up our instructors before the air got weaving, said awakenings being nobly borne by our tutors. They realised that we were an irresponsible but keen bunch of *quirks* (service nickname) and there was a war on.

Atmospheric conditions at the aerodrome were ascertained by holding aloft a silk handkerchief; if it remained limp or fairly so, we flew – if it flew, we didn't! Piloting a Boxkite was a novel and exhilarating experience because one was neither on, nor in, the machine but sort of in front of most of it except the elevator. One sat on a tiny wickerwork affair attached to a framework built out from the leading edge of the lower main plane – it seemed to be a long way out too – and from this airy perch, with legs outstretched, feet on an open-air rudder bar out front, firmly grasping the joystick to starboard and engine switch to port, we made our early attempts at flight, and actually flew!

When airborne there was absolutely nothing but lots of space and air, between one's seat and the ground below; the view looking down between one's outstretched legs was definitely bird's-eye and the completely unrestricted 'look around' quite fascinating, as was also the discovery to most of us that the horizon was terribly important and always at one's eye level. The instructor sat on a few wooden laths behind the pupil, slightly higher so that he could lean over and grasp the joystick – he could also reach the engine switch, but had no physical control whatever over the rudder bar moved by the pupil to instructions shouted into his ear above the din of an unsilenced engine's exhaust.

Boxkites were equipped with one 'instrument', a drip-feed oil pulsator which one watched as closely as circumstances permitted – say,when flying level or straight ahead. If the oil was seen to be dripping regularly and at the correct rate of flow then one knew the engine was getting its quota of oil and should be OK, but if there were pauses in the visible oil supply then one nosed to earth immediately with engine switched off and landed as best one could.

The Gnome rotary engine ran at full pelt and one's speed through the air as well as the niceties of landing were governed by a switch one flicked on or off, thereby blipping the engine for more or less momentum as required. If one paused too long between blips one ran the risk of losing the engine, so care had to be taken during this vital operation.

Stalling a Boxkite was dangerously easy and at the low heights we flew of 100 to 200 feet, a distinct hazard, as the space required in which to recover from a stall simply wasn't there. The margin of error between stalling and flying speeds was so narrow that one could not truthfully term that margin a safety factor! Of this we *quirks* were blissfully unaware as we meandered around on the fringe of both safety limit and aerodrome feeling, as we were, on top of the world at that particular spot, even during those so early hours at dawn and in the softness of a tranquil evening the sheer delight of those ambling early flights was indescribable.

So calm was the air as we practised that when executing our 'figures of eight' and flying dead level we'd pass through our own backwash of disturbed air when crossing over at the centre of the eight from one loop to the other; we'd get mightily bumped whilst doing this and the old Boxkite would wobble and heave uncomfortably, but that was good flying.

To qualify for one's *Brevet* or 'Ticket', one had to carry out quite a programme, consisting of take-offs, landings, left and right hand level circuits, a climb to a minimum height (or higher) with a barograph in a sealed box slung around one's neck, execute good figure eights, and finally *volplane* or glide in with engine dead and hand held well away from the switch, then make a smooth landing and come to a standstill within thirty yards of official Royal Aero Club observers who were on the ground watching one's flight. All this required pretty good judgement, yet the surprising thing was the large number who passed the tests with flying colours.

We were taught to fly and judge our speed by capital F: Feel and capital S: Sound, a sense of balance and the noise made by the air whistling through wires and around struts. Never, we were told, NEVER rely on instruments; a sensitive seat and delicately tuned ear were much more reliable! A total flying time of six hours and twenty-four minutes, of which one hour and six minutes were flown solo, accounted for my *Brevet* and during my tests I, being light and small, attained the terrific height of seven hundred and eighty feet – a Hendon Boxkite record which stood for some considerable time!

After Hendon came Eastbourne where there were more advanced types of aircraft to be flown before being posted to an active service station as a fully qualified operational pilot, with between twenty and thirty hours total flying to one's credit. The advanced types consisted of Blériot monoplanes and Curtiss biplanes, but there was also a sprinkling of Boxkites, Maurice Farmans and Caudrons. It was here that I went through what I believe still is a truly unique experience. I am pretty certain that no pilot has ever purposely spun a Blériot and got safely away with it, nor have I heard of any unintentional spins followed by one-piece landings. In fact I am convinced of the impossibility of spinning a Blériot and coming out whole because the machine was so slow in responding to the controls. The reason for this was its reliance on warping the wings when manoeuvring – it lacked the more sensitive ailerons. Wing-warping was a cumbersome strong-arm job. I know it called for considerable effort from myself, a mere five-feet-one-inch of pilot, but even taller and heftier men with longer arms and in consequence greater powers of leverage have told me that flying Blériots was hard work. As for anyone being able to control a spinning nose dive, I am sure that no wing-warping aircraft of any make could be expected to obey instructions in such a circumstance!

AN AIR MECHANIC'S DIARY

By R. A. Lovell

There were three of us who, having passed a medical examination in Whitehall, presented ourselves at Hendon Aerodrome, where we were given a trade test and three arithmetic sums before being told to report at Victoria Station three days hence. One of us had been given the rank of Leading Mechanic and he was entrusted with a railway pass for all three of us (we other two were graded as Air Mechanic 1). We were told to make our own way to Sheerness Dockyard, which we duly did, without any escort or other authority. That was on 19 September 1914, long before the days of Crystal Palace as a recruiting depot. We were housed in the naval barracks in the dockyard where we found about thirty others who had similarly joined. We underwent drill for about six weeks, under Captain Owen, Sergeant Muggeridge and Corporal Rossiter, all of the RMLI. I shall never forget the kindness and help we received from the old salts, most of whom were lost in the North Sea a few weeks later when the cruisers HMS *Aboukir, Hogue* and *Cressy* were sunk.

One of my early memories is being measured up for my uniform, which was a No. 1 suit of fine blue serge, a No. 2 suit in rough serge and a working suit of white ducks as well, of course, as the usual underclothes. All of these were a free issue but each replacement after that had to be paid for by ourselves. Pay was 4/- [20p] a day for an AM 1, of which 1/- [5p] was deducted each week for 'breakages'.

We slept in hammocks which were slung over the mess tables at night. Another early memory is being interviewed by the Master at Arms (the 'jaunty' or 'crusher', I cannot remember which) who asked whether I would drink my ration of rum or take the money, in lieu, which amounted to 14d [6p] for each two days.

After around six weeks a number of us were posted to the Central Flying School at Upavon in Wiltshire, then commanded by a Captain Paine RN, where we underwent instruction in rigging and in splicing under Lieutenant Breeze. In those days engineer officers, and indeed all specialist officers, did not have the executive curl on their rings. It was while at Upavon that I enjoyed my first flight, in a Henri Farman, piloted by Captain Hubbeard of the Royal Flying Corps. The flight sergeant there never forgave me for speaking directly to an officer but got his own back by detailing me to scrub the floor of the hangar and by making me spend hours in the open air of Salisbury Plain washing engine parts in petrol. In due course I was posted to No. 1 Squadron, which was being formed at Fort Grange near Gosport, from whence we went to Dover and then to France in February of 1915 to relieve Commander Samson and No. 2 Squadron, which moved on to Mudros in the Greek Islands. It was while in Fort Grange that I was hit by a propeller, whilst trying to swing it, on an Avro with a Gnome engine. I remember being visited in bed by Captain Courtney RMLI and told that I was the first person to have been hit by a propeller and live. Both Captain Courtney and my first CO, Longmore, became air chief marshals of the RAF later on.

I served in France until November of 1917and finished my service in South Devon on DH 9s when the war was over. My official number was 490 (until we were all bundled into the RAF, when 200000 was added on). I am very proud of that number which shows that I was one of the first 500!

A Letter from Flight Sub Lieutenant Leslie Chivers

My very very dear Dads,

So you're home again at last. I bet you had a ripping time, eh? Now to tell you about my Solo trip, which I completed yesterday. I should have wired you both but arrived back too late.

The morning dawned calm but wet, miserably wet, so I had no idea Ballooning would take place, however I was informed I must be ready to do my Solo by 12.45. Hurrying over lunch I was on the spot to time. The Balloon was inflated by 1.20 so I boarded her and rose. (Still raining at 1.25.)

On rising to a height of 2,000 I was enveloped in a cloud, the earth being quite invisible. I continued joyfully for half an hour then valved down to 500 feet with the intention of taking observations – hoping to find out where I actually was and in what direction I was making. Unfortunately at 500 feet the clouds still obscured the earth, I hadn't the slightest idea where I was but continued my course for another twenty minutes at the same altitude. Then thinking it wise to descend still lower lest I should be making seaward, I dropped to 300 feet and discovered I was just over an immense wood.

Bye the bye, it was still raining and the floor of the basket was slightly awash, result wet feet, don't mistake me I said wet feet not cold feet; as a matter of fact I felt perfectly happy and calm. The rain made the balloon very heavy – though I made repeated attempts to rise by throwing out bags of ballast it was useless and I continued to descend right into the heart of the trees. It was very unfortunate and somewhat unpleasant being bumped from tree to tree, but I stuck it for some while in the hope of rising, but in the end decided to rip the Balloon hoping to fall between the trees (fir trees).

Instead when all the gas had left the envelope I hung (in the basket) suspended from the topmost branches. 'Some game Eh?' However, I still felt 'very bright', being *absolutely* unhurt which I consider Providential.

As there was no one about I threw my trail ropes over the side of the basket and climbed down fifty feet to Earth. A telegraph boy passed by at that moment and told me I was in Addington Park, three miles from Croydon. Fortunately within a half mile there was a Convalescent Depot with 100 soldiers in camp so this boy took a message from me to the Commanding Officer who *at once* sent *eighty-five* men to my assistance. 'Some Squad'.

Well, to cut a long story short, between us we commenced to fell this giant tree and haul it down with the end of my trail rope which we had secured halfway up. It was rather a job but I was anxious that as little damage as possible should be done to the Balloon, and when we did eventually bring it down I found scarcely any damage had been done. I quite expected it to be torn so I felt very cheered.

The men worked awfully well and to cap the lot the CO lent me a lorry to take it to Croydon and then up by rail. The officers then took me to their quarters and treated me most royally. Have just written to thank them for all their kindness. They gave me a most succulent tea.

I wondered how the CO here would take it, but he was most awfully nice, assuring me the bad landing was really quite excusable owing to the miserable weather. So now I'm as happy as a lark, as fit as a fiddle, and as sound as a bell.

Hoping to see you Saturday

Ever your loving boy,
Leslie

Captain R. C. Swales
On 30 July 1912 John Edmonds was granted Aviator's Certificate No. 262, qualifying at Eastchurch on a Short Biplane. *Flight* magazine of 3 August 1912 records:

> *First Marine Private Gets Certificate. The first private to qualify for the Royal Aero Club certificate at the Naval Flying School at Eastchurch is a 'soldier and sailor too', Private J. Edmonds, of the Royal Marines. He has been serving under Commander Samson, and used one of the Short biplanes.*

Edmonds qualified as a pilot two weeks before 'the Father of the Royal Air Force', then Major Hugh Montague Trenchard CB (Certificate No.270), who had been a difficult pupil and was considered a poor pilot.

During the next two years, Edmonds remained at Eastchurch, except for the period May to December 1913 when he embarked in the cruiser HMS *Hermes*. She was an old light cruiser which had been converted to carry seaplanes. Private Edmonds joined her on the day she re-commissioned after conversion. During the remaining months of 1913 a series of successful seaplane launching and recovery trials were held in her. *Hermes* became the embarked HQ of the RFC Naval Wing and in July 1913 she participated in the annual naval manoeuvres to demonstrate the new capability of aerial reconnaissance at sea.

Clearly, not all this period was embarked. *The Aeroplane* magazine of 13 November 1913 records:

> *At Eastchurch Naval Flying School much flying has been done, despite the weather … Thursday was a very busy day as most of the machines were out for tuition flying and cross-country trips. The pilots flying included: Capt Lushington, RMA; Capts Courtney and Barnby, RMLI; Lieuts Davis, Miley and Osmond, RN; Eng. Lt Briggs RN; Asst Paymaster Finch Noyes, RN; Sub Lieuts Rainey, Marix, Pierce, Young and Littleton, RNR; Petty Officer Andrews RN; Ldg Seaman Bateman, RN; and Private Edmonds [sic], RMLI.*

It is interesting to note that among these early naval aviators, some of whom would go on to illustrious careers in flying in the First World War, Private Edmonds was the most senior by date of qualifying as a pilot.

On final disembarkation, just before Christmas 1913, Edmonds and the rest of the Eastchurch squadron were transferred to the books of HMS *Pembroke III* and the administrative HQ Naval Wing moved to Sheerness. Through 1914, Edmonds still appears in the ranks of active pilots at Eastchurch.

The *Aeroplane* of 30 April 1914, p.507 notes:

> *Their Majesties' Aerial Escort. At Eastchurch [on Tuesday 21 April] …
> Comdr. Samson, RN (BE No.50), Eng. Lieut Briggs, RN (Blériot No.39),
> Lieut Osmond, RN (Caudron No.40), Lieut Littleton, RNR (Sopwith No.27),
> Sub Lieut Peirse, RNR (Avro No.16), Sub Lieut Rainey, RNR (Short No.3)*

and Pte Edmunds [sic], RMLI (Short No.34), all flew to Dover and flew over
the Royal Yacht at their Majesties' departure for France. … On Thursday …
Lieut Osmond, RN (Short No.65) … and Pte Edmunds [sic], RMLI (Short
No.34) were scouting. … On Friday, Comdr Samson (Short No.10) … and Pte
Edmunds (Short No.2) were out.

Flight of May 1914 reports from the 'Royal Aero Club Eastchurch Flying Grounds'
the following activity for the last days of April:

Tuesday – The following made a fine flight to Dover, flying over the Royal yacht
in harbour before leaving for France and returning [seven machines led by Cdr
Samson and including] 34 Short, 50h.p., Private Edmonds, RMLI.
*   Wednesday – Fine morning, storm midday. … The following were scouting*
nearly all day [four machines including] Short No 34, 50h.p., Private Edmonds,
RMLI.

Private Edmonds was similarly recorded as airborne in the Short No.34 on the next
two days and also in the following 1914 editions of the magazines when 'Quite a lot
of scouting was done' from Eastchurch. Edmonds, as usual, was the only private
among a group of pilots who were commissioned officers.

On 1 July 1914, the day the RNAS was formed, Edmonds was advanced to
Leading Mechanic. On 20 July every serviceable naval aircraft was launched to fly
in formation over the Fleet Review at Spithead and Edmonds was surely one of the
pilots. Two weeks later Britain declared war on Germany and it appears that
Edmonds' active flying career came to an end as the RNAS went to war. In late
August Flight Commander Samson was ordered to take his Eastchurch (Mobile)
Squadron over to the Continent, initially to support the RM Brigade at Ostend. In
his book *Fights and Flights*, published in 1930, Samson commented on this
operational deployment:

the aeroplane men … were about seventy in number … I may add that among
my aeroplane men were five or six whom we had taught to fly at Eastchurch. The
whole lot were a splendid set of fellows, and were in fact the finest body of men it
was possible to command. Practically every one of them had been personally
selected by me, in the early days of Naval aviation, out of volunteers from the
Navy. Never once were we let down by our men, and both in France and the
Dardanelles they worked like slaves … They were the very pick of the RNAS,
which means that they were absolutely second to none. I must mention some of
their names … [among a list of fourteen names – nine RN, five RM – is that of
Leading Mechanic John Edmonds].

Air Commodore E. L. Gerrard
At Eastchurch we found an extraordinary mixture of personalities: Frank McLean

was an astronomer and coal owner, with a conscientious objection to a bank balance. He thought it to the general benefit that money be kept circulating: aviation helped a lot in putting his theory into practice; of course astronomical expeditions to the South Seas helped, and he had other devices. Mr Cockburn was flying instructor; Lord Egerton acted as a test pilot until we were sufficiently advanced to do our own testing. We offered our necks for nothing (we had little else to offer) so the Government had a really cheap do. We four drew our pay of course; mine was five shillings a day. Lord Egerton was one of those very quiet people who often have unsuspected qualities. One day he was to test the machine from the top of the aerodrome; he proposed to take off uphill, at a row of trees only a few yards away. We protested that he ought to move further back. He said nothing but put her at the trees, which he just failed to clear. There was an almighty crash; he escaped with a shaking and a few bruises. He strolled back and told his men to bring up his own machine which he put on the same spot and again charged at the trees; this time he cleared them by inches. He showed less emotion over it than many a golfer who drove out of bounds and tees up to have another slash at it. On a previous occasion he had had a crash and a broken strut had been driven into his leg, a car was rushed up to drive into hospital, but he simply sent for his own car and drove himself to hospital, seven miles!

Egerton was quiet, but an even quieter one came to stay within for a few days, no less a person than Wilbur Wright. He listened intently to everything *we* (mere children in aviation) had to say, but scarcely ever spoke. There was a story told of him that when he visited Paris soon after making the first ever aeroplane flight, a banquet was given for him. After several speeches in which he was referred to as the Bird Man, he was called on but dissented; however they insisted; at last he got up and this was his entire speech: 'Ladies and gentlemen, you call me the Bird Man. The only bird that talks is the parrot, and he's a durned bad flyer!'

A very high proportion of our own pilots are of this quiet type, introverts I suppose you might call them. They liked doing things by themselves and not having to talk about them and impress people. The extrovert, who is a bit of an exhibitionist, wants a lot of people around to see 'how wonderful'! You can distinguish the two types, while extremely young: the latter will show you everything; they are our actors, actresses, and politicians. The former include many thinkers, scientists, and explorers. They say his friends had great difficulty in persuading Newton to publish his work. I spent an evening with Shackleton, the polar explorer; he never spoke unless spoken to. I found it hard to believe when quiet little Ball became one of the notable VCs of the war. I flew down about 100 miles (a considerable distance for those days) to ask him about it. He said, 'It's quite simple, you dive and come up underneath him, put your gun like that, and fire.' Simple for him perhaps!

The air had a great attraction for stammerers also, possibly because there would be long periods when they need not talk. We had about half a dozen of these on one course at the Central Flying School. One guest night, after a very good dinner, I arranged with a couple of others to herd them all together around the fire; the chorus of *ers...ers... shs...shs...* and chin waggings was a wonder to behold.

To return to Eastchurch; in addition to Short, who at first built under licence from Wright, and then on his own designs, there were three or four amateurs designing and building, mostly at weekends. Professor Huntington, the metallurgist, built a machine of wood and not, as you might expect, of metal. It was too heavy. It was only after several months of charging about the aerodrome that, at last, after hitting a hard bump, he was flung in the air. We were all immensely pleased. Another 'charger' was not so fortunate. When he hit the bump (it was an ancient cart track) the machine went base over apex and the would-be pilot was quietly ejected on his head. After the debris was removed, I saw his chauffeur diligently examining the ground where it had been. I walked out and asked him what he was looking for. He said, 'Well sir, the governor usually has a lot of sovereigns in his trouser pockets!' Ogilvy was building himself a smaller and faster Wright with a view to competing in the Gordon Bennett race to be held at Eastchurch in the summer of 1911. He put up a good show but was much outpaced by the French Nieuport, which won at 76mph. Ogilvy was also busy designing an instrument to help the pilot to maintain the most appropriate speed when climbing, gliding, etc. Up to then we had no instruments. His first air speed indicator consisted of a flat plate which, under air pressure, compressed a spring and moved a finger on the dial. He was brave enough to fit it to my machine and come with me for a trial. I put the machine through various evolutions while he noticed the readings; suddenly he grasped me by the shoulders and shouted in my ear 'Good God, we're stalled, push her nose down!' We certainly were near stalling point, but that was intended to give his instrument a good testing.

The Naval Director of Compasses, Captain Creagh Osborne, was also very brave and took infinite pains to provide us with an adequate instrument. The ordinary naval compass was quite useless for our purpose. The vibration started the needle swinging; also it took a long time to steady after a quick turn. He soon overcame the vibration difficulty, but the other problem was less tractable. If he made it too 'dead beat' it ceased to be a compass. If he made it too lively one might, if there were no landmarks of steady on, chase the needle round and round and never get anywhere. Many times he arrived with a smile on his face and his little box under his arm saying 'I think we've got it this time'. Eventually he produced an excellent instrument.

Clark-Hall, the Gunnery Officer at Sheerness, designed an excellent bomb-carrier for us and fitted of a bomb sight of sorts; he put us a long way ahead of the Germans in this respect. They carried their bombs in their laps and threw them overboard when they thought the appropriate moment had arrived. The first practicable wireless telegraphy set was designed by Basil Binyon, and the first interrupter machine-gun mounting by G. V. Fowler. None of these officers received any sort of recognition or reward, although after the war civilians were awarded hundreds of thousands of pounds for apparatus which had proved useful. The same applies to Shaw, a naval warrant officer attached to us, who designed and made the first dual control for flying instruction. His idea was rapidly copied all over the world.

This brings us back to our first arrival at Eastchurch. The two machines provided for us by Frank McLean were biplanes with plenty of wood and wire about them. The pilot sat on the leading edge of the lower plane with a sort of ladder sticking out into space which carried the rudder bar. The passenger sat close behind the pilot embracing him with his legs. Behind the passenger was the engine. When under instruction one had, of course, the back seat, and by leaning forward one could reach the control lever which worked the elevators and ailerons; the rudder bar one could see but not reach, so that the pupil never touched the rudder bar unless he was in the air by himself. The rudder is, of course, used to maintain lateral stability as well as steering. This led to serious trouble for my first pupil. I taught him all I could under the circumstances and then despatched him on his first solo. He made a couple of nice circuits, and quite a neat landing. I was beginning to think I was something of an instructor when suddenly he opened the engine and charged straight at where we were standing in front of the sheds. We scattered and he crashed into a shed, breaking his thigh and doing a lot of damage. I helped to set his thigh; it required an astonishing amount of force. By then I was convinced that, so far from being a star instructor, I was just a washout. However, when he was able to tell his story, my self-esteem recovered slightly. It appeared that, finding he was not precisely head-on to wind on touching down, he had pressed the right rudder bar harder and harder in the effort to turn to the left, helping with the engine when the rudder was ineffective. I asked him why he pressed the right rudder bar rather than the left, and he said he thought he was riding a bicycle.

Shaw's dual control soon became available and that sort of difficulty was resolved. That, and one fatal accident, were the only mishaps which occurred with the large number of officers I taught. The pupil in the fatal case was really too old and set [in his ways] to learn to fly. Being very senior, I could not force him to wear a belt. Coming into land towards the sheds, he badly overshot the mark, put the nose down steeper and steeper and fell out. I had another elderly pupil who made the same error, but he was wearing a belt and managed to pull the nose up just before it was too late.

David S. Simpson

On 25th [March] Lieutenant Oliver flew the Borel to Leven. This was an uncomfortable flight, as the windscreen had been removed to give an increase of about 3mph.

Manoeuvres began on 1 April. The aircraft were trolleyed down the beach and launched into a choppy sea. For the next few days they co-operated with the torpedo boats HMS *Nith* and *Ness*, scouting the area of the Forth for submarines attempting to penetrate the estuary ahead of the 'enemy' force. Despite fog and wind a couple were spotted near the May island and Bass Rock. Manoeuvres then carried on without mishap, other than a submarine ramming the schooner *Tartar* on its way into dock. The personnel returned to Dundee, to temporary buildings, an uncompleted slipway, and, now the weather had improved, the luxury of two newly-arrived stoves to a hangar.

On 7 May, in glorious sunshine, Gordon landed his flimsy aircraft in Saint Andrew's Bay amidst the bulk of the visiting battleships HMS *Dreadnought*, *Agamemnon*, *Bellerophon* and the light cruiser *Blonde*. He was invited to lunch on *Dreadnought* and introduced several of her officers to flying.

In fair weather a period of regular flying began. This was confined mostly to the coastal area between Montrose and the popular Saint Andrews. Activities included practice with submarines, observer training, photographic work and a steady effort to advertise aircraft and their use, which was not always entirely successful. An attempt to carry Commander Fane of the *Vulcan* to visit ships at sea was frustrated when Short 74 refused to leave the water; a not unusual occurrence in full view of the busy estuary. At least one flight concluded with a seaplane being towed back to harbour by a passing destroyer.

Gordon and Kilner flew Shorts 74 and 75 to Aberdeen to take part in the Naval and Military tattoo. Kilner hit some debris on landing; fortunately fishermen beached the seaplane before it sank. Accidents were few and minor in result, CPO Russell's helmet being blown off his head and fortunately missing anything of value on the way back. Kilner's engine caught fire on the way to Saint Andrews, luckily extinguishing itself during a rapid descent.

A remarkable number of flights, usually by Short 42, ended up at Saint Andrews. These flights proved to be so popular with summer visitors and townspeople alike that, to avoid the aircraft being damaged while parked, it was agreed that a temporary station be set up on the Bruce Embankment by the West Sands. This site had hangars for two aircraft and one seaplane, the town's price of £5 for the preparation of the site being found acceptable. It was also convenient for machines from Montrose who found the lengths of hard golden sand an attraction.

On 23 May 1914 the German light cruiser *Augsburg* paid a courtesy visit to Dundee, providing an aerial photo opportunity as a change from taking the rail bridge and Wormit. On 10 July King George V and Queen Mary paid an official visit to the town. The naval and air bases got a visit of their own when Churchill arrived by pinnace from the Admiralty yacht *Enchantress*. He was met by the duty Sub Lieutenant and, after the customary formalities, proceeded to inspect the base, machinery and the site of the new slipway. The Royal visit delighted all except the suffragettes, who chucked something towards the Royal Party from a convenient roof. The art of dropping anything from a height was still rudimentary, and that, coupled with the ladies' restrictive clothing, ensured no harm was done. A possible attempt to blow up Dudhope Castle at the same time was foiled when wind extinguished the candle at the end of the fuse.

There was a break in the holiday season when, in mid July, aircraft from the station took part in the Spithead Review, B Flight from Dundee being under the command of Squadron Commander Gordon. Aircraft were slow to return; by 28 July Short 42 was the only aircraft on the station. Gordon and Kilner made full use of it in the summer weather, visiting the Territorial Force Camp at Buddon Ness, participating in exercises, giving lifts and making their presence felt locally. Meanwhile the Norwegian pilot Lieutenant Gran was preparing to cross the North Sea from Cruden Bay near Aberdeen to Stavanger in Norway, in an 80hp Gnome-engined Bleriot monoplane.

This pleasant period was soon to end. By 30 July the submarines and *Vulcan* were at sea, armed and heading for Rosyth. Guards appeared on the rail bridge, telegrams came and went. When war started the station was put on a care and maintenance basis, but this situation did not last long after the sinking of ships off the Forth. Four Shorts arrived to carry out submarine patrols, mostly between Montrose and May Island on the Forth with sorties out to sea. Aircraft on hand at various times included Shorts, Wrights and probably Small America Flying Boats.

Zeppelins were a little beyond the reach of these machines. The nearest approach came one snowy night when L14 attempted to attack Edinburgh. Hunting the Forth for a target in this miserable weather the captain noticed that the town was on the wrong side of the estuary, realised he was over the Tay, and gave up the whole thing without disturbing anybody.

Captain R. C. Swales

Samson contrived to remain in France and Belgium until February 1915, leading a mixed RNAS force of aircraft (now re-named No.3 Squadron RNAS) in the air and an innovative unit of armoured cars (the 'Motor Bandits') on the ground. Jointly planned and executed operations by the aircraft and armoured cars introduced a new, ground-breaking method of warfare. During this period Edmonds is recorded by Samson as being present as his 'personal servant', but he was clearly more than just a batman. A typical 'stunt' by this pioneering unit was recorded by Samson when, in October 1914, Flight Lieutenant Marix, RNAS, had been left with an armoured car party guarding an unserviceable aeroplane in hostile territory:

> to a man of Marix's disposition a long wait was rather boring, so he had set off to see if he could come across any uhlans who might still be lurking in the neighbourhood. He took with him eight men, including Private Edmunds [sic], my servant, and Gunner Allen, one of our old Eastchurch Marines, and went towards a château in which uhlans were reported to be. Placing his party so that they surrounded the building, he advanced towards it with Edmunds and Allen. Before he got within 200 yards of it more than twenty Germans dashed out, some mounted, others on foot. He opened fire and gave chase. … The chase resulted in the death of one German and the capture of the officer and one trooper, who surrendered. The officer was very angry when he saw the small numbers of the party who had defeated him.

Samson had a high opinion of certain men in his force. He later recalled an armoured car patrol in Belgium:

I took … the 3-pounder [gun] lorry and two armoured cars. [Lt] Warner acted as gunlayer to the 3-pounder, a job he kept throughout; he was a very fine shot, and would not let anybody else fire it. Armourer's Mate Hughes and Gunner Platford were his chief assistants, and Private Edmunds always used to come as well. With this doughty four one felt confident to take on anything.

John Edmonds was advanced to Petty Officer Mechanic on 1 January 1915. The buccaneering exploits of 3 Squadron with the BEF came to an end when they returned to England in late February of that year and were ordered to deploy to the Dardanelles to support the Mediterranean Expeditionary Force in the Gallipoli campaign. The advance party under Samson's command was established ashore on the island of Tenedos by 26 March. Bombing of Turkish positions began on 2 April. Edmonds remained with the RNAS on Tenedos and, later, Imbros until September 1916 when he returned to England. The next part of his service is recorded as being at RNAS Cranwell, a main training base, from September 1916 to December 1917, during which period he was advanced to Chief Petty Officer Mechanic 3rd Class on 30 April 1917.

On 31 March 1918 CPO Edmonds' naval career ended when he was transferred to the Royal Air Force, which formed the next day. His entry in the RM Medal Roll shows that he was awarded the 1914 Star and Clasp (for his service, under enemy fire, with No.3 Squadron) and the British War and Victory Medals. The 1914 Star was issued to him on 24 July 1919 at 38th Training Squadron, Tadcaster, where he was serving with the RAF. His other two medals were issued to him personally and his Clasp was issued to him on 8 November 1921. It is probable that he had by this time left the RAF.

In 1930 Air Commodore Samson noted of his early 'aeroplane men' from Eastchurch:

I am glad to say that a large number of these men now hold His Majesty's Commission as officers of the RAF; but not one ever received adequate advancement.

John Edmonds, the RMLI private who led the way in those early days of flying was not among those who were commissioned.

Air Commodore E. L. Gerrard

We four came under the Admiralty for all purposes but the nearby senior Naval officers took a great interest and encouraged us. Admiral Prince Louis of Battenberg often visited us and brought VIPs with him. Once he brought Prince Henry of Prussia and it fell to me to take the Princess into the air. While the machine was being prepared, we chatted and she asked me what I did if my passenger became seriously frightened. I said I would pretend there was something wrong with the machine and land as soon as possible. I ensconced her in the machine and we started off. The engine began spluttering and I landed at once. She expostulated with tears in her eyes that she was not a bit frightened. However, we were soon off again and all was well. I knew the Admiral, having served in his flagship in the Mediterranean. Captain Godfrey Paine visited us so often that we decided to make him one of us and taught him to fly. Although above the usual age for such capers he did very well. Later he became Commandant of the Central Flying School on its inception.

Being a simple-minded person, when planning my flying teaching I put first things first and last things last and fitted in the rest. This was the general method of teaching for about four years until Smyth-Barry reversed things and put last things first. When I heard of it I said 'The chap's mad' but after a few seconds reflection I said 'I withdraw that, the chap's a genius'. It is easy to be wise after the event and, of course, everyone realises now that a pupil on one of his early flights might – perhaps by some error of his own – find himself in a difficulty to cope with which required an advanced knowledge. Smyth-Barry gave him this advanced knowledge before his first solo flight. He was one of my pupils at the CFS in 1913, perhaps the best I ever had. He had learned all I could teach him before the end of the course, and I allowed him to do pretty well as he liked. At that time I often went to Farnborough to take delivery of a new machine or to try out de Havilland's latest design. He liked getting outside opinions on machines, both from a flying and a service point of view. I liked all his machines and had few criticisms to offer, although he would put the rudder bar at one's extreme reach. Other designers did the same in spite of our protests; we nearly lost one of our star fighting pilots doing a simple roll over his own aerodrome. He was rather short in the leg and not very firmly strapped in. He slipped a little in his seat, lost contact with the bar and the machine got out of control. He managed to climb up and get at the rudder bar with his hand! His reputation as a stunt pilot was certainly deserved.

One day in 1913 I took over a new type of machine and started off to the Central Flying School at Upavon. I had no belt and felt rather unhappy from the start, but thought I would get used to the thing. The weather deteriorated and I was nearly thrown out several times, often I had to drop the control stick to pull myself back into the seat and then hastily grab the stick again I was bathed in sweat and fear when I landed and told my Flight Sergeant to put the machine in the darkest corner of the shed and allow no one to touch it. One day Smyth-Barry came along and asked to try it. I said 'Certainly not!' but he pleaded and I thought, 'After all, he is as good a pilot as I am, and a second opinion would be valuable'. Knowing Smyth-Barry, I made him promise to fly the thing carefully in the exact manner I laid it down. Off he went and did all the things I had told him not to do. However, he landed safely and I merely looked at him with all the reproach I could muster. He said, 'You know Major, I felt much safer flying that machine dangerously.' Well, I had got my second opinion. We measured up and found the centre of gravity was too far aft and, to compensate for that, the tailplane had been chocked up until it was an even greater angle than the main planes. The machine was definitely dangerous.

I did one fine piece of flying by accident. The competitors in the round-Europe race in 1911 were due at Dover one fine sunny day so I thought I would hop down and see them arrive. The part-owner of the Dover aerodrome had bragged to me what a fine aerodrome it was. On arrival I saw that all was clear, so I need not bother much about the come down into a fine aerodrome. It was a day of marvellous visibility, I could see right into France. I switched off the engine, and started circling with the intention of touching down in the middle of the aerodrome, but too late I saw that this would not allow me enough room. The engine had gone beyond recall, I could only wriggle and twist to try and gain a few yards, she went swishing along the ground and finished up in the very corner of the aerodrome – so-called – with one wing just touching a tent rope and the other just touching the hedge. The officials and people came running up, clapping and shouting 'Magnificent landing'. I hoped they would continue shouting, not because I deserved applause, but so that they would not hear my hammering heartbeats!

I got my own back on that blighted part-owner later, but that is another story. Never again did I bother about scenery when arriving at a strange aerodrome, but I was deceived once again by bad advice as to landing ground. I was taking Mr Winston Churchill from CFS Upavon to Portsmouth where he had official business as First Lord of the Admiralty. The position of the landing ground at Gosport was correctly described to me, but I was told that the grass was rather long and the ground rough near the edges. I would be quite all right in the middle. Well, I landed precisely in the middle, but did not see a sheer three-foot hole until I was practically in it. The undercarriage was wiped off. This was doubly ignominious for not only was Mr Churchill passenger but I had taught him to fly. For an instructor to wipe off the undercarriage in the presence of a pupil was one of those things simply not done.

The only other spot of bother I had was en route to the 1912 army manoeuvres in a Nieuport. I was to spend the night at Oxford, where there was an adequate landing ground. On arrival with a nearly empty petrol tank, I was horrified to see hundreds of people completely occupy the landing ground. I had not enough petrol go off elsewhere, so I made a couple of dummy landings close over their heads. Fortunately, a few intelligent people realised the situation and cleared a lane for me, and I touched down successfully. I asked what the dickens all those people were doing and was told that two pilots had been killed there the day before. They had heard I was due, and had come out to see me killed! Next morning I started out for the manoeuvres, but had got only to about 1,000 feet when a connecting rod broke. I had to select a field in a hurry, squeaked in nicely between a couple of trees, and found I was coming across the lands of ancient plough. There was nothing to be done about it; I must just wipe off my second undercarriage. It was Friday the 13th. I sent a wire to Gregory saying it might have been very serious were it not for the date!

We were fortunate in starting flying at Eastchurch at that particular period. Had we started much later they would have been so much less to discover, and much of the feeling of high endeavour would have been lost. On the other hand, had we began much earlier, the chances of survival would have been against us; chiefly because the catastrophic loss of lift on a curved plane when it reached a certain angle of incidence was not appreciated. I think we owe this knowledge to the Nieuports. A machine might be seen to be flying quite steadily and then suddenly dive to earth. If you asked what had happened you were told, 'Une chute mortelle!' This was the name given to the occurrence, and no other explanation was available.

I think it was the prospect of breakage and the *chute mortelle* which influenced the very early pilots to fly so low. Our instructor Cockburn, for example, had never been above 200 feet, until I took him to 400 feet when he was my passenger on my 'passing out' flight. He gave me a push and shouted 'Much too high!' We arrived as new brooms and immediately adopted the opposite view. Our argument was that the higher you go, the more time for recovery if something could happen. There was also the tactical aspect; a reasonable height seemed called for. Engine failures were still numerous, ten to fifteen minutes was an average sort of flight. Of course, the knowledge that something was likely to happen every few minutes kept you all alive. As engines, and our knowledge of them, improved our flights got longer. I think that we could have captured all the records except speed, that is to say: Climb, Duration and Distance. We were busy on other things, however, and the Admiralty had prohibited participation in public contests. This was a wise decision, though disappointing to us at the time. For example, I was offered a 'mount' for the round Britain race of 1911, and would have accepted if permitted. I watched the start at Brooklands, and saw my mount dive into the ground before it was clear of the aerodrome. A brilliant young naval officer lost his life flying a similar machine when flying privately.

I was very proud of my pupils at the CFS. And when Henri Farman came to England, I asked him to come and see them. They did their stuff, and I asked him what he thought of them as compared with the old-time pilots. He said, 'They are very skilful and I congratulate you, but they have not the sense of apprehension of the old pilots.' That makes you think! On consideration, I think this sense is inborn, though of course it can be developed. A person lacking a sense of danger in the air (and on the road) is the more dangerous in that this lack may be concealed beneath a high degree of skill and judgement. When I asked Henri Farman whether he would like to try one of our machines, he picked one out and started off. Soon he disappeared into one of the numerous folds on Salisbury Plain. I was beginning to feel anxious, when he suddenly appeared only to disappear again; this porpoise-like performance continued until he landed. His undercarriage wheels had never been more than one metre from the ground. He commented favourably on the maintenance of the machine. This was an aspect not often appreciated; all praise went to the pilot. I was always very fortunate in this respect: our engine mechanic (Chapman) took infinite pains. My RE Corporal at CFS loved his engines; it was positively emotion-raising to see him fondle a piston as he placed it with extreme care in the engine he had just overhauled. I think I forgot to mention that the seven-cylinder Gnome engine prepared by Chapman for my Endurance flight ran non-stop for four hours thirteen minutes. This simple flight obtained a lot of publicity as it was the first air record brought to England.

Part Two

Home Waters

FROM CANADA TO THE RNAS

By James Steel Maitland

I was sent to the Royal Naval Air Service unit at Chingford, Essex, and duly commissioned a RN Probationer Sub Lieutenant. The uniform was naval, and we were all very proud to be in the Senior Service, so superior, we felt, to the military equivalent, the Royal Flying Corps. At Chingford we Probationer Officers under Instruction were somewhat strangely called *quirks*. We were instructed in all aeronautical matters by senior officers RN, until we could qualify as solo flyers on light aircraft and our rank as sub lieutenants was established, so that we could be passed on to other stations for more advanced flying suitable for the RNAS.

Organised entertainment was evidently not considered necessary for such a small (and select!) company. Only local civilian efforts were available, occasionally, and Chingford was not particularly productive in that line. Zeppelin raids were frequent, the Zeppelins flying at great heights and doing some damage, but at heights quite unattainable by our light aircraft.

I only had one incident in the air at Chingford. We were trained on Boxkites, which could reach about 50mph. but could obtain no great height. Then we went on to Maurice Farmans and the Avro. The latter – a biplane – was of a more advanced type, fitted with a Gnome engine. This was a 9-cylinder, air-cooled, rotary engine, which made flying more practicable. The accident occurred while flying solo in an Avro. Another learner was in another Avro, and we were the only two in an empty sky. I was up at some 4,000 feet, and he was flying below me. In the Avro there were two 'blind spots', one immediately in front of and slightly above the pilot, the other in a straight line behind and somewhat below him, so that each pilot, in a certain position, could be blind to the other for a very short period of time. I had decided to descend and had turned round about. He crashed into my tail plane, leaving me no rudder or elevator. I had no control of the steering, though I could manoeuvre the wings, almost as though I were in a modern glider. I had time to switch on the engine, thus lifting the plane on to the level, and succeeded in making a good landing at the 'drome'. There the fire engine and other rescue teams had been alerted. I was sent up again at once, and made a successful flight and a good landing. The other plane had its propeller smashed but all the other controls were functioning. The pilot landed in a field some twenty miles away, and he never flew again. I understand that up to this date this was the first time in RNAS history that a collision in mid-air ended without fatal consequences.

After Chingford I was transferred to Calshot for experience in all other more advanced machines including Short seaplanes and larger flying boats of more advanced design. During my instructional duties I was detailed to pay particular attention to certain VIPs sent to get the 'low down' on flying boats or other craft of some importance. On one occasion my instructions were that the 'personage' was to be given every help to fly seaplanes, although he was a little over the age to start learning but was very keen indeed. I spent hours on him. He learned all right to fly but could never learn to 'land' on the sea, and he wrecked many a good machine and must have cost us thousands of pounds. Unfortunately, I had to admit that he was impossible and he was transferred to being an observer. He gained the DFC for some courageous feat with the RAF in the East. His name was Wedgewood Benn, afterwards Lord Stansgate, and he was the father of the one who now bears his name.

After Calshot I was posted to Lee-on-Solent. This was a very pleasant change, right on the south coast of England, and excellent headquarters in some of the requisitioned fine houses of that district. I even had the added attraction of a WRNS secretary. My rank was raised to that of Flight Commander until the RNAS and the RFC in 1918 became the Royal Air Force. Our uniform became military in style, the cloth being RAF blue. Soon afterwards, when in Paris, I was treated with considerable suspicion; the uniform was strange and suspect.

AVIATION IN THE GRAND FLEET

By P. R. Masson

I drifted into the job of relief pilot – always in Light Cruisers – when the regular pilot was on leave or getting over a ditching or crash. It was good experience but rather trying as I was never in a ship for more than a few weeks and hardly long enough to 'bed in'. From the RN point of view I was an outsider. The RN officer is a magnificent type of man, downright keen on his job and as genuine as one expects a sailor to be, but he has lived his life acquiring standards and an etiquette.

Eventually I was posted to the good old *Undaunted* permanently. Mine was the first aeroplane and was a source of interest, joy and pride to everyone in the ship. For months we had trouble censoring letters until a notice was posted. In those letters, that aeroplane had become the most marvellous contraption and even the pilot was the most wonderful fellow. The sailor is nothing if not generous in his sentiments and never does things by half. It took weeks to 'bed in' but the *Undaunted* was a very happy ship. Lieutenant Commander Nuthall was First Lieutenant. The MO was a character and so was Commander Sillince, the Chief Engineer. Also there was Geoffrey Elliott, Lieutenant RNR, from the P&O. Because he was a gentlemanly, peaceable sort of man we called him 'Bloody Jeffrey'. We were in the 7th Light Cruiser Squadron with HMS *Carysfort* for Flagship, together with *Penelope* and *Aurora*. They called us the 'U' boat, but I think no one minded very much.

We soon had the first fly-off and everything went off very well. It was Lieutenant Commander Nuthall's job to pull the release cord that let me loose and I got to know his familiar figure crouching in the slipstream waiting for my signal. He lost a few hats over that job. They sent a senior man over from HMS *Furious* for the first time and at one time I thought he was going to do the flying off himself. Eventually, he looked after the arrangements on deck and it should be put on record that there was never a hitch and I must have flown off scores of times. Ourlongest period at sea was about six days and, if not flown off for any special job, I always flew off the morning of the day we were coming in, usually as dawn was breaking. We could only fly off once each trip because we had to fly to land and be loaded on board from a lighter. Also we had to fly off before the ships' guns were fired as the aeroplane would not stand the concussion of a naval gun. Once we tried leaving the aeroplane. The forward gun was not fired but when No. 1 Starboard gun was fired I saw something dark fly overboard and soon found that it was the side of my Camel.

Soon after I joined the *Undaunted* we sailed out of the Firth of Forth to come in to Scapa Flow. That meant I had to land at Smoogroo, a small airfield on the north side of the Flow, west of Scapa Seaplane Station. Before long I got to know the Orkneys well, but at the time I had never set eyes on those wild and rugged islands. There were several days which I used studying the charts for all I was worth and it was a good thing I did, because there was no chance of even a glance when flying a Camel, especially in bad conditions. They woke me at 2.30 am to fly off in fifteen minutes. In ten minutes I had dressed, drunk a cup of tea and eaten two eggs and was walking forward to the flying platform in my flying kit. In the chilly half-light of dawn my enthusiasm for flying was not too great. The sailors huddled up in their 'lammy' coats in the bucket seats behind the guns looked up from the penny dreadfuls they were reading by the light of a dim blue light with a sympathetic expression. According to Naval regulations we had to wear a life-belt always. It consisted of a tube like the inner tube of a motor cycle protected by a stocking affair. Normally this was worn deflated round the waist with the tube for blowing up sticking up in front just below the chin. I wore a thick and heavy flying leather coat, helmet, goggles and a special Perrins lifebelt outside, which contained a bottle of compressed air which could be released to blow up the belt by bending it over to break the seal. On top of all this there was a Very pistol on a lanyard and I was still short of the heavy fur-lined thigh boots, which never appealed to me as a good thing to swim with. But it was cold at times without them and many times I had no feeling or life left in my legs after an hour or so. I carried my uniform hat. Besides the sailors manning the guns, I saw the MO hanging about muffled-up looking miserable and ill-used. A boat was manned and it was not too cheering to know that the MO and the boat were for my benefit. With so much gear on I fitted into the cockpit like a snail in his shell. Having a last word with the First Lieutenant to learn our position, I would give the usual 'Petrol on', 'Switch off', 'Suck in' and, after a few turns, 'Switch on' and with any luck the engine roared out as it did. Once I had 'got my revs' the engine was throttled back to tick over. The mechanic who had swung the propeller would scramble down his ladder leaving my whole twenty-one feet clear. While I worked my controls to make sure all was free, the sailors posted at the wings would cast off all lashings, leaving only the quick release. Full throttle and a wave to the First Lieutenant and the machine bounded forward and I was off. On this occasion I had nothing to do but make for Smoogroo and land. In some ways it was a wonderful feeling to be up in a world of one's own with nothing but sea as far as the eye could see. We carried petrol for four and a half hours.

Almost as soon as I had got to 10,000 feet looking for the Orkneys, I saw a heap of murk where they ought to be and knew I was 'for it'. A first approach directly for the centre was soon abandoned. There are hills there over a thousand feet – the Old Man of Hoy the highest – and they were all in that black heap and even if a level keel could be maintained there was too good a chance of hitting a hillside. Many times I had practised flying in cloud and with a Camel. It was pretty well impossible and these excursions invariably ended in a spin which was all very well with a few thousand feet below the cloud. My next move was to fly well south beyond the worst of the cloud and come up the channel hoping to get some help from the buoys. Conditions got worse and worse and I had to get down to a few feet off the sea to keep it within sight. At first a few buoys were spotted but they were of little use, except to let me know I was starting up the channel. I soon lost them and had an hour of nightmare flying doing violent turns when something dark loomed up ahead and spotting little rocks and islands which were pretty hopeless for landing. Eventually I flew over Scapa seaplane base and across a neck of land and saw some houses and a church with the top of the steeple in the cloud. All this time it was raining torrents which did not help visibility. I knew the church and town must be Kirkwall so doubled back to pick up the north shore of the Flow and followed the shore west. I spotted an airfield which could only be Smoogroo. It was half flooded but without a second's hesitation I turned steeply, shut off the engine and touched down just where grass began and water ended. There was little run and to make matters worse my engine roared out full bore either because of a short or more likely because I had let the pressure off the 'blip' switch which cut the engine out. It is not possible to alter course once the wheels are down more than about half a degree but a hangar lay straight ahead and in I went while the ambulance people leaped for their lives. There were two machines inside, so when I had finished there were three wrecked machines. I crawled out with nothing worse than a bruised knee. They told me they had heard me for about an hour and had the ambulance ready. They had no messing arrangements here and it was hours before I got away on a lighter. An engineer at the pier doing some work there had heard the crash half a mile away. He supposed 'he was finished', which I assured him was not correct. This day broke all records in another way. I had had those two eggs at 2.30 am and never a bite until dinner at Scapa seaplane base where I had to go to get another Camel. What a dinner! And the rum punch! Starvation must be a terrible thing.

FLYING BOAT EXPERIENCES

By C. P. Bristow

At Lee-on-Solent, although there were a number of forced landings, I can only remember four crashes with one fatality. In one of these crashes a young Canadian friend of mine named Gwyther took off parallel to the shore in a F8A flying boat. These small craft had a tendency to veer left when taking off due to engine torque, and this had to be allowed for. Unfortunately, he did not correct sufficiently for this and found himself skidding along the grass on the cliff top. It was a nasty crash, splintering the aircraft. He sustained head injuries with broken arm and ribs and was some considerable time in the naval hospital at Haslar where I visited him. The fatality was also in a flying boat. The trainee pilot put the aircraft into too steep a descent when coming down to alight on the water and it went out of control, falling

400 feet into the sea when he was immediately killed. From that height it was like falling on granite.

I became very friendly with a boy from Muswell Hill, called Robert Woolnough. We were the same age and had similar tastes and interests, so on our off days we would go out together. As flying was our most important occupation, lectures were reserved for bad weather days when flying was impossible. There were not many of these, so off days were few and far between. When we had completed the required number of flying hours, Woolnough and I, together with several others, were told to report to Calshot for training in the use of Lewis guns and the dropping of 16lb bombs. Calshot Spit is a long narrow promontory of pebbles pointing eastward at the western entrance to Southampton Water. One of Henry VIII's coastal protection castles stood at the end, commanding the entrance to the Solent. Calshot had been developed as a seaplane base with two large hangars and a slipway to launch machines into the calm waters of Southampton Water. The station consisted of wooden buildings used as dormitory blocks, messes, lecture huts and an administrative hut with a parade ground in front of it. Naval tradition was paramount and the station was run as a ship, with the White Ensign proudly flying from the flagstaff. When asking for leave, it was 'going ashore', and an afternoon off was 'make and mend'. We marched more quickly than the Army, saluted differently from them and could buy tobacco and rum more cheaply. Calshot was at the back of beyond, its only access being a narrow country lane. Our main communication was by picket boat from the landing stage by the castle, across to the other side of the Water and up the River Hamble to Warsash. As we were to be only briefly stationed at Calshot, we were housed in a barrack block at Warsash. This was a pleasant place, up a slight hill with a nice mess and recreation room and views over the Water and all the comings and goings of the various ships of wartime. On one occasion we saw a big cargo ship being towed up to Southampton, with a waterfall pouring off its bows and all pumps working full blast to save it after having been holed by a mine in the English Channel.

Every day we assembled at Warsash jetty at 8.30am for a picket boat to take us across to Calshot. We waited for the most senior officer who was always last on and first off. There would usually be about twenty of us going over for the day, returning at 6.00pm. Our time at Calshot was spent in a few lectures on the Lewis gun and bombing, and putting into practice what we had learnt. After lectures, therefore, we were taken up in a Calshot Spit, sitting behind in the observer's seat. Here we could wind away a plywood panel beneath our feet, revealing the ground or sea below, and a bomb-sight had then to be adjusted in relation to speed and drift. The pilot was directed to fly over the target and when it came in line with the sights, we pulled a catch which released a 16lb dummy bomb from the rack underneath. It was fascinating to follow it down from about 800 feet at ever increasing speed. First it seemed to lag behind a little and then, if lucky, when near the ground it would shoot forward onto the target, a small area of about twenty feet in diameter marked by stakes. All this took place near the station over Fawley, a large area of waste ground and marsh which was ideal for our practice. Now, of course, it is covered by a large oil refinery and a new village with hundreds of houses.

For gunnery practice we chased in the air another Short 225. Round the observer's cockpit there was a large ring which would swivel round so that the gun could be fired in all directions. Normally there were two Lewis guns coupled in parallel so that both could be fired at the same time, but for our exercise they were substituted by a camera gun. This special device took snapshots on film instead of firing bullets. The sights were the same as on a real gun and our pilot had to manoeuvre to get near the opposing aircraft – fifty to a hundred yards if possible. When it was in the sights, the trigger photographed it against a 'spider's web' of concentric circles and across showing dead centre. Several shots at varying angles were taken and later that day on the ground we saw the developed results.

On one dull boisterous day, when it looked unlikely that there would be any flying, Woolnough and I decided to play truant. We hired a sailing dinghy and sailed up to Burseldon, under the road and railway bridges, up to the deserted higher reaches of the river. Here we anchored, had a swim and then a snack in the pub by the bridge. In those days there were very few boats at moorings so we had plenty of sailing room. Today it is almost possible to walk from Warsash to Burseldon from boat to boat. On our return to Warsash we visited the pub on the hard, The Crab and Lobster, where they had a pool in which were live crabs and lobsters. We pointed out our choice and it was fished out, cooked and served up to us for a delicious crab supper. Fortunately, our absence that day was not noticed and it has become an outstanding memory for me.

It was on a short weekend leave that I took the train from Swanwick to Southampton and on to Cardiff, leaving on Friday and returning late on Sunday, getting back to Southampton at 6.30am on Monday morning. Unfortunately, I had caught influenza and when I got back to Warsash that evening, had to stay in my twenty-four-bed dormitory until the following Friday. I found that I was quite ill and felt awful and totally remote from the life of the station. At the end of a week I got out of bed and, although weak, was right again a few days later. This must have delayed my time at Calshot to some extent, but even so, I was there only for about five weeks. I still have happy memories of it and like to return and find some things unchanged.

THE MAXIM BATTERY ARMOURED CAR FORCE

By AM1 Stammers

1915

1 January: W. R. Burdett and myself enrolled in the Scott Maxim battery Armoured Car Force. Put into reserve squadron and proceeded with route marches, sleeper shifting, parade ground preparing at airship shed Wormwood Scrubs, our headquarters and recruiting and training centre. Called out with various other ratings to join a detailed section at Oxted, Surrey. Proceeded to Oxted, arrived at

night with Lieutenant Dearmer in charge. Police found us billets in Limpsfield one mile distant. Parade 8 o'clock next morning.

Detailed to No. 9 Squadron, carried on with training, etc. During stop at Oxted we visit range, etc., and take part in several route marches in snowstorms, etc. Learn to pilot Scott Maxim Sidecar with passenger.

Start for headquarters 5.30 in the morning. No. 9 Squadron only arrive about 11 o'clock in Jeffry lorry and kit, no room in machines for us. Myself being on guard night previous I fell asleep. Review of armoured cars and Scott Maxim by Sea Lord in Hyde Park just after arrival. Dismissed for the day. Parade Talbot Works 9 o'clock the following morning.

Following a fortnight at Headquarters we embark for Weybridge, Surrey. All with machines, etc. Police found us billets here but thought we had an allowance of £1.1s.1d a day, I should think. Rotten they were, we shifted to different ones same night, from the pan into the fire. Here they thought our allowance was twenty-eight shillings per week and charged us that. Again we shifted to much better digs recommended us. Very satisfactory indeed.

D. Section (Burdett and myself in the section) and machines ordered to headquarters under Sub Lieutenant Booth, some arrived some did not till later. Burdett was detailed for the wireless car and stopped at Weybridge and occupied same billet. In C Section now, Lieutenant Peacock. Thus we were separated

D Section arrived at Talbot's and paraded next morning. Some of the squad were detailed to Squadron 13, till then the reserve squadron, now being made an active service squadron under Lieutenant Commander Lord Tollemache.

Squadron training, action semaphore, etc. Physical drill, lots of it. Company drill and squadron drill, lots of that too. Machines overhauled and re-kitted, toolkits, etc. All have hopes of active service somewhere.

Squadron 13 proceeds to Ascot, Berks with machines. Lots of excitement. Machines stored in Royal Hotel stables. Royal Hotel officers' quarters and Squadron HQ. Parade ground racecourse in front of Royal box. Three parades per day, physical drill 6.30, full kit 8 o'clock, afternoon parade 2. Extra evening parade on account of stopped leave 9.15. All in billets 10. Pickets parade streets to see everything kept in order and everyone in on time. The residents arrange concerts for us, very good. Much grumbling against stopped leave, several open demonstrations against it. Motorcycles, private ones, observed and made prisoners much against owners' wishes, to prevent leaving village.

Sub Lieutenant Archer, transport and billeting officer, conceives a wonderful (?) plan of putting us into barracks and making us as uncomfortable as possible and hopes that it will work. He is ably assisted by his fellow conspirators CPO Balchin and co. The barracks they picked for us are the quarters picked out for the stable boys and horse grooms during race week. The quarters' beds and mattresses not having been used for over two years are properly lousy and filthy. Indignation and disgust arose on everyone's lips; even the other officers would not come near the hole. We were provided with soap and pails, etc. and ordered to turn everything out of our (perhaps) new digs and wash them out. Someone had some cigarettes, we smoked till they were gone and started making the most terrific din and threw as much out of the windows as we could shift. Windows and all went down, someone found a hose and the place was flooded out and soaked generally.

Chief petty officers tried to rule the mob but no use – they did not want barracks and they meant it. That evening everything was in chaos, petitions were drawn up and the medical officers who had inspected them when they had been looked upon as suitable army quarters consulted. 'No barracks' was the cry even of the residents themselves who liked our boys, and remembered how the Army fellows fared. The petition of the squadron and the residents' petition went up to the Commander. He held a parade and, in front of us, when no one could say anything except him, tore them up and said, 'I mean you to go into barracks'. Some wag shouted 'stables, you mean' and was heartily supported.

For this we were all forbidden to leave the village or talk above whispers in the street. We hung about everywhere and made various demonstrations until it came to the notice of a retired Army major or colonel, I forget which, 'God bless him', who made a row and reported the whole circumstances to the proper quarters. He dared our Commander 'Dear old Jolley' to proceed further in the matter. Eventually some of the heads came down and washed out the idea and the strict rules, unnecessary ones laid down in spite. The mattresses and other filth in the stables stopped where we left them and the pails and so too. So ended the barracks' scheme. All the committee aforementioned got the severe bird and knew it and dried up severely. The CPO concerned nearly lost his life through it. Someone had a bar of iron and dark spot on a dark night, so dark that he missed him, worse luck, but it taught him to stay in at night.

JOURNAL OF A WIRELESS OPERATOR

By Phillips William Norman St Clare

A few days prior to the opening of hostilities, I found myself, at the age of sixteen years, with wonderful notions of what a war would be like. I was a Boy Scout and considered myself a hardy veteran in campaigning. Scouts were asked to volunteer for either of two duties, viz, coastguarding or ambulance. I volunteered for both and was accepted. The day on which Great Britain declared war on Austria, 12 August 1914, I arrived home from my clerical duties in Torquay to find I was wanted for coastguard duty that night and was to report to the station at 7.30pm. Highly excited at receiving this intelligence, I am afraid I gobbled rather than eat my dinner and, changing into my scouting togs, reported at the station a good half hour before I was expected. There I found several more of our troop, some coming off duty and others, like myself, just reporting. CPO Pearce, the stern but kindly official in charge, received us well and lectured us as to our duties, making us quake in our shoes as he pictured the awful responsibility we were about to take on our young shoulders, and the frightful consequences of any inattention to duty on our part. Things appeared a bit better, however, when we learned that a thoroughly competent bluejacket would accompany each of us on patrol, and when I finally set off on my own duty at 8 o'clock I felt that Lord Kitchener himself was but small fry compared to myself on my first commission for HM Navy.

Our patrol along the cliffs in the twilight was very pleasant indeed, but much as I should have liked to have returned with a handful of captured spies, we never met a soul. My blue-jacket companion, who though I believe had a feeling of contempt for the fighting power of the scraggy youth trailing alongside him, beguiled the time with anecdotes of his life afloat and ashore and planted within my breast the first seeds of love for all things 'Navy' that has since grown so great that no living soul on earth can ever hope to crush. I decided then and there that when my turn came it should be served in the ranks of 'those that go down to the sea in ships', even as our family history shows my forefathers had so decided. I never did another coastguard patrol as a Scout, but those two short hours decided my future for the next five years at least, a career I dread to think I might have missed, but for that one night's duty.

LIFE IN BLIMPS

By AM1 A. H. Gamble

Blimp is the name given to a small type of dirigible airship employed by the Navy for scouting and other purposes. It was designed after a type of airship originally made by the French. Owing to the submarine activities around our coasts by the enemy, a large number of these airships were made and put into commission to combat the menace. In appearance the airship is a long pear-shaped bag of gas with a car slung underneath it. The length of the gasbag, or the envelope as we call it, was about 170 feet and the car was no bigger than a good sized rowing boat. The envelope was made of ordinary balloon silk treated with aluminium dope to give it a silver appearance and to prevent it soaking up moisture. It was inflated with hydrogen to a pressure of thirty-five pounds per square inch, whilst in the bag were two pockets, called ballonets, one fore and one aft. These could be inflated with air from the propeller, so that by inflating the fore ballonet you could push the gas aft, and vice versa when the aft ballonet is inflated. On the envelope, near the stern, are two tail-planes by which the ship is steered. The car is slung from the envelope by steel wire, eye-spliced to swivel rings on the car and to rigid rings affixed in large fig leaf patches which are glued with a rubber solution to the envelope. These patches take the whole weight of the car. If one were to lift these patches vertically they would easily be removed by hand, but as the pull on them is horizontal with the side of the envelope it would take many tons to remove the patches. The boat-shaped car has seating accommodation for three persons and is made of three-ply board, strengthened where necessary. In the rear is the engine rig, a Rolls Royce six cylinder 75hp engine driving a pusher propeller.

To prepare the ship for flight it is blown up with gas to the required pressure. The petrol tanks, which are torpedo shaped, and interlaced one on each side of the envelope, are filled with petrol, approximately fifty gallons each. The engine is then warmed up slowly for ashort period to ensure that it is working properly. On the engine being stopped the landing party is ordered to handle the ship, that is to say spread themselves out fore and aft on the four guys, two starboard and two port, allowing about eight men to handle the car. They then lift up on the car and the men on the guys walk the ship ahead to the aerodrome. When a suitable spot for take-off has been reached the ship is halted. The process of ballasting up is then carried out, when the car is lifted and the men on the guys ease up or slacken. Ballast is either taken in or thrown out as required, so that the gas bag will just lift the car from the ground. The engine is then started, the landing party lifts up on the car and lets go the guys, and with the elevators slightly up the ship is driven away up, always into wind. On reaching about 400 feet you straighten out, for it was at this height that our patrols were mainly carried out. The ship is steered to compass and answers the helm very quickly in normal conditions, but in heavy winds or gales the ship is very buoyant in the air and is quite difficult to handle.

After completing your trip the signal is given to land by you to the landing party, who are formed up on the landing ground with their backs to the wind. You then blow air into the forward ballonet driving the gas aft and making the nose heavier than the tail. Then after driving down with the elevators depressed, towards the landing party to approximately thirty to forty feet, you straighten out, shut down the engine and drop your trail rope. On seeing the trail rope the landing party pile themselves on it and gradually haul you down, catch your car, man the guys and walk the ship back to the shed.

P. R. Masson

After landing at Scapa seaplane base station (which was famous for its hot rum punches) they certainly put me right with the world. They lent me pyjamas and I went to my bunk with a feeling that I had never visited such a happy place. Altogether, I spent months at Scapa Flow. In many ways it was a fascinating place. Bleak, stormy and windswept, but at times strikingly beautiful, especially at sunrise and sunset. In June, sunrise and sunset almost merged and it was never completely dark even at midnight. There is a little island of rock in the middle of the Flow on which seals could be seen. It enjoys the name of the 'Barrel of Butter'.

We lay off Flotta and the whole coast was rugged cliff and heather clad hills beyond. Once I saw a golden eagle and cormorants; gulls and gannets were common. We had walks on Hoy and played golf on the Calf of Flotta on a course made by the fleet. Each hole carried the name of the ship that was responsible. You could just tell the fairway from the rough as there was a little less heather. The greens were not as good as the fairway on a real golf course. Once Geoffrey Elliott and I played in a high wind with sleet storms most of the time. We wore sea boots and sou'westers and tossed up or took it in turns to lift the balls out of the waterlogged holes filled to the brim with icy slush.

I never managed to get to the top of the Old Man of Hoy. We were usually at four hours' notice and they did not like us to get too far off. Once three of us reached a little mountain tarn. The other two watched me have a swim, although it was

February with snow about but a beautiful day and the water felt good. Later I missed my identity disc but found it where I had undressed when I could get there again, four months later.

Sometimes we had weeks when it was too stormy for leave boats, and fishing, reading and 'caulking', i.e. sleeping, were the only pastimes. There were plenty of fish; I never caught one fairly but foul-hooked one in the back once or twice. Sometimes we had sailing exercises and I learned what a wonderful boat the naval whaler is to sail.

Stromness and Kirkwall were the two important towns but they were surprisingly small and there was little of interest compared to walking the moors. On one occasion, the Paymaster and I walked about six miles through the heather in sea boots to buy lobsters. A fisherman took us down to a cave below high tide. He took off the padlock and opened a door and it was like bedlam let loose – there were scores of huge lobsters striking at each other. They had their claws tied but as we trudged back with two large lobsters each slung over our backs I hoped those lashings would not come adrift. We found a twelve-mile walk through heather in sea boots was sheer punishment long before we had finished. The crofters on some of those small islands seemed desperately poor and lived in primitive conditions but they could be embarrassingly hospitable. Once, two of us stopped for tea at one of these crofts away on the heather with only a track leading to it. We had to step down to enter the only room. My friend sat on the only chair while I sat on the bed. The woman, looking the picture of trim efficiency, plied us with bannocks and butter and kept filling our cups with delicious tea. The only snag was that a simpleton with the mentality of a child of five grunted and did somersaults on the bed behind me. As he weighed about twelve or thirteen stone and was a powerful man, I had my work cut out to look unconcerned and get on with the bannocks. She did not want us to pay anything after all we had eaten.

After we had been out for five or six days on convoy and had an uncomfortable time, Scapa Flow seemed like a haven of peace and comfort. Just before I joined the ship they had come in with masses of ice covering everything aloft. One of the guns was choked with ice and after they had poured a couple of buckets down the barrel and thought it was clear they fired it. The breech blew out and killed the gunnery officer and one of the crew. Often we did not know, when going to sea, whether we would come back to Scapa Flow or the Firth of Forth, but I was always told to which base I had to fly. Twice I flew off without getting our position when there was some urgency and conditions were a little exciting and we could not communicate with the ship. It was not quite as important as it may sound because after an hour or so the position of the ship was of little moment. On both occasions flying SW brought up landmarks and after a while we knew most of them all up the East Coast; St Abbs Head, May Island, the Bell Rock and, farther north, the Tay Bridge, the Tay estuary and Moray Firth. Scapa Flow was large enough for flying off.

I was sent off once to look for a torpedo but never found it. For some reason mishaps seemed to occur more in the Flow than at sea. Once I saw, through a telescope, old Jackson from the *Carysfort* sitting on his tail and looking very forlorn.

The engine had sunk leaving the tail sticking up and he had climbed up and sat on the rudder turned flat. It was strange looking at him through a powerful telescope when he was six miles away and looking as though only 200 yards. One of the battle-cruiser pilots, flying off the platform fixed on top of the big guns, crashed on the deck and killed a marine. Still another fell into the 'ditch' right in front of the ship. They had not time to stop the ship's propellers as the ship drove right over him. To the surprise of everyone they picked him up intact although his machine had been cut to pieces by the ship's propellers. I saw him the same day and some wag asked him, 'And did you get wet?'

Occasionally the whole fleet put to sea when there was thought to be a chance of the German fleet being out. On one such occasion we had a four-day storm, which forced us to reduce speed. It was a magnificent sight to see the other ships at times almost completely covered in water and spray right to the funnel tops and, at other times, exposing some of the keel. It was a very uncomfortable time on board even if it filled us with glee to think the big capital ships were getting it in the neck. We had an old-fashioned harmonium in the wardroom and one night it broke adrift and made a fearful mess. Water washed about our quarters and in theWardroom it was mixed with shrimp paste, pickles and jams from a smashed cupboard. Four men were lost overboard in the fleet and out of twenty-four aeroplanes only one was able to fly afterwards. Mine was broken-backed and unfit to fly. I had seen green seas over it and aeroplanes are hardly made for that. Some ships had lost every trace of aeroplane, even the trestle that held the tail in some cases. HMS *Aurora* was one that came in with the flying-off platform as clean as a board and it caused me some satisfaction because we had had some heated arguments when the *Aurora*'s pilot had fitted wire lashings and I had argued for ordinary rope.

C. P. Bristow

Our time had now arrived to be posted to operational stations, so we were provided with our orders and railway passes. I was posted to Felixstowe with a Canadian named Pearce, but Woolnough was sent to Torquay, at which we were both disappointed. Pearce was a large, mild-mannered man who perspired a lot. As it was nearly summer and quite warm weather this was noticeable, and probably why I remember it. He and I sallied forth to London, found a hotel and the following day took a train to Felixstowe, getting there in the evening and booking in at the Felix Hotel. We walked down to the seafront that night in the black-out and we both fell into a shallow trench in the chalk, probably dug for a temporary shelter in air raids. Felixstowe air base was on the shore of Harwich Harbour – a wide stretch of sheltered water with many warships and other craft at anchor. It had slipways for launching seaplanes and flying boats. Later in the war I was to get to know it the hard way by accident but, for the present, Felixstowe didn't appear to want us and told us to report to Westgate-on-Sea.

So we returned to London, taking two days on the journey to Westgate, visiting a couple of London theatres on the way. We eventually got there and were impressed by this small friendly station, situated in a pleasant residential seaside town. It was placed at a strategically important position at the east end of southern England and nearest to occupied Belgium. It was also at the mouth of the Thames approaches and at the north end of the Straits of Dover. Further south and west the Channel was dominated by the British on the north coast and the French on the south coast. To the north of us were the seaplane bases of Felixstowe and Yarmouth. There was also a large RFC station at Manston, three miles to the south, but we acted independently of them, except for protection against enemy raids when we sometimes patrolled together. In these cases the Navy took the leadership, as the overall commander of the area was the Admiral of the Nore, based at Chatham. Our CO at Westgate appeared to plan all our movements, which involved everyone at the station. Our task was to patrol this area of the North Sea and bomb any U-boats we found. We were armed with three Lewis machineguns and were classified as fighter-bomber seaplanes. Both the CO and the second in command were pilots, but did very little flying, so patrols were the responsibility of the sub lieutenant pilots, flying regularly with six commissioned and four petty officer observers. The observers were responsible for bombs, guns and wireless and the pilots for flying and navigation, and also for keeping an eye on engine performance.

We soon found out that this was to be a serious active service posting, and that we had been sent to replace four young officers who had been killed in two seaplanes in an engagement with seaplanes from the German base at Zeebrugge. This was our first real indication that confronting the enemy was going to be a dangerous business. The air station was at the east end of the promenade with two hangars and two slipways leading down to the sandy beach. High tide came right up to the seawall and slipways. Ratings' quarters and recreation huts were behind the hangars, whilst officers' quarters were in a terrace of three-storey houses in a private road. This was right next to the station with a broad front lawn down to the promenade. Our mess was in the centre house, which had big French windows on the ground floor and balconies to the first floor bedroom. This room was occupied by the CO, with my room directly above on the second floor. I lived here until May 1919 when I was demobilised. A feature of these houses, and typical of Westgate, was a covered verandah at the back facing south, looking on to the road and the front entrance. We often relaxed there, rather than on the north-facing sea side and lawn.

There were ten of us pilots, all about eighteen or nineteen and all flight sub lieutenants. The CO and second in command were both full lieutenants. The CO, Gerry Livock, was aged only twenty-one, but a veteran with three years' flying experience. The second in command, Pearce, was a married flight lieutenant of thirty-two. The first lieutenant was a lieutenant RNVR, a South African of about forty, a bit of a mystery to us all, who smoked strong South African tobacco. This last came in cotton bags, looking like dried grass and gave off a distinctive and strange aroma. The doctor was a sandy-haired Scot, aged about forty. The padre had served in the Navy his entire career; he was fifty and smoked an enormous pipe. Additionally, there were three sub lieutenant and eight petty officer observers, who flew with us as Wireless Operator/Gunner/Bomb-aimers, all wearing their half-wings. The station had ten Short 184 seaplanes and one single-seater Hamble Baby fighter seaplane. With their big wing-span of sixty-three feet, the 184s' wings were folded back when they were in the hangar, but we always had two standing on beach-trolleys ready for instant action. They stood on the tarmac outside, charged with petrol, 600 rounds of ammunition and one 230lb bomb on the rack underneath the fuselage. There was a radio station with two tall masts at the base, and on the low cliff at the east side was a lookout and signal point with mast.

Phillips William Norman St Clare

My name eventually being called, I passed by the Marine Guard at the door and found myself in a cold uncomfortable looking room. Before me was a long wooden bench, its surface littered with books and inkpots. Five piles of documents and signal pads were placed at intervals also and behind each pile sat the figure of a bluff old sea-dog. I stepped quickly up to the table before, saluted and stood waiting.

'Your Christian name?' demanded the person on my right.

'Phillips, Chief.'

'Why call me "Chief"?' came next.

'You are a Chief Petty Officer,' I replied.

'Umph! Surnames?'

'William Norman St Clare.'

'Are you a Scout?' queried another officer.

'Yes, Sir,' I joyfully replied.

Next a Lieutenant Collinson, whom I afterwards found to be a schoolmaster, put me in a whirl with a mass of educational questions from which I eventually escaped to answer another inquisitor. This officer wanted my statement of aerial knowledge. My practical career in this direction up to this date consisted solely of making numerous toy parachutes from tissue-paper and strawberry baskets while at school, toys I may say I succeeded in floating for miles at a time. This statement highly amused us all and I felt more at ease.

'Anything else?' asked the airman.

Suddenly I remembered the lists of vessels and other things I had spent so many hours compiling and learning, so drawing myself up I said quietly,

'Yes Sir! I can give from memory all published data concerning the various air navies.'

The officer stared at me for a minute, then laughed and said, 'Really! That is fine. And how did you learn such things?'

'I made lists and studied them, Sir!'

'Why?' he asked sharply, standing up.

'I thought it would come in useful.'

'I see,' he said and, then opening a large book and turning over a few pages, suddenly asked, 'You said "any published data" I think? Then please state shortly what you know of Germans airships.'

I told what I knew and he checked each statement by the book. When I had finished he said, 'You are a little out of date on some points, but far better than I ever expected. I think we can send him to the doctor now.'

The others assented and I retired joyfully from the room and followed a petty officer to the Sick Bay as Naval surgeries are called. Next I had a lively half hour's knocking about and testing by a small bespectacled doctor and was finally told to get some lunch and report back about 3 o'clock. Outside the Sick Bay I asked the petty officer if he thought I had a chance.

'Yes,' he replied and then, grinning broadly, added, 'So have the other sixteen.'

Three o'clock came and I fell in with the other fellows, whom I noticed had somehow decreased to the number of twelve. We waited expectantly while, after some minutes conversation with a couple of officers, a CPO walked over to where we stood, carrying in his hand a paper, evidently a list of names. Clearing his throat he began to address us.

'Attention, you boys, to what I have to tell you. The names I am about to read out are those of the five boys selected for training by the Admiralty's Special Selection Board. They are to be enrolled on the books of the Royal Navy, not for the duration of the war but four years' colour service from the time they are eighteen and for four years reserve after completion of their colour service.'

My name was among the five.

A Contemporary History

Another section of the work of the RNAS has been the defence of his country against hostile raids. From time to time this matter has aroused some criticism but only in reference to the quality and quantity of the material at the disposal of the service. Squadron Commander Butler, Flight Commander Bone and Flight Lieutenant Cadbury, amongst others, acted as strafers of Zeppelins and, in combat with German aircraft, showed great determination in defending this country against aerial aggression, particularly in the difficult art of night flying.

As a model of combined operations in which aircraft, submarines, destroyers and light cruisers all took part, the raid on the German fleet in Schillig Roads, Cuxhaven, on the morning of Christmas Day 1914 would be hard to beat. This was apparently the first occasion on which seaplane-carrying ships were present in action. Three such were present, having been escorted to an agreed upon rendezvous. These vessels launched from their decks seven machines which not only made valuable reconnaissance flights over the Heligoland Bight but also bombed several points of military importance. All machines returned safely after being hit in several places by shrapnel. Three pilots ran short of fuel and were unable to complete the journey back to their parent ship, but such a contingency had been foreseen and submarine *E.11*, commanded by Lieutenant Commander Martin

Naismith, was waiting close inshore to aid any machine in difficulties. (Naismith was later awarded the VC, after brilliant services in the Dardanelles.) By his coolness and courage he rescued all three pilots. Most people are now familiar with the story of the British seaplane in the Battle of Jutland in 1916. Sir David Beatty, within a few minutes of the first reports that enemy warships had been sighted, ordered the seaplane carrier *Engadine* to send up one of her machines to scout in the required direction. The order was given at 2.45pm; at 3.08pm the plane was well underway and at 3.30 the first reports were received from him in the *Engadine*. Sir David in his report congratulated Flight Lieutenant Rutland, the pilot and Assistant Paymaster Trewin, the observer, on their achievement. Lieutenant Rutland was awarded the Distinguished Service Cross.

GREAT WAR EXPERIENCES

By F.J. Rutland

I do not propose to discuss the Battle of Jutland here, except so far as it concerns aircraft. In HMS *Engadine*, we went to sea to carry out a sweep of the North Sea, because we had indications that at least a portion of the German Fleet were putting to sea. We left the Firth of Forth on the afternoon of 30 May 1916, having a rendezvous with the Grand Fleet at Scapa at the Long Forties, a point about 100 miles east of Aberdeen. We were never to reach there; suspicious smoke reported by an advanced cruiser, HMS *Galatea*, resulted in an order to send up a seaplane to report. I got away in a Short 164, No.8359, with Trewin as the observer. We got off in undisturbed water, sighted the enemy and sent our reports. They put in some extremely accurate anti-aircraft fire, but we took little notice of this. We got our report to *Engadine* and although it was arranged they should be passed by signal to *Lion*, the battle-cruiser communications were so badly organised that she would not answer our call, but the signals were picked up by a light cruiser and passed on.

Here was perhaps the turning point in the Navy's appreciation of the use to which aircraft could be used in conjunction with warships. Unfortunately, about an hour after getting away, and just when I was on my way south to sweep for the enemy battle squadron, I had a petrol pipe fracture. I landed and repaired this, then the ship came up and I was ordered to hoist in. I asked permission to go on, but this was refused. We could have been of great use had we gone on again; unfortunately as the *Engadine* could not effect communications with *Lion*, the Captain decided it was better to hoist the plane in for the moment. Later the sea became too rough to hoist out planes. We got off at sea; we had established inter-communications between plane and ship in action, for the first time in history. It was the fault of the Navy entirely that we were not used to better effect. Their point of view was that we could not be relied upon, due to so many failures, and inability to get off at sea, except in the most favourable circumstances. They would not accept us until we were 100 per cent perfect.

The Commander in Chief's attitude to aircraft is exemplified in his action regarding HMS *Campania*. She was at anchor near the seaplane station, and did not get the signal to get under way. It is difficult to understand why this was not discovered at the time, as it is usually the duty of the flagship to get a confirmation of such a general signal from all ships. Thecaptain of *Campania* saw the fleet as they passed his anchorage and made a signal asking for permission to sail. It was not until then that Jellicoe knew she was not there. She was ordered to join, but by this time she was so far astern of the Fleet that the Commander in Chief ordered her to return to port. *Campania* was a large ship but she could not maintain a speed of more than 14 knots. This was her only real disadvantage. It seemed to have escaped the Commander in Chief that, even if she were 100 miles astern, her aircraft could still operate with the fleet. She had one great advantage; seaplanes could be flown from her decks. She carried fourteen, all equipped with wireless and with thoroughly trained wireless operators. Many of the mistakes at Jutland would have been averted had she been present. Jellicoe was not air minded, one would suppose, but this is not so; he was just incapable of adding to his organisation any unit that was not as I have stated before, 100 per cent perfect.

We kept our station on the beam of *Lion*, all through the action, until the advanced units of the Grand Fleet went into action, when we went to the assistance of the disabled heavy cruiser HMS *Warrior*. We really had ringside seats, and saw the *Queen Mary* blow up, with my great friend Freddy Shealth, who was the Director Officer, whose duty it was to fire all guns from the control top.

Phillips William Norman St Clare

The training that we underwent at this period was mostly in the nature of signalling. Classes were formed and we spent an hour or so under each instructor in turn. We were told all about the practice and theory of magnetism and electricity with a few sidelights on their application to wireless telegraphy. We learnt semaphore signalling and gradually mastered the Morse alphabet. Once that was done, we ran on to using buzzers, flash lamps, heliographs and flag-wagging. I thought that almost finished signalling, but we next turned our attention to naval flags (a subject I soon mastered) and foreign and colonial ensigns (which I already knew). Running an even course, with this came other sundry items such as storm and weather signals, danger signals, Zeppelin signals, star shell and Very light SOS codes, and such things as the lighting laws for different type of vessels at sea.

There are one or two incidents which can be written of our short stay in Roehampton. The first of these was the end of the daily bathing parade. Our ablutions took place in the centre of a field and the baths used were really very broad tins with only six-inch sides. The water being cold and the centre of the field distinctly airy, we eventually prevailed upon those in charge to have the bathing place moved to the edge of the field by the gate. This was done andeverything was as well as could be when one day, without a word of warning, the gate opened and admitted to our midst a very pretty young lady. I leave the picture to your own imagination, merely stating in passing that we boys completed the first hundred yards in nothing and during the second we burnt the wind.

The young lady referred to was, by the way, the only member of the fair sex we had the pleasure of talking to during our early training, but as she was an interested and frequent visitor it will be readily understood that she was doubly welcome and appreciated, and was none other than the young and beautiful Lady Sybil Grant. Before we finally left she presented us with a mascot in the form of a huge pure white Pyrenean mountain dog.

The result of the no smoking order is interesting from the point of view that, whilst on joining the Navy, fifty per cent had never smoked, within a few weeks of joining the whole camp could lay claim to be moderate smokers, and increased our sins in this direction in equal proportion to the drasticness of the future orders. Where the cigarettes continued to arrive from was a cause of great anxiety to our officers. I suspect that someone must have broken bounds pretty frequently. It was nothing out of place to climb to the uppermost branches of a tree, to escape the eagle eye of the law and have a quiet smoke. However, as our CO afterwards said, 'Boys will be boys, and I should not have loved them half as much, had they never defied my instructions'.

Shortly before leaving Roehampton, the 'no leave' order was rescinded and we were allowed 'ashore' once a fortnight for a matter of sixteen or so hours. This time, however, was none too long for a journey to my home nearly 250 miles away and, on the first occasion on which I did the trip, it made me much the worse for wear, suffering as I was at the time with a swollen face and a bad attack of neuralgia. Before my next leave, however, different regulations were in force to my advantage, and I was able to put in a few hours well needed relaxation in my beautiful Devonshire home.

Twice during my first few weeks I had managed to take a trip away from the camp, but on each occasion the journey had terminated with a startled experience. The first of these started with a visit to the airship shed at Wormwood Scrubs, together with a couple of dozen other fellows, undertaken by our commanding officer, in order to explain and interest us in our duties. Things went exceeding well and we were wonderfully interested in the large airship berthed in the shed and everything that we were told about it. The lecture coming to an end, we were mustered and marched out into the open. I was the last to leave, and carefully pulled the iron door behind me as I passed through. The next moment I heard the most appalling noise I could ever imagine, and was thrown violently forward on to the ground. When I recovered I found that the huge airship had exploded, blowing half of the roof away, and killing three men who were standing near. Many others were injured, and I could not help thanking my lucky stars I had got that door closed when I did.

The second escapade took place during a visit to Kingsnorth aerodrome, at that time the leading airship station in the country. We had started out quite early in the morning for the long run down to Chatham by naval cars and, after a thoroughly enjoyable journey, arrived at the aerodrome and were shown a thousand wonders. Airships larger than the inflated one I had seen at the Scrubs were here and, after an enjoyable tour round, we were taken out on to the landing ground to witness an experiment about to take place. A small type of airship was resting there and we were surprised to see that the gondola was nothing more or less than an ordinary two-seater aeroplane, complete with wings, etc. The idea of this, as it was explained to us, was that the airship should float about over London by night andthat in case of a raid by hostile craft the engine would be started, the balloon cut free and the aeroplane find herself already on the spot and into the thick of it. It was a mad, brilliant and brave idea, and I thought highly of the two officers I saw climbing into their seats.

Our Talbot days were by far the most instructive and interesting. Several trips were undertaken to places like Hendon and the Marconi Works at Chelmsford, that were either in use or in course of construction. We saw much of our old friends from the Scrubs here also, as well as of that gallant band of sportsmen who formed the armoured car squadrons, who at this time were being disbanded and re-enlisted into the RNAS. It was the proudest thing in the service for us then even now to be known as friends and confreres of an armoured car man. They have a lot to be proud of, alas, unwritten, like many other gallant deeds.

Whilst we were on the heart of London everything connected with us was as a ship at sea. Talbot Motor Works had become HMS *President 2* and we had aboard our own quarterdeck, cabins, mess decks, officers' quarters, wardroom, and galley. To go out through the gates was to 'go ashore' and a lorry taking men ashore was always 'the liberty boat'. We were divided into Port and Starboard watches, did our duty watch just as the sailors do, and took our time from the ship's bell. There was a ship's office and guardroom, the latter ruled over by the 'Jaunty' and 'Crusher' as the Master-at-Arms and his assistant have been called from time immemorial. The Captain held his Divisions each morning and the defaulters had to 'doff caps and get yer bleedin' 'air cut', just like any other AB in His Majesty's Navy.

Strictly and wonderfully Naval was all about us and we soon learned to love it. Of course, there were a few things we found objections to, one for instance the early morning deck-swabbing parade. Trousers rolled up above the knees, bare feet treading on the cold concrete flooring, we dodged beams of water directed from many fire hoses as we scrubbed for dear life the already spotlessly clean decks. This procedure was also carried out in the lecture rooms of an evening, leaving behind a permanently damp atmosphere. Shortly after our arrival at Talbots the experiment had been pronounced a success and fifty odd men (eighteen to twenty-year-olds) who had been receiving wireless instruction elsewhere were drafted into our section to join us in our training. The Admiralty also called for another hundred boys whom, needless to say, they received in a few days, and this expansion of personnel required quite a number of extra instructors to train. The increasing number of instructors made our illicit love of the fragrant weed more difficult to satisfy as no longer were you sure that the petty officers were engaged elsewhere as you were when only two were over us.

At the top end of the recreation ground was a large mound of earth evidently used in pre-war days by the spectators as a vantage point from which to watch games in progress. About a dozen of us were very much attracted by this mound, so much so in fact that, during the small grey hours of each morning, the rest of the camp would have been surprised to see at the back of the mound a party of boys but lightly clad hard at work with picks or shovels, digging a way into the interior of the mound.

A fortnight later certain boys would be wanted by such and such an instructor of an evening, but not a sign of them could be found. Yet when the nine o'clock roll call was called everyone was present. Interrogated, the offenders stated on oath they had been on the camp all the evening, and had never thought of breaking bounds. The CO, Lieutenant Tomlinson, thought different. He was not the kind of man to doubt a fellow's word, yet on the face of things something was wrong. The camp had been searched from end to end without a sign of the boys. They must have broken bounds. Sentries were posted at more frequent intervals around the camp for several nights and one evening roll call was held at 8.30 instead of nine. No one was absent. The boys were dismissed and at 9.10 a second roll was called. Eight boys were missing. The sentries were ready to swear that no one had climbed the eight-foot-high railings, so those eight missing boys must still be in the camp. A systematic search was organised, but not a boy was found. The CO by this time was getting wild. He knew they had not left the camp but, somewhere within it, were those eight boys blissfully ignorant of the fact that a second roll had been called and their absence noticed.

Suddenly he had an idea and with a few words to a petty officer who remained behind, the CO led his staff in a direct line for the mound of earth. Four members of the ranks of men, who were in the know, gasped with relief as they saw the CO and his followers climb up the mound and scan the camp from its summit. Their secret was safe. Suddenly the terrific peals of the fire bell awoke the silence, and the very ground on which the CO stood seemed to open up as out of the earth a few feet from where he was standing appeared one by one, eight excited and anxious boys, ready to help save the station from destruction by fire. They were followed by a heavy cloud of tobacco smoke. Further inspection showed a wonderfully camouflaged doorway giving lead to a roughly furnished but nicely made dugout, littered with cigarette ends. The CO withheld his judgement. He was a sport and realised it took all his cleverness to find them out. Instead they had to put in an hour each evening filling in the dugout and when that was finished no more was said. It is perhaps worth mentioning that each of those eight boys received many little favours afterwards for no apparent reason at all, and all received promotion.

THE DESTRUCTION OF L53

By Flight Lieutenant S. D. Culley

The Zeppelin was the great 'bogey' weapon of Kaiser Wilhelm and his army staff in the First World War. It was employed before the war as a political weapon and the claims for it were, as is usual with such things, far greater than justified. Although the Zeppelin was available from the very start of the war, it was not from the political aspect very different to the claim made by Hitler for secret weapons, which were going to blast the British off their islands towards the end of the Second World War. However, several Zeppelins were destroyed by even the very inefficient aeroplanes available at the beginning of the war, when they were used as offensive bombing craft over Britain, so the airship was very quickly relegated to its proper function as a means of reconnaissance for the German Navy.

In this role there is no doubt that the Zeppelin was a most useful aircraft, if expensive. Operating over the North Sea it could remain in the air for long periods, day and night, and was able to report on the movements of ships over vast areas of that important sea. The only British aircraft able to operate at any distance from Britain was a flying boat, and that was so heavy and slow that the Zeppelin could practically ignore it. The main base of the Zeppelins was in northern Germany, and they were of particular annoyance to the British Harwich Light Force, which operated from Harwich under the command of Admiral Sir Reginald Tyrwhitt. Although some cruisers in the Grand Fleet were fitted with very small fighter aircraft, none of the ships of the Harwich Force had been so fitted, so that the ability of the Germans not only to report on every movement of the Harwich Force, but even to bomb the ships (admittedly without anything more than a nuisance effect) was particularly galling to the admiral. He therefore put the problem to the famous Commander (at that time Colonel) Samson, whose headquarters was at Felixstowe, and requested that he should devise some way of dealing with this great nuisance.

It so happened that in order to give the flying boats of Great Yarmouth and Felixstowe greater range, a lighter had been designed especially to enable a flying boat to be warped aboard. The lighter was towed behind a destroyer to wherever the fleet might be going on patrol and, at an appropriate moment, the flying boat would be launched from the lighter, take off from the water and proceed on its mission, returning to its base in the UK by air. It was decided to experiment by fitting a small land fighting aircraft to one of these lighters. The aircraft chosen was a famous Sopwith Camel, which had the particular ability to climb quickly to what were then considerable heights of 20,000 feet. The original Camel for this special purpose was fitted with skids, not unlike ordinary skis, and these were designed to run along troughs fastened to the deck of the lighter. The destroyer steamed at its highest speed, about 30 knots, and thus ensured airflow over the deck of sufficient speed to give the aircraft immediate lift when released. When all was ready according to plan, the trial was made. Typical of that great character, Colonel Samson himself insisted on being the first pilot to try the idea. It was not successful. As soon as the aircraft started to lift, it appeared to become out of control and plunged into the water immediately in front of the lighter, which swept over it. Naturally everyone expected this to be the end of the career of Colonel Samson, but not at all; he was recovered intact and as he was hauled into a boat his only remark was 'That was no damn good, we must do it better next time'.

For the next experiment it was decided to fit a flat deck with a Camel on its ordinary wheeled undercarriage. A young pilot, a Canadian in the Royal Air Force by the name of the Lieutenant S. D. Culley, who had had experience of deck flying in the Grand Fleet and who was then stationed at Great Yarmouth, was chosen as the pilot. The experiment, which was made on 1 August 1918, was a complete success. The Camel was prepared for its defensive role and the standard Vickers machine gun and all its accessories were removed. In place of the single Lewis gun fitted in the top-plane of the aircraft it was decided to fit two such Lewis guns, as it would not be possible for the pilot to make any change in them during flight and it was essential that the greatest possible firepower should be available for the very few critical seconds in which they might be called upon. The guns were fitted with two ammunition 'pans' of ninety-seven rounds each. The Royal Navy destroyer allocated for the operation was the same as had carried out a successful trial, HMS *Redoubt*, commanded by Commander Holt DSO RN. The lighter *H5* (as the craft was officially called), with the Camel fitted, was taken out with the Harwich Force on the evening of 5 August 1918 for its first operation, but the weather the following morning was unsuitable for its operations and the force returned to Harwich. On the evening of 10 August, Harwich Force again left on an operational sweep of the south-eastern part of the North Sea and the Camel was again taken out, as were a number of flying boats on other lighters as well as a number of motor torpedo carrying coastal motor boats (CMB), which were carried in the various ships of the Fleet. It was therefore rather a large force which found itself the next morning in the south-eastern part of the North Sea not far from the German and Dutch coast.

At dawn the CMBs and the flying boats were launched and the flying boats then attempted to take off. However, the water was so calm that, without exception, they all failed in their attempt and finally had to be hoisted into the respective lighters for an ignominious return to port when the fleet had finished operations. The motorboats set off on their prescribed sweep in the hope they might meet some ships of the enemy.

AM1 A.H. Gamble

At the beginning of 1917, I was sent to take over one of these blimps as engineer/observer. The crew consisted of three of us: wireless operator, pilot and me. We operated from near Milford Haven in South Wales and our work was mainly to patrol the Irish Sea, St George's Channel and the south coast of Ireland. A typical patrol was from St David's Head, across Cardigan Bay to Bardsey Island to Black Rock on the Wicklow Coast and down to Tuskar Rock on the extreme south-east corner of Ireland. From there, we went back across the Bristol Channel and homeward via Lundy Island. These patrols were carried out each day, except when fog or gales prevented them. The average daily patrol was from ten to fifteen hours per day. We used to welcome a change in this programme, especially when told off for escort duty. We would escort a convoy of merchant ships laden with valuable cargo for America, from Bristol Channel ports right out into the Atlantic, zig-zagging in front and then circling above the ships whilst naval surface craft patrolled on each flank. After leaving an outward convoy we would usually pick up American troopships and would escort them around the south of Ireland right up to Anglesey. This, of course, was not as dreary as patrol work. Patrolling at 400 feet when the visibility was good, we could survey easily fifty square miles out to sea so that you could keep your eye on surface craft to prevent them from being attacked.

On one occasion we were watching a tramp steamer making up the coast of Ireland about twenty-five miles distant when a German submarine appeared on the surface preparing to attack. It sighted us as we turned our nose towards it and before we could get within ten miles of it, it had dived below to the bottom. When we arrived over the spot some ten minutes later only large dirty patches where she had touched bottom were visible. Following the direction of the patches, we bombed in front of the foremost patch with no result. However, by signalling to various patrol craft, they managed to get a ring round the area. They located her with sounding apparatus and sank her in the early morning. On another patrol off the Cornwall coast we received a message of submarine activity in Mounts Bay. We patrolled the bay for some hours before spotting the wake of a periscope which soon disappeared. We dropped a bomb and managed to bring a quantity of oil to the surface, then signalled a motor lighter and led him over the target to put paid to it with three depth charges. Unfortunately we were unable to get a good view of the result as a heavy mist had been gathering, and to prevent getting a severe shaking from the explosions, we had to climb to 1,000 feet. We had been recalled to base two hours previously and, because of the mist and staying with the attack as long as possible, this made our journey back very tedious. We were practically snow blind, riding on the white crest of the clouds for three or four hours. Next day we received confirmation of the sinking of the submarine.

I think the most adventurous part of my life with the airship was spent in Ireland from early 1918 until about August of that year. We were sent across to near Wexford to make ourselves a nest of our own. In a huge park many trees had been felled and, instead of a shed, we tied the ship up in this avenue, the wood around being its only protection. To fill the petrol tanks I had to scale the trees on either side while the landing party pulled the ship over to me. Unable to get much gas sent over to us we had to wait until the sun shone on the envelope to swell the gas and give us lift before we could get out on patrol. In the cool of the evening, of course, when we returned to land we would be very heavy and landing was difficult. To assist us on our journey home one night, three German submarines gave us a good shelling. The cheeky bounders were only about two or three miles from Tuskar lighthouse and the lighthouse keeper watched them; needless to say we did not go for them because we were such good targets.

The only time we returned from Ireland would be to have a newly overhauled engine fitted, as these engines had to be replaced after 150 hours flying. It was on patrol from here that we bagged our second submarine near the Saltee Island, off Waterford harbour. We spotted a nice little oil track moving slowly on the surface and bombed just in front of it and holed her. We invited by signals an American destroyer to come over to us, which she did, and when she saw the objective proceeded to finish the job by dropping seventeen depth charges, and disturbing the ocean a bit with pieces of submarine and crew.

The envelope of the ship was fitted with a ripcord, by means of which one could rip open the gas bag and deflate it in case of emergency. Unfortunately, this emergency arose one night in Ireland. When a terrific gale sprang up suddenly and the ship was torn from the moorings, I had the painful necessity of scuttling her by this process. This resulted in packing up the damaged outfit and returning to Pembroke by tramp steamer. On arriving at Pembroke, I found out that out of six ships in commission there four had been condemned as unfit for flying. It had been discovered, happily without any casualties, that German agents had been working successfully to get at the aluminium dope with which the ships were treated, so that the fabric of the envelope had become rotten. I had only arrived a few moments before I was ordered to go temporarily to one of the two ships still in commission.

P. R. Masson

It is difficult to describe conditions in a storm at sea but one interlude is worth relating. The Gunnery Officer and I had just left the bridge to make for the wardroom and something to eat. The wardroom was right aft and all watertight bulkhead doors were shut so we had to make our way aft along the whole length of the deck. Lifelines were rigged – simply a rope running fore and aft with running bights to hang on to. We tossed up for positions and I won. The idea in tossing was that the winner could go last and the first man would get to the hatch, give a kick and by the time the second man arrived it would be just open so he could pop in with less chance of getting a wetting. We must have waited ten minutes while nearly every sea swept over the ship from the starboard side and poured over in great masses of green water. The chance came at last and off he went and I followed twenty yards behind. I saw a sea coming and stopped running and just hung on for my life.

When the sea had gone I saw his rope hanging free. I could not stay there so went aft and kicked on the hatch. While I was waiting for it to be opened I saw what looked like a bundle of old clothes hanging over a rail at the stem. I ran across and towed the bundle through the water left from the last wave. The hatch was just being shut again but it was soon re-opened and we bundled in. Beyond being breathless and knocked about the gunnery lieutenant was all right and had no idea what had happened. It was one of those cases where it was quite possible he had been washed overboard and back again.

Apart from the actual flying off, the stickiest part of our job was the landing conditions – we never really knew what we were going to get. One morning they flew me off very early and it turned out to be one of those sparkling mornings when it was a sheer joy to be alive. I soon found May Island, looking like a fairy island on a blue carpet with the whitewash of the coastguard station fairly glistening. Besides a keen appreciation of the upper world of my own I had a keen sense of anticipation regarding a good breakfast (and they were good at Turnhouse) and a day ashore before my ship came in late in the day. Even from May Island I could see that things might be awkward and my jubilant feelings were soon dampened. The whole of Edinburgh and the surrounding country was covered in a dense white woolly layer of morning fog which was surprisingly level. About six or eight feet of Arthur's Seat stood out like a rock in the sea. The tops of the cantilever of the Forth Bridge stood out in the same way. I flew up and down studying this grim situation. The hills in

Fifeshire offered a crash landing but no breakfast. There was petrol for about a quarter of an hour. I flew to and fro between the tip of Arthur's Seat and the Forth Bridge and once, within twenty feet or so of the rock, a soldier waved to me. I had landed at Turnhouse scores of times and so knew the relative positions well. Treating the matter like a chess problem, I made the best mental calculations I could, first of the direction and force of the wind and, secondly, of the exact point where I should enter the fog to just make the landing ground, gliding nearly a mile for every thousand feet. Having spent long enough on this little mathematical problem and knowing it was no good putting the matter off, I got into position, throttled down until the engine was just ticking over and nosed down, with my hand on the throttle ready to open out and zoom up if I saw anything ahead. I intended putting my wheels down if I saw grass below me and taking a chance on what I hit while slowing down. I got lower and lower. My altimeter showed that I was fifty feet underground and I knew something had to happen soon. Without warning I saw a hangar frame pass my wing tip a few feet away and knew I was near the ground so flattened out and to my complete astonishment heard my wheels running over frozen ground. It must have been one of the best landings I ever made and as I taxied back the hangars came into sight. The anticipation of breakfast came back full bore. Some of them referred to those oatcakes as congealed porridge but they never tasted better to me.

No doubt this account sounds as though it was a grand spree for the fleet in general and for us flying men in particular, but if the Germans would not come out there was nothing we could do about it. The fact that we were there mattered and, for us flying people, we may have had a lot to do with the end of the airship raids. Once they sent me off after an alleged enemy seaplane. It was a good day with ragged fleecy white clouds so that I could get my height quickly and unobserved. For a time I could see nothing in the air except these ragged clouds and the fleet through the holes now and again. Eventually, I saw two planes far below me and I thought 'Here's my chance and this is what you were trained for'. Taking advantage of all the bits of cloud I got near and dived down on to their tails with my thumbs on the gun triggers – all this according to the book. I even came down the sun so that they could not see me. Just as I was about to let go I saw with a cold chill that they were British and I was very annoyed with them about it at the time. We had always been told how important it was to keep a look out behind and I had a practical lesson that day. Although I flew up behind then and fifty feet away in formation, neither of them saw me although I stayed there for five minutes. Being much faster I meant to get some satisfaction out of the meeting so climbed to about 1,000 feet above them and ahead and dived down immediately ahead and had the satisfaction of seeing them sit up as though they had been bitten.

That time I had a bad time getting back. It may have been that dive but one of my cylinders cut out and a little later a second and a third. The rotary engines, with such a lot of weight revolving, had to be perfectly balanced. Each of the nine plugs at the head of each cylinder had to be perfectly matched for weight. My trouble was that the leads to the plugs came adrift – they were simply wires which led up from the centre behind each cylinder. In spite of the infernal racket and vibration I kept going because I had to. I could not make height but kept it much better than I expected. Coming in over the Bell Rock I studied it, not so much as a landing place, as there was nothing but the lighthouse on a rock, but with the idea of ditching close and swimming for it. However, when I saw the waves nearly going over the top of the lighthouse, that idea did not seem so good, so I kept on for the coast of Fife. Having got there, I thought I might as well see how far I could go, keeping a look out for landing places as I went along. I succeeded in getting all the way to Turnhouse, dodging across the Forth when it got narrower. They told me afterwards that the engine was nearly dropping out and every instrument was broken with the vibration. I knew about the instruments and was not really surprised about the engine. At that time they were rather strict about us landing at Donibristle and not Turnhouse when coming in from sea. If the machine had been fit to fly off they would not have said anything, but this one was not. I had to go before the CO over this as there was little excuse, especially when I had had to cross the Forth and go a little farther to reach Turnhouse. I simply told him there was a good breakfast at Turnhouse and nothing at Donibristle. I think he was pleased at my tribute; anyhow I heard no more about it.

AIRSHIP INCIDENT

By Wilfred E. Jones.

In October, 1917 I enlisted in the Royal Naval Air Service as an aircraftsman. After a preliminary training at the Crystal Palace and Fort Tregantle, Cornwall, I was drafted to one of the largest airship stations in the country, Goonhilly Downs, a dreary and desolate tract of unbroken land within a few miles of the Lizard and Land's End. The country is, for the most part, open and bare but about half a mile from the camp there are dense woods, admirably suited for the purpose of mooring out the smaller type of airship when no accommodation can be found for them in the main sheds.

On the night of 15 December 1917 I was one of a party of six detailed off as 'gas guard' to the airship SSZ 15. The weather for some time previously had been on its very worst behaviour and, consequently, the ground surrounding the woods was nothing more than a quagmire. The airship was positioned in a large hollow, six feet deep, to allow the car to rest in, leaving the envelope just above the surrounding ground. The pit was fully a foot deep in slimy, sticky mud, and it was no unusual thing to find one of your gumboots missing when walking or, rather, paddling through it. The two coxswains in charge arranged for us to work in watches, two hours on and two hours off. My companion and I took the first watch and everything went well, the pressure being maintained without any difficulty at all. Here I might add that the first and foremost duty of a 'gas guard' is to see that the air pressure in the envelope is maintained at a certain figure, registered by a clock-like instrument fixed in the car, known as a manometer. He is also responsible for the well-being of the airship, seeing that the guy-ropes are firmly secured to the trees, and that the car is well weighted down with ballast bags.

The method of keeping up the pressure is as follows: a small hand-blower is fixed some few yards away and connected to the envelope by means of a fabric hose twelve inches in diameter so that when the pressure is decreasing the blower is started, thus pumping air into the proper chambers inside the envelope which is duly registered by the manometer. We came off duty at 8.00pm, and tried to get 'forty winks' in our bell tent, but it was too cold to sleep, and we were not sorry when the time came to relieve our companions. All went well during the night, there being scarcely a breath of air, but towards three o'clock on the Sunday morning the sky became overcast and threatening and a slight breeze sprang up, which necessitated re-securing the guy ropes. Our fears and anxiety as to the condition of the weather were not without reason, and when my companion and I went on watch at 6.00am a stiff breeze was blowing which caused the ship to toss and roll about like a vessel in a stormy sea. In addition to this, the pressure was now going down very rapidly, which so alarmed the coxswains in charge that they decided to report matters to the duty officer at the camp. At first we put the decreasing pressure down to a leakage in the valves, but learned afterwards that the rolling of the ship had gradually torn a hole in the bow of the envelope – a fact which I was to be very thankful for, as the following events will show.

Before going, one of the coxswains said that one of us should sit in the car and keep an eye on the manometer continually, as the pressure was fluctuating so considerably, and also to make additional ballast. I agreed with my companion that he should work the blower some few yards away on the bank whilst I occupied the pilot's seat. I installed myself in the car, which was sunk down into the pit below the surface of the ground, but, what with the intense cold and wet (it was now raining steadily) and the continual rolling, dipping and plunging of the ship, my position was far from being an enviable one. But still worse was in store. Suddenly, without any preliminary warning, a terrific gale burst upon us. I learned afterwards that in scientific terms it was known as a 'cyclonic suction', blowing at over 60 miles an hour and its occurrence in this country is very uncommon. The first effect it had upon the airship was to uproot the car and dash it wildly against the sides of the pit, which were luckily in an extremely soft and muddy condition, thus leaving the sides of the car undamaged.

Almost simultaneously she shook herself like huge dog and shot upwards, ripping the guy-rope attachments off the side of the envelope like paper. Imagine, if you can, my horror. Here was I, quite a novice of the service, alone in an uncontrollable leviathan of the air, and absolutely helpless. I raised myself from the bottom of the car, where I had been thrown after the first jolt, and looked over the side. Never to my dying day shall I forget the sickening sensation that went through my whole system. It was still dark and raining very heavily, so that I had great difficulty in discerning my position. A terrific crackling and tearing told me that we were dragging our way through the trees. No sooner were we clear of the branches than another sudden gust caught us in its grip, and the next minute we were dashing headlong for the ground. The realisation of this proved too much for me and I swooned off into unconsciousness. I have a very faint recollection of feeling a terrific thud (probably caused by the car striking the ground, mercifully without exploding the two 100lb bombs with which she was armed), and the next minute I found myself thrown into the mud, clear of the car.

My mind was in a very confused state, but it did not take me long to decide to get away from the wreckage. I struggled to rise but could not, as when I was thrown out of the car I had caught my legs and feet in the wire suspensions, and was now held captive by the monster. Misfortunes never come singly, and in a few seconds the gale again increased in fury causing the airship to career off wildly across the open ground, dragging me with it. Over and over I was tossed like a cork in a raging storm, helpless. The terrific thuds and bumps as I came in contact with the ground were something cruel, nearly driving me to distraction.

Never in all my life shall I forget that journey. Every now and again I would find myself engulfed in the folds of the envelope, and to this day I still have a remembrance of the horrible stench of the stale gas in my nostrils. Gradually I could feel my strength ebbing away, and I felt that surely the end must come soon. Trivial incidents during my youthful career came crowding through my brain with hideous distinctness and rapidity. I could even picture the salvage party from the camp hunting about among the wreckage for my mutilated remains. I felt myself floating away into space, where, I knew not. A sudden gust of gas from the envelope overwhelmed me, and I remembered no more. When I regained consciousness I found myself lying on my back in a field, and upon looking round I could see, although but dimly, my late captor, some hundred yards distant, being carried away rapidly with the wind. My thankfulness knew no bounds; at last I was free. Although these happenings could only have occupied a few minutes, to me it seemed a veritable lifetime. I tried to get up on to my feet, but stumbled down again, the very effort causing me excruciating pain. I lay still for a few minutes trying to collect my scattered wits, but my brain was in a hopeless jumble and I could scarcely bear to think. Eventually, I managed to get up, and tried as well as I possibly could to crawl away from the scene of my misfortune.

Truly I was in a pitiable condition. What with my clothes badly torn, my face and head bruised, and caked all over with mud; I must have cut a grotesque figure. I would have rivalled a scarecrow of the most ragged order. I felt numb and stiff in every joint, and could have sworn that every bone in my body was broken, but a rough survey soon eased my mind considerably on that score.

It was now pouring in torrents, so I commenced to make my way, feeling more dead than alive, towards a light that I could faintly see in the distance, and great was my joy when I discovered that it belonged to my fellow gas guard. Never was a meeting more hearty and welcome. He had seen the ship become uprooted from the pit and carried away on the wind, and had immediately secured a lantern and followed in the same direction, as he jokingly said, 'to pick up the pieces'. With his very necessary assistance, I eventually succeeded in reaching the camp and was very quickly installed in hospital.

The other gas guards had given notice of the unfortunate happenings, so that things were prepared for our arrival. I was sobbing and trembling all over as though

I had the ague, and the hospital orderly told me afterwards that my language almost set their water afire. I was cleaned up and fitted out with dry clothes, so that by the time the doctor arrived on the scene I was feeling slightly better. He was a thorough hard-headed Englishman, not easily roused as a rule, but I shall never forget the excited way in which he subjected me to a most careful and minute examination. He could scarcely believe it possible for anyone to have undergone the knocking about that I had and still be alive, or at least sound in wind and limb.

He prescribed absolute rest and no food of any description for a few hours. But I am afraid that the former part of his prescription was not strictly adhered to, because I received visits during the morning from all of the officers on the station, and they made me feel as though I had done something great. To me it was not a case of having done something – it was a case of having been sadly done.

Later on in the day I was able to leave the hospital looking a perfect study in bandages and, a few weeks later, save for feeling a bit shaky, had completely recovered from the shock, though the sight of an airship even now sends a shudder through me, as I recall that awful experience.

C. P. Bristow

The day after I got to Westgate, I was told by the CO to get more familiar with Short seaplanes and to take up one of the older ones and practise taking off and landing in the local environment. He also ordered one of the petty officers to come with me to gain experience as an observer. There was a strong breeze and a choppy sea, which made takeoff a bit easier, but landing more difficult. We made three circuits, taking off towards the shore and turning out to sea for three or four miles, before heading back to land for the descent. I timed this for touch-down about half a mile out, in order to give sufficient distance from the shore for the next take-off. On the fourth time the floats hit the wave tops and we started to slow down and settle when, suddenly, the fuselage turned over and the slowly revolving propeller scythed off the fronts of the floats, and we came to rest with the tail right up behind. I told my passenger to get out quickly and move on to the rear of one of the floats to counterbalance the weight of the engine, and I did the same on the other float. As we had lost the buoyancy of the front of the floats, it was only the rear three compartments that were keeping us afloat and I was concerned that the fuselage might turn right over and then we would slowly sink. Fortunately, the station motor launch was not far away and, in about five minutes, appeared alongside and took us off. I tried to get them to get a line up to the tail and so pull it down and stop the body turning right over and becoming waterlogged. But this proved impossible, and when the wreck was taken in tow it did eventually turn over. The only way to salvage it was to lift it out of the water, which was quite impossible for our small launch. Help was summoned from a naval vessel lying off Margate and this came to the rescue, lifting our wreck out of the sea by crane. It was eventually delivered to the air station as a complete write-off, with only the engine and a few other components salvaged.

This was my one and only crash and I suspect that there was a weakness in the two front struts, which failed due to the bumping on the rough sea. I reported to the CO immediately I got ashore and he took it very mildly, asking for a full report in writing. After that my new colleagues were very sympathetic and no-one seemed to blame me for the accident as they could all imagine what it would have been like had the engine failed far out to sea. Regardless of the accident, I was detailed at once to take my turn in patrolling, fully armed, over our area of operations.

Life was not arduous at Westgate and discipline was light. When not flying, we had to stand by on the station in case more seaplanes needed to be launched. If the weather was bad and flying not possible, we could sometimes get into Margate, which was about three miles to the east. We got there by train or bus, or occasionally walked if feeling energetic enough. The theatre there kept going throughout the war, and sometimes we went to evening performances. During the winter months Westgate Town Hall staged dances for the locals twice a week in a small ballroom, and a few of us enjoyed going to these. There was a good local dance band and we all joined in the traditional dances, the Lancers, military-two-step, the veleta, waltzes and many others. Inevitably we got to know some of the local residents and found them friendly, but careful of their young daughters. On occasion we went over to Cliftonville, where the largest hotel sometimes arranged dances. Alternatively, on non-flying days, we sometimes raised a couple of teams to play football, or even did some cross-country running.

The White Ensign was hoisted and lowered each day with the appropriate bugle accompaniment, as in all Naval establishments. If we were caught out in the open during this ceremony, we had to freeze to attention and salute, but if possible we dashed for cover to avoid it. The amalgamation of the RNAS and the RFC, forming the new RAF, took place on 1 April 1918, but both services continued much as before, in their own uniforms and traditions but mixing some personnel. Ranks were changed to the new ones gradually and new uniforms in khaki were chosen and made up as the existing navy and army styles wore out and were replaced. I ordered a new khaki RAF tunic and trousers from Gieves, but only wore them occasionally, continuing to wear my original naval uniform when flying.

We were always conscious of the menace of the German seaplane base on the Belgian coast near Zeebrugge. They were equipped with monoplane seaplane fighters, which although faster, were not so seaworthy as ours, but their greater speed gave them the advantage in any conflict as our station knew to its cost through losing two seaplanes in combat. So we generally patrolled in pairs, accompanied by two fighters from Manston air station. These flew above us, weaving about trying to reduce their speed to our slower pace. They didn't like this duty much and shot off home on return when in sight of land, their endurance being only half of ours, so petrol would have been low by that time. There were a few occasions when, by careful collaboration and timing with Felixstowe, our patrols met out at sea and made a sweep together over our area. This was primarily to make a show of strength to the Germans, either visually or through them hearing our wireless. On one occasion my observer gave me the headphones, saying 'listen to this', and I heard a lot of chatter in German. Speech on the wireless was at that time in the experimental stage, our communication being always in Morse code.

We didn't fly very high, usually at about 1,000 feet, so it was not necessary to wear warm clothing. I always wore my monkey jacket and leather helmet, over which I put on a collapsed lifejacket, which could be inflated instantly by pressing a lever on a miniature air bottle inside. I sometimes wore goggles, but these were not often needed because, in the front cockpit behind the massive engine and radiator, the full force of the slip-stream was not felt. I had to lean right or left to see straight ahead, but that was only necessary when taking off or landing. On patrol I was usually looking around or downwards to identify any sea or land marks and to check my compass course.

Our operational area covered the southern North Sea up to Shipwash, and east to Belgium as far as Sandettie, together with the Thames approaches and the Strait of Dover. Duties on patrol were primarily to search for German submarines or mines. On one occasion I went far towards Belgium, back to Suffolk down the shipping channels and out again to the open sea for four and a half hours before turning back to Westgate, getting back with little petrol left and an enormous appetite. I always carried a chart of the southern North Sea and the Dover Straits in a frame, a watch, a bottle of water and a haversack containing a tin of pemmican and some chocolate, in case of having to come down in the sea and being adrift for some time. The observer, sitting behind, had his headphones, a book of call signs and pencil and paper for recording messages. Importantly, he also carried a small plywood box holding two pigeons for emergency messages.

Flight Lieutenant F. J. Rutland

I think the story of the sinking of the *Warrior* should be included here, because it was here I performed the act for which I was awarded the Gold Albert Medal, and although my family knows I have this, I am sure they are hazy about the episode.

I can start by saying that at no time was I in any danger, but here is the story. On the evening of 31 May, *Warrior* having come through the mist, found herself, together with her sister ships, within 500 yards of the enemy battle-cruisers. These ships opened fire at point blank range, and literally blew the flagship, HMS *Defence*, out of the water. Fortunately, at this moment, the *Warspite*, one of our latest and finest battleships, was struck aft, and her steering gear was temporarily put out of action, with the result that she came around in a large circle which carried her between *Warrior* and the enemy, effectively masking their fire, but not before *Warrior* had sustained many casualties, and was on fire in several places. The enemy again disappeared and, in poor visibility and confusion, the *Warrior* came out to the westward and met the *Engadine*. As we now had no duties, we asked if we could be of assistance, and were told to stand by her. Later we took her in tow, the weather got bad during the night and the stem of *Warrior* sank lower in the water as each hour passed. At daybreak it was decided that she could not possibly reach port and preparations were made to abandon her, and take off her officers and ship's company. It looked as though we were too late, as there was now a fair sea running.

HMS *Engadine* was a cross-channel steamer and was fitted with huge rubbing strakes all round the hull, to facilitate going alongside jetties. Without these we could not have stayed alongside for the period necessary to take on board her 900-odd persons. The crew lined up as though at drill, thought that they would have to swim for it, and discarded pieces of shell that they intended to keep as souvenirs. We got alongside by a superb piece of seamanship, and the order was given to abandon ship. Our officers and men lined the ship and grabbed each man as he came across, until he was safely inboard. Because of the large numbers, on so small a ship as ours, it was decided to get all able-bodied personnel first, and send them below decks, thus leaving the decks clear for the wounded. Each ship had put out all the fenders they could muster, and a great many of these were hazelwood, bundles of sticks wired together. These were mostly broken up by the working of the two ships together, davits having been sheered from their supports, and we were holed in several places, though all the holes were small. The noise of rending steel was terrific and only orders shouted in your ears could be distinguished.

The wounded were passed over, six at a time. Practically the last stretcher was being passed over when the wounded man in it slipped out of the side and fell between the two ships. I was a few yards away and at the same time two officers and the captain of *Warrior* were passing to *Engadine*. Several officers and men jumped on the netting or bulwarks as though to go down after him, and the Captain at once shouted an order, 'No one is to go over'. I looked down, and realised that no one even intended doing so; such a feat was impossible. The poor fellow had fallen through the gap between the rubbing strakes and the *Warrior*, this gap being open at the moment, preparatory to the ship taking another charge at the *Warrior*. The man was supported by the broken hazelwood. I decided it would be a matter of seconds before he would sink through them, and decided that nothing could be done.

I went on for a few moments helping the wounded, but then found that the poor fellow, though still between the ships, had come far enough forward to be rescued without real risk. Two men had put a bowline in a piece of rope, and were trying to lasso him. As he was three feet below the rubbing strake, the ship's side could not touch him, so he had escaped injury. I had the position weighed up in a second. I ordered several men to hold the rope, slid down it, and then swam to the man and brought him to the rope, put myself in the bowline and, holding him my arms, told them to hoist away.

We were nearly to the deck when I saw the hawser that was holding the bow being paid out and cutting across my lifeline. I saw the wire cutting though my rope and, looking at my unconscious man, I thought, sorry me lad, we've got another dip coming. I apparently had the same habit then as later, for I spoke my thought aloud and many people heard me. Old Hancock, the captain of the ship in peacetime, was serving as a lieutenant RNR. Seeing my predicament, he put the engines ahead, and told the captain, 'Rutland's over the side'.

Two minutes later we were aboard and the ship was clear. I had calculated everything except the hawser, and I am still mystified as to how my 'lifeline' got between the hawser and the ship but, of course, I had no hand in placing it as it was already in position when I arrived. After all that trouble the poor fellow died of his wounds. Apparently it was known that he only had a short time to live.

We proceeded to Rosyth where we had been reported sunk. The *Lion* had seen us on her beam, until the melee which surrounded *Warrior*, and thought we had got mixed up in it too. We landed our wounded and later our *Warrior*'s ship's company and the many men who had died. The captain made a speech on the dockside and it was not until then I found anyone had taken notice of my rescue. The captain gave me such a boost that I became embarrassed. Sometime later I received the Gold Albert Medal, for this, and the DSC for my flight at Jutland. I looked up the Navy List and found no man living held the Gold Medal. Fewer than twenty had been awarded the Bronze Albert Medal and approximately three or four the Gold medal posthumously. I was indeed awed. The only point I want you to remember is everyone had come through a great battle and the reaction had set in. On top of that their ship had sunk. Under such conditions, it is no wonder that my act was to receive such recommendation and reward.

Flight Lieutenant S. D. Culley

Soon after dawn the crew of the Camel lighter went aboard from the destroyer and quickly had everything prepared in the event of the usual patrolling Zeppelin putting in an appearance to see what this rather large assembly of ships was up to. It is not therefore very surprising when the flagship received a message from the Admiralty about 8.00am to the effect that an airship was cruising somewhere in the vicinity of the Bight of Heligoland, and they should keep a lookout for it. The crew on the lighter were duly alerted and, from then on, everyone throughout the fleet was scanning the skies to find the hoped-for victim of the new weapon

At about 8.30, Culley suddenly saw the Zeppelin in the sky at a great height – estimated then to be about 10,000 feet. After that things moved very quickly but with absolute precision under the calm direction of Colonel Samson in the lighter and Commander Holt in HMS *Redoubt*. Soon the lighter was approaching full speed, and with Culley already in the cockpit, the extremely tricky operation of starting the engine by means of swinging the propeller by hand was undertaken. The airman who had been appointed for this work was a magnificent type of man, tall and powerful and absolutely calm. He was fitted with a special belt around his waist, which was anchored to the deck at a point which just permitted him to reach the propeller. He performed this operation with a 30 knot wind in his back as though nothing exceptional at all, and as soon as the engine started he carefully pulled himself back by the anchor cord, unclipped the hook and disappeared below the deck, leaving now only Colonel Samson visible with his head just showing to give the pilot of the all clear signal when he was completely satisfied that the aircraft could take off.

Culley then pulled the release fitted in the cockpit of the Camel and after a run forward of less than five feet the Camel literally leapt into the air and was safely launched. The time was precisely 8.41. The weather was perfect and the excitement was intense throughout the whole of the Harwich Force. It was equal to the excitement of a Cup final at Wembley. As the sole actor and reporter in the operation we shall have to leave the narrative now to the pilot Culley to describe.

Before I pulled the quick release toggle in the cockpit of Camel N 6812, I had of course pushed the throttle forward to give maximum revolutions. With the release, the thrust one felt was quite considerable and it is perhaps more correct to say that the Camel took itself off rather than I did. Within a few seconds I found myself over the superstructure of HMS *Redoubt*, which was towing the lighter by a line of some 600 fathoms long. I was therefore well satisfied that the engine was giving me its best for climbing. It was a fine sight to see the rest of the fleet spread over the water below, but my anxiety was to find the Zeppelin again, for it had been some minutes since I'd last sighted it. I was fortunate in picking it up very quickly and from then on my eyes hardly left it, except for brief glances at the instruments to ascertain height, direction and the behaviour of the engine.

The Zeppelin appeared to be very high indeed, and still the size as when I first observed, which was about the size of one's little finger. I surmised therefore when I reached about 5,000 feet, that she had started to climb quickly, and this was bad news to me for she belonged to the very latest type of Zeppelin in a class known as the 'Height Climbing 50s' which were reputed to be able to out-climb any aircraft then available in the Allied forces. However, there was nothing for it but to continue to climb as fast as possible, always in the direction in which the Zeppelin appeared to be moving. There was no question of trying to make an interception as one could not make any attempt to work out a plot. So I climbed 12,000 and 15,000 feet and already I could feel the little Camel beginning to be sluggish on its controls, indicating that it was feeding the height. At one moment the engine coughed, and this change in the rhythm of its song had an immediate reaction in my heart. However, it went on again beautifully and never again gave rise for any worry.

Finally, when I was about 18,000 feet I realised I was getting very much more on a level with the Zeppelin and I then saw that it was changing course and it appeared to be turning out to sea again, after having been cruising east more or less towards its base in Germany. I therefore turned after it, somewhat depressed, for I realised that at that height I would have little or no speed advantage and almost certainly it would escape. But fortunately I'd made a mistake and it was not long before I realised that the Zeppelin had turned directly towards me and I was then almost at the same level. With a relative speed of over 120 knots, it was not long before the few miles which is separated us was reduced to nothing and I saw that I should meet the aircraft head on with it a few hundred feet above me. I had been given strict instructions in writing by Colonel Samson that I must climb above the airship and dive on it in attacking as there was practically no defence from above.

But it was obviously now or never, and in a few seconds I had the huge bulk of the Zeppelin looming ahead of me. I could see the control car and the engine gondolas with their propellers turning, and I pulled the small Camel back into an almost stalled position and, as the Zeppelin came over me, I pulled the trigger of the two Lewis guns on the top plane and heard them rattle off their charges. As I passed under the belly of the airship I saw a large dark object drop and disappear below, but of course there was no possibility of following it. It was probably the only survivor of the Zeppelin, who was reported later as having been picked up by German search vessels, having descended the 19,000 feet by parachute – certainly a record for those days.

After the guns ceased to fire, the little Camel fell away completely stalled and out of control. There was absolutely no possibility of watching the airship and I had to devote the whole of my attention to bringing the aircraft out of the spin into which it had fallen. This took several thousand feet. Finally I had it on an even keel and looked back to see the airship sailing along majestically as though nothing had happened at all. I was about to turn again to my controls when suddenly, at three widely dispersed points, there was a burst of pure flame. Within a minute at the most the whole of the airship except for the tail portion was a mass of flames, which died out almost as quickly as they appeared and the great metal skeleton framework with the smoking, but not burnt out, tail part still with the flag flying, dropped rapidly in one piece but with the back of the skeleton broken about one third of the distance from the nose. The great airship L.53 disappeared below into the haze taking with it over 30 German crew. The time, I was told later, was 9.41, just one hour after I taken off from the lighter.

After seeing the complete destruction of the airship, I realised that this would not be a very healthy place to be in, for certainly the German monoplane seaplanes, which had a very good performance, would be in the vicinity soon, so I again put on full throttle and descending fairly rapidly I flew more or less west well out to sea but parallel with the Dutch coast, which I could see dimly to port. I knew I was getting fairly short of petrol, and must of course have used more than normally, for the engine had been at full throttle for over an hour. I began therefore to think about where I might end up in the event of not finding the fleet again at the rendezvous near Texel lightship which had been hurriedly arranged before my departure. I had not, perhaps strange to say, a good map with me, but only a very small scale atlas map which I had torn out of some book and which showed up on one small page the whole of the Dutch coast from the German border to Belgium. I had been able to make a rough mark on the map as to where Texel lightship should be and as I began to pick up points of the Dutch coast from height of 5,000 feet at which I was now cruising, I realised I must turn out to sea. I was somewhat comforted by seeing quite a number of, presumably Dutch, fishing boats on the water, but out to sea there was a complete cover of a very thin but effective veil of mist which prevented me seeing anything at an angle. As I turned out to sea, my engine stopped and I knew then that I had used the whole of my petrol in the main tank and I had only a few gallons in a small reserve tank left. I therefore throttled down to the minimum revolutions in order to keep airborne as long as possible. Shortly after this, I saw what appeared to be two very much larger fishing boats further out to sea, and I thought they might perhaps be Dutch naval ships, so I made for them descending the whole time. In a few moments I entered the very thin veil of mist and emerging found that the two fishing boats were in fact destroyers and I suddenly saw the whole of Harwich Force steaming in perfect order.

Phillips William Norman St Clare

Several hours after leaving London and after much juggling with trains and names, Jones and myself found ourselves covering the last lap of our train journey and finally alighted on to the platform of a quaint old country station of Helston, Cornwall. Here, a Crossley Tender labelled 'R.N. MULLION' picked us up and tore off along country lanes before we had time to take stock of the town at all. It was only a matter of minutes before we turned into a lane scarcely wide enough for the vehicle itself, and finally past a sentry box to the Admiralty Road and so to the air station. Mullion aerodrome is situated in a central position on the Lizard, that massive promontory of hard even ground which forms the heel of the Cornish boot. A few miles west of it is the village of Mullion, half a mile or so inland from the sea. Helston, the largest accessible place of importance, is seven miles due north. Thus the aerodrome was more or less isolated from outside interference and, being on an absolutely flat expanse of land, was in an ideal situation as regards landing operations.

The first object which met the eye of new arrivals was the massive airship shed towering high above everything else at one side of the camp. This was the second shed erected here, the first having been blown down by a gale, steel girders collapsing like matchsticks before a perfect hurricane. As is generally the rule, all the workshops lay at the base of the shed. Between those and the officers' quarters was the parade ground and quarterdeck, boasting a tall mast and flaunting the White Ensign over all. A little distance from all this was the gate by which we entered, the guardroom and garage, Petty Officers' hut and messroom, the men's messroom and huts and, lastly, the canteen. The personnel of the station was about seventy all told, all skilled workmen, among whom were included Messrs Ellis and Russell, old Talbot Boys to whom we were handed over to be made comfortable.

We had some opportunity during this period of finding out a few things about the neighbouring country and one evening decided to walk to Mullion and have a look round. The first sign of habitation we discovered was the village of Cury, just a scattered array of thatched cottages and farms. From here we followed our guide along some of the most delightful country lanes and eventually landed at Mullion village. It was a typical Cornish village of one main street with two or three cobbled alleys leading off. A few modern houses intermingled with rose-covered cottages made an alluring picture. There are two churches, a school, an inn and a temperance hotel with accommodation for summer visitors, quite a few of whom choose this ideal quiet spot for a perfect rest.

Ellis and Russell were old friends of ours, birds of a feather in fact, for we four had been punished together one evening for playing billiards instead of doing duty watch. We soon learnt from them just how matters stood. Russell was the only man flying owing to Ellis's ship having come to grief a few days before our arrival and being now in the process of re-rigging. The two ships were Coastal No. 10, still flying, and Coastal No. 9, out of commission. Coastal No. 8 had started off from Kingsnorth to fly around the coast to Mullion, but half way had met trouble of some nature and come down at sea, only the wireless operator being picked up from the wreckage alive. England had, in those days, a lot to learn about lighter-than-air craft. While Russell was in the air, Ellis who was in charge, kept a W/T watch in the wireless station they had jointly erected. The two ships had never flown at the same time owing to the shortage of wireless personnel, to which we were a welcome addition. The duties of the aircraft at that time were to search around for mines and report anything out of the usual they happened to see. They had no fixed patrol but worked in conjunction with two destroyers, HMSs *Boyne* and *Foyle,* in touring around the coast and as far out to sea as they thought convenient, altogether a not very exciting outlook. The usual method of procedure when a ship was to fly was to call up the duty destroyer and inform her of the fact, about two hours before the ascent. The wireless station being at that time only a rough affair, this made it necessary for most messages to and from airship and station to be sent via the destroyer, great satisfaction ensuing should a message be sent and received direct. The airship wireless supplied was a Type 52 (about 40 watt) set with a range of fifty-sixty miles. Its short range was mainly responsible for the difficulty in reception of signals. A 350-watt Marconi, quite a powerful set, was provided as auxiliary, but was more often than not useless owing to the difficulty in starting the engine in the intensely cold air. Thus the *Boyne* and *Foyle* met with a lot of extra work much to everyone's annoyance. Seven or eight hours in the air without landing was thought quite a long patrol at this period of the war, giving sufficient time for the aircraft to have a general look round the vicinity and return before dark. Nothing seemed to be done in a very business-like manner as far as flying was concerned, which we were told was due to the strange views held by the CO, a major in the Army, who had little faith in the usefulness of the craft.

Owing to the shortage of men in the wireless department, no watch had been kept when there were no ships in the air, but the advent of Jones and myself allowed of a better business footing. Ellis, a very capable man to be in charge, immediately mapped out our duties. Coastal 9 would be flying again in a few days and then both ships would be on patrol at once. On non-flying days we all four took a turn at wireless watch from six in the morning until six at night. The last on duty at night had also to take the press news at midnight. On flying days Jones and I did the land watch between us until the ships had both landed. In the event of an emergency flight after both Russell and Ellis had flown then either Jones or I undertook it to give them a rest, and also to generally act as relief operators on the ships.

All this was put into operation at once, and everything went as well as could be expected. Non-flying days were quite a bore, watch having to be kept on the wavelength used by aircraft and very few messages were heard, none directed to us. A few merchant ships (using a higher wavelength) would jam through effectively when they sent in our vicinity, but on the whole there was very little doing. It took but a very little while to get fed up with this sort of thing and we all hoped it would not last long.

The coastal or coastal patrol airships were at that time about the best known type of non-rigid airship. The envelope or gas container was of a capacity of 170,000 cubic feet and to this huge balloon was slung a gondola to seat five men. This gondola was by no means a strong or comfortable affair, being nothing but a framework of wooden stays and wire suspension covered over with canvas. A top cover of three-ply wood divided into five sections supplied the different compartments as follows: coxswain, pilot, second officer, wireless operator, engineer. The second officer acted as observer when flying, but as he was seldom taken, the brunt of his work fell on the wireless operator.

An engine was fitted at either end of the car. As a general rule they were a 220hp Renault aft and a 100hp Berliet forward. Communication between one seat and another was made either by walking along the top of the car, an exceedingly dangerous business, or sliding along a two-inch rail at its base, holding on to any part of the car which would hold your weight and prevent you from falling into space. This equally exciting method of taking a walk becomes mere child's play with practice. These airships could carry one 230lb bomb and four or five 100lb bombs, although considerably more was managed on some occasions. They were, moreover, fitted with two Lewis machine guns on the gondola and one was sometimes on top of the gas chamber, reached by a shaft through the envelope.

August 1917 was a red letter month for both Russell and me, for it was during this month, and just a year since my arrival, that we both received the news that we were to take over ships and begin flying. It was well worth the long wait for we were exceptionally fortunate in being chosen for this commission. Both the ships to which we were allotted were of an entirely new type but recently invented and expected to prove wonderful buses. Long before their arrival, rumours began to drift through of the supposed capabilities and everyone on the station was highly excited awaiting their advent.

Russell's arrived first in sections and the riggers were set to work on her erection. Being the first of a new type to be erected on the station she took quite a fortnight to rig, this being rather a long time for a non-rigid airship. My own bus arrived later and practically completed her erection within a few hours of the former. The airships we saw gradually gaining semblance in our sheds well offered to bear out all that was said of them.

They were given the name of SS Zeros, as they were really a glorified edition of the SS (Submarine Scouting) airships, which had proved so efficient an addition to the aerial Navy up to this time. They differed greatly from the airships already at Mullion, being of a smaller capacity and seating three instead of five. They also differed from their mother type the SS. The envelope held 70,000 cubic feet of gas and was pear-shaped or streamlined. On the sides of this envelope were slung two huge petrol tanks. The gondola, or car, was of entirely different construction to anything hitherto invented, being nothing less than a long narrow boat, fourteen-feet long by twenty-two feet in width, curving off to a point at the front and rounded astern, evidently designed for working on the water, a thing unheard of at the time. The car was strongly built of three-ply wood and fitted with a copper keel. There were three seats, the wireless operator forward, the pilot amidships and the engineer aft just before the engine. The engine selected was a 75hp Rolls Royce driving a four-bladed propeller.

It really was amazing the amount of gear carried in or about the car. The engineer's seat was a stool, underneath which were divers accumulators and tool bags. Either side were mounted a Lewis automatic machine gun, though one of these was afterwards substituted by a drift meter when dual control was fitted. Then there were various engine switches and lighting set. To overhaul the engine whilst in the air, the engineer was compelled to climb out on a rail projected from the side of the seat, gaining further support by leaning on suspension wires. On this rail, and a similar one on the other side, were bomb racks. Two more bomb racks were slung between his seat and that of the pilot amidships. This seat was a conglomeration of the wheels, switches and meters all necessary for the proper propulsion of the craft. Then came a locker which was afterwards utilised for more instruments and then came my own seat in front. Underneath the padded seat was a battery box containing four Fullers block accumulators for the transmitter, an additional one for the receiver, one for the ship's lighting, and one large one for the flash lamp. One side of the seat held a large sachet for carrying my code books and the other side held a revolver and a battery of Very light cartridges of various colours. Above these were lighting switches. A Lewis gun was mounted on one side and a camera on the other. From a bar in front of the seat there arose a signal halliard ending somewhere up near one petrol tank. To this bar was also affixed a writing desk for taking down messages, several lights and a compass. Two huge bulls eyes, red and green, were mounted on their proper sides of the vessel and a white one astern. These were also under my control. Further in the bows were slung a wireless transmitter, a receiver, a pair of relays and all their various switches. Either side of these were fixed two aerial wheels containing a wireless aerial several hundred feet in length on one side and an auxiliary on the other. The wire descended through an ebonite tube to the underneath part of the car to where it was attached to a heavy lead weight. By an arrangement of wheels in my seat this could be lowered or wound in at will.

This made the seat nearly full but room was still found for eight large size pans of ammunition for the guns. After I had taken my seat and tightened myself in with several lead covered code books, room still had to be found for a box of camera slides (half plate) a large signal flash lamp, a full complement of Naval and international signal flags, a book of signals to use with same, a pair of semaphore flags, thermos flask, food and numerous other things. It was a full house I can assure you.

AM1 A.H. Gamble

It was during the first week with this ship that I experienced the hardest tussle with a gale. We were well out into the Irish Sea when we were recalled to base, but the gale was on us very quickly. We headed into it on our homeward journey and had a stern struggle to round the rocks off St David's head. Struggling in between the gusts we swayed to and fro from the towering rocks 800 feet high and it was only by turning our nose dead into wind that, yard by yard, we crept away. Slowly we battled on into St Bride's Bay but whilst there the gale was so intense we could hardly make one knot. The pilot became alarmed and wirelessed for a landing party to be sent out in lorries to intercept us. After still struggling on, the gale changed direction slightly and we drifted broadside at terrific speed over the aerodrome. Then came the excitement of landing. We had numerous attempts to get down. In one attempt the trail rope got looped up. After freeing it on our ninth attempt, the landing party, which included every available man on the station, pulled on the rope, and eventually brought us down with a crash, in which fortunately we only received a severe shaking.

For this gallant work the skipper received the DFC and for his perilous work of freeing the rope the wireless operator received the DFM. I was told, as soon as I had had a meal, to go and examine the engine and clean the plugs etc., and refill the petrol tanks for the next day's flight. However, I was glad when my old ship was re-commissioned and we sped back again to Ireland, to take up our duties there afresh. Considering the amount of flying I took part in, from 3,000 to 3,500 flying hours with these ships, I would like to pay high tribute to British aircraft engineers, for the performance of the engines that came under my care. The defects that occurred in flight were remarkably few, beyond a few sooty plugs and one or two magneto defects. The only real trouble experienced was when a bottom water joint gave out one Sunday morning over the Bristol Channel. To repair this we had to descend to the surface. We alighted on a choppy sea while I proceeded to make up the damaged joint. Whilst I was doing this a patrol boat, which had been standing by us, lowered a dinghy and rowed to our assistance. The sailors rowed with such gusto that they nearly cut us in half! After filling the radiator with sea water, drawn by a canvas bucket which we carried, we then prepared to ascend again. After bailing out the waterlogged car, and throwing out all ballast we found we were still too heavy to lift, as we had to valve gas to descend to the surface. The only thing left to lighten the ship was to drop one of the 230lb bombs into the sea with the safety catch set at safe. This we did and, to ensure its safety, I tied my handkerchief around the safety vane. As we rose from the surface I gazed after the departing bomb with mixed feelings, but nothing happened and we joyfully ascended to resume our patrol.

To carry out repairs on an engine whilst in flight one had to clamber out on a two-inch rail, and to be able to work with two hands one had to rope oneself to the engine struts, for if your feet slipped into the sea you would go. I mentioned a canvas bucket; this had three hundred feet of line attached and it afforded us many a fine bit of sport. We used to fish with it; when I say fish I mean that we would hover round a fishing smack, drop the basket and it would be filled up with some nice fresh caught fish for the ship's crew breakfast the next morning. We once hovered over farmsteads on Bardsey Island and all the villagers came to view us. We put half a crown and a note in the bucket for some eggs, lowered the bucket and had it filled up with some nice fresh eggs. Unfortunately, when hauling the eggs the wireless operator loosened a small fire extinguisher from the side of the car, and it fell among the folk on to a dog's back and killed it. The fishing afforded a little diversion from otherwise tedious patrol duties. It was a glorious life, healthy, and adventurous, and I was pleased to have been able to serve my country in such a manner.

S. D. Culley

Moments later I was diving on HMS *Redoubt*, which I could see was already stopping, putting the lighter crew on board, and preparing a small rowing boat for my reception when I dropped into the water. While this was going on I paid a visit to the ships of the rest of the fleet hoping that my petrol would last. Thanks to the great efficiency of Commander Holt and the ship's company, I was very soon making my landing approach and dropped into the sea almost literally in the arms of the whaler's crew. The aircraft was of course somewhat damaged about the wings but did not sink and by means of the collapsible derrick (which had been designed for the purpose) the faithful little Camel N6812 was hoisted aboard the lighter and brought safely back to Britain. It is now in retirement in the Imperial War Museum in London, having been selected to be a permanent record of the famous Camel which brought such destruction to the enemy air force, and ground forces also, on many fronts in the First World War. And so I was able to play my part in this most excellent example of a combined operation between the Royal Navy and the very newly born Royal Air Force, which had been in existence for just over four months.

While Cully was airborne Harwich Force continued on its naval sweep, unfortunately without the help of the flying boats as scouts, and dependent only on what information can be obtained by the CMBs. But no enemy naval ships were encountered and soon the CMBs had returned and been picked up by the fleet ready for the return to the rendezvous fixed for the Camel. Naturally, every man above decks kept a lookout in the heavens as well as on the surface of the sea and, as time went on and nothing was seen, it is natural that some anxiety was felt. However, in due course the great flame in the sky was observed by the fleet and a cheer went up as it was felt certain that the flame could only have meant that the Zeppelin had been destroyed.

When Admiral Tyrwhitt saw the flash in the sky he turned to the officer of the watch and asked 'Who is here who knows his hymn book well?' The officer, having been a choirboy at one time, stated that he did. The Admiral then asked the number of the hymn commencing 'O happy band of pilgrims'.[1] This necessitated the production of a hymn book and the hymn was duly found. A signal was therefore made to all ships in the fleet, calling their attention to the hymn. As a result, being a Sunday, ships' companies of the fleet sang the hymn heartily. It was appropriate also for their point of view as Harwich Force was often referred to as the 'Happy Band of Brothers' and also the 'Light Affliction'.

As time went on, and the Camel did not return, the Admiral became worried as to whether the flame seen in the sky could have been the Camel and not the Zeppelin. He made a signal to Colonel Samson asking if he thought this possible. The answer was 'certainly not'. In the end, of course, their doubts were laid to rest with the sudden appearance of the Camel. When Culley boarded the destroyer he was told by Commander Holt that he would have to stand on the aft gun platform alone as the whole fleet was going to pass by *Redoubt* in line astern led by *Curaçoa*, the Admiral's flagship. And so it happened, notwithstanding the danger from submarines. *Redoubt* remained stationary and all the ships of the Harwich Force with decks lined by ships' companies, passed in review, cheering the pilot of the new service who had given them such a display.

C. P. Bristow

The procedure for getting ready for take-off was as follows: pilot and observer both climbed the small wire ladder from the port float, stepping on the bottom wing and then into their seats. The plane at this stage was resting on its floats on a beach trolley and six waders pushed it down the beach and into the sea. The engine was then switched on and there was a handle at the side engaging the crankshaft of the big 12-cylinder Sunbeam engine, which took two men to turn, providing the engine had previously been warmed up. It would then start by turning a magneto by hand whilst, with the other hand, giving a quick turn to the valve of a compressed air bottle; this fed through a small pipe into the cylinder, giving the engine a jerk and starting it with a roar. The engine then was opened sufficiently to move the plane on its floats and taxi out far enough to turn into the wind, which was often offshore so that it was necessary to go a good distance to enable the plane to clear the land once it became airborne. On patrol, the plane was loaded with 80 gallons of petrol,

---

1. *Oh happy band of pilgrims,*
   Look upward to the skies,
   Where such a light affliction,
   Shall win so great a prize.

a 230lb bomb and 700 rounds of ammunition. All this in addition to three guns, the crew with possessions and the plane itself, weighed about two tons; with this total weight and the drag of the plane it was necessary to build up to a forward speed of 25 knots to get the floats to rise on their flat bottoms and enable the tail and its float to rise, so putting the aircraft into a level position. Once level it quickly became possible to increase speed further and so get the floats to skim across water and the wide wings to take the weight; the `feel' of the wheel control then increased and at 45 knots, by gentle pressure on the joystick, the plane became airborne. With an increase of airspeed the plane climbed quickly to its cruising height of 800 to 1,000 feet and the engine was throttled back slightly until descent. The propeller in front was coarse pitched, four-bladed, six feet and four inches in diameter and made of mahogany ply, a magnificent piece of workmanship.

On the dashboard in front of the pilot were compass, airspeed indicator, altimeter, lateral bubble indicator, engine rev counter, oil pressure gauge and water temperature gauge. The lateral indicator had a curved glass tube with a bubble to indicate that the aircraft was level. This was actuated by centrifugal force so that when doing a perfect turn the bubble remained central. It was, however, possible for this to happen whilst the compass was slowly revolving, so, to be sure of a straight course in grey conditions, it was important to keep both compass and lateral indicator steadily positioned. The other essential instrument was the altimeter. This was activated by air pressure like an aneroid barometer and varied from day to day, always having to be reset at zero before taking off. Once, when turning from the east near the Belgian coast down into the Straits of Dover, I got caught in a thunderstorm at about 2,000 feet. Hailstones bounced off the wings, so I had to change course to get out of the storm area and finally alighted at Westgate in sunshine. When taxying to the shore I saw that the altimeter reading was 400 feet, so great and sudden had been the change in air pressure.

We had a much longer endurance airborne than most other aircraft, carrying enough petrol to remain aloft for at least five hours. As our over-ground (or over-sea) speed was 55 knots, we were able to cover a large area in one patrol. Bad weather was our main concern, but we managed to fly in most rain and murky conditions, although we didn't like them. We flew in low cloud and mist when visibility was not less than two miles, but it was very unpleasant in such circumstances, as once airborne and a few hundred feet high there was no defined horizon, the sea and sky being blended together. Once airborne, we were quickly out of sight of land and there were few sea marks to help navigation, so accuracy in taking compass bearings and timings, and making the correct allowances for speed and direction of wind, were essential or we could easily get lost. Navigation was dependent on the correct application of this information mentally, as there was no provision for written calculations. This was the job of the pilot, as well as flying the aircraft. Often we would fly for three or four hours without landmarks and eventually make a landfall hopefully somewhere near the calculated place. All the time in the air was rather tense and there was always a sense of relief when we got back.

The observer kept wireless watch, being constantly in communication with our station, as well as using his eyes continually to survey the sea below. It was his job to identify such sea marks as there were, the few lightships still left on station, or any particular marker buoys, but mainly he had to look out for submarines and mines. He controlled the twin Lewis guns on the moveable ring surrounding his seat and the bomb-sight under his feet, together with the bomb-fusing and release controls. He also had the two carrier pigeons in their plywood box, which were trained to return to the loft at Westgate and were our last line of safety. On our return from patrol, when about ten miles from home, I would signal him to fire a few bursts from the guns and release the pigeons. This gave both him and them some relief and exercise. I had one observer who, in his exuberance, shot through one of my flying wires, but the pigeons always survived and managed to get home after their launch high up in the air.

There was plenty of variety, if not excitement, in every flight. The weather changed continually and was a major factor in all our movements, and no one day was the same as the next. The aircraft, too, were always a problem as the engines were not very reliable and frequently went wrong. However, we had a good staff of riggers and engineers, who took a pride in their work and were as keen as the flyers to keep all the seaplanes operational. There was wireless contact with the station for a distance of up to sixty miles. Radio messages, by Morse code and headphones, were received on a crystal and transmitted on a one-valve battery with a copper wire aerial, trailed 250 feet long from a reel underneath the plane. When descending, the observer had to wind this in quickly, because we were soon down from our average cruising altitude of 800 to 1,000 feet. Then our wireless contact naturally ceased, so if we came down on the water our pigeons were the only contact with the station to give information of our position.

After a few weeks I became quite proficient at manoeuvring the large Short 184, both on the water and in the air and I believe that I became one of the CO's 'blue-eyed boys'. He allowed me to fly the new Fairey 260 when we received two on the station. He also let me fly his pride and joy, the single-seater fighter seaplane, the Hamble Baby. This was exciting because it was half the size of a Short 184, had a Gnome Rotary engine, and needed only the lightest pressure on the controls. Taking off, landing and flying were a joy. It had two machine guns on the top plane fired by a button on the wheel control, and it was exciting to dive on to a target moored on a raft and blaze away with both guns, before pulling out of the dive.

Apart from these, I flew several planes of the Short 184 family. They were both heavy and slow. The floats had to be large enough to support two tons weight and not to be submerged too deeply, which would prevent rising when gaining forward speed to take off. Although of the same design, they were built by different makers and some were older models, so they all had their individual characteristics. There were one or two favourites, which I preferred to fly. All were very noisy and, after sitting behind the engine for four hours, it was a blessed relief to get down and have some peace.

The state of the weather was always on our minds. Bad visibility, fog, high wind or rough sea all prevented flying, and the weather was constantly changing. We sent a weather report to the Admiralty at Chatham two or three times a day and they collected information from various sources, producing a daily weather map of the south-east, which was made available to ships and air stations throughout the area. When I took my turn as duty officer for the day, I had to go to the 'Lookout' on the low cliff and record the weather signs, then make a forecast for the next four hours, and this was all telephoned to Chatham. During daylight and at any times when machines were flying, there was a man on watch at the Lookout station and all movements out at sea or in the air were recorded. On one occasion I was standing looking up at a DH9 from Manston, which was heading out to sea, when it suddenly dived and I was horrified to see the starboard wings collapse, followed by the fuselage twisting, being spun by the thrust of the port wing. It dived into the sea about a mile out and I could only think of the two men in it. I sounded the alarm and sent our launch out to see if they could be rescued, or if any wreckage could be salvaged, but by the time it got out to the position there was no sign of anything. I reported the event to Manston, and the sequel was that I had to attend an inquest at Sheerness, where the pilot's body had finally drifted, as I was the only witness to the accident.

The highest I ever managed in a seaplane was 5,200 feet. That was in the N1782 – one of our oldest and tried Short 184s, which had just had a thorough overhaul. The CO asked me to take it up on a test flight, not too far as it wasn't armed, and not north-east towards possible enemy interception. Another pilot, Jack Prescot, came with me and we took off, heading north away from the coast. This was an excellent opportunity to see just how high we could go, so I kept climbing, slowly turning into the Thames approaches. At 5,200 feet I found that the plane would not go higher without stalling, which meant a dangerous loss of speed. At that height we felt quite safe in flying over land with the sea not far away on our left, and as it was a clear day we had a wonderful view of Kent and Essex, and the whole of the Thames estuary. We turned south near Shoeburyness, leaving Southend pier behind and crossed Sheppey, heading east for home, descending over Manston airfield and gliding down to Westgate with the engine off, touching down in Westgate Bay. When we got ashore after the usual taxying up to the tarmac on a beach-trolley, I was told that the CO wanted to see me urgently. He asked where I had been and what I had been up to, as he had received an urgent signal from the Admiral at the Nore, asking about a strange unidentified aircraft flying at a great height over the coast, and the Shoeburyness guns wanted instructions. I explained and I think that was the end of it. But Jack Prescot was impressed and, being something of a water-colour artist, he painted a little picture of the seaplane and entitled it 'Happy Memories'. I have kept it all these years and it is hanging in my bathroom.

Whilst thinking about these events, I must refer to one which illustrates the effect that changes in weather conditions made on our flights. During the winter of 1918 we had a fall of snow which lasted many days and it was very cold. The day after it became clear and sunny and I was detailed to go on patrol alone to cover the shipping lanes between the Tongue and Sunk light vessels. It was a lovely clear sunny morning and I left expecting to be away for about two hours. The wind was from the south-west, so it was necessary to taxi out at least half a mile before turning towards the shore to take off, this to ensure that there was sufficient height to give at least 100 to 200 feet clearance when crossing the shoreline before turning north out to sea. I could see the shoreline for two to three miles towards Reculver and Herne Bay, but as I looked I could see it disappearing into a black wall, which steadily swallowed everything as it advanced over the sea and land. A huge bank of mist was moving rapidly east and I realised that I should soon be lost in it, so I turned sharply back to Westgate and alighted before the wading party with the beach-trolley had returned up the beach. They were surprised at my sudden return and not pleased to have their quiet smoke disturbed. But they waded out to me again with the trolley and wanted to know what was amiss. Before they had got the plane on the trolley they quickly found out. Suddenly everything was blanked out in thick mist and I was very thankful that I hadn't been caught out beyond the North Foreland, with the Kent coast blotted out in that thick fog coming down into the Straits and the English Channel.

Armistice Day came to us at Westgate out of the blue. We awoke as usual, wondering what the weather was going to be and if flying would be possible. It was dull and overcast with low cloud and didn't look promising. To us the war was a continuing state with which we had become familiar in all its danger and periods of boredom, and was now an inevitable part of life. It had started when we were at school and after four years of fluctuating fortune, the thought of its end seemed hardly possible. That day we were having breakfast in the mess when the CO told us that he had just received a signal from the Nore advising all services that hostilities would end at 11.00am, as the Germans and their allies had surrendered. Therefore, with immediate effect all operations would cease and there was shore leave for everyone except those engaged in essential services and duties. It was obvious that some sort of celebration was necessary and we thought first of getting out all the seaplanes. But that would hardly be fair as it would mean that most of the ratings would be required to handle and service them, and anyway the CO vetoed it. So we decided to go over to Manston for lunch to meet the men who used to fly with us as escorts.

Phillips William Norman St Clare

SSZ14 had meanwhile made her first test flight and was undergoing some minor adjustments. Since 2 September 1917 was a sports day on the station and as Russell particularly wanted to participate in some running events, he asked me to take a flight for him in Z14, which was now ready for a further trial. This I agreed to do for I was most anxious to see what flying was like in the new busses. So I accordingly reported to Lieutenant Elliot, the pilot, and we prepared to ascend. Following the usual custom we took our seats in the shed and waited to be carried out. As it was only a test flight, I carried no codebooks as wireless would not be needed. However, we took a few pans of ammunition and a bomb or two just in case of emergency. Food and all unnecessary stuff were likewise dispensed with. The landing party was the smallest I had seen up to this date, consisting of only twenty men. These men, after being told off for their different jobs, unlashed the ropes which were holding the airship securely down, lifted off the sandbags which were hung around the rails and slowly hauled us into the open. It was a totally different feeling to that I had experienced on the other ships. The car being only a few feet high made it possible for me to lean out and almost touch the ground on which we rested. After the usual balancing up to get in flying trim, the engine was started and we ascended, rising at quite a steep angle immediately and continuing so until we reached a thousand feet above ground. Here we flattened out and circled round the station watching the landing party fall in and dismiss.

After a few preliminary circles around the aerodrome we drew up almost to a stop above the wireless cabin and hung against the breeze. Here I stood up on my seat and signalled by semaphore that everything appeared OK, and that we were proceeding for a run over the sea. It was a queer sensation, that signalling. In other vessels one was securely hemmed in up to the waist by the sides of the gondola, but on this Zero one had no arm space unless you actually stood up on the seat, balanced to the roll of the ship. It felt for all the world as if I was up the standing on air, the sides of the car finishing less than a foot higher than the seat on which I was standing. The signal being acknowledged, I sat down again and the ship headed for Penzance. We crossed the cliffs at Mullion Cove, giving a cheery wave to the people visible in the hotel grounds and then followed along the cruel looking rocks, past Poldhu, Marazion and St Michael's Mount. We stuck around a bit over Penzance and I flashed a 'Good luck' in the direction of the seaplane station. Then, waving adieu to the numerous people visible, the ship glided over the peninsula, crossed the cliffs and out to sea. Here the engine was opened full out and we 'ripped' along.

By this time I had made one or two good discoveries, among them being that I was experiencing the joys of flying for the first time. This may seem strange in face of the fact that I had already completed well over a hundred hours in the air, but it is nevertheless true. Aeroplane flying is delightful, I had found that out quite early, but you must go fast in an aeroplane, else you'll drop. Goggles must be worn to protect the eyes when looking around and windscreens hamper the view. If an object attracts your attention, you can only circle around and investigate. Now all these faults are missing in an airship; you can go slow, you needn't wear goggles, and you can hover. I decided quite a long time ago that an aeroplane pilot has never known real flying until he has been in an airship during flight. To this I now add an amendment to the effect that flying in a Zero airship is the thing. Getting away from size and effectiveness and looking solely from the point of view of the real sensations of flying I am confident by long experience that nothing at present invented gives the sensations experienced so much like those of a bird as Zero flying. She can go fast. She can go slow. She can hover with noiseless engines. She can go high or low. The altitude record is over 10,000 feet whilst the capabilities of low flying can be counted in inches off the ground with a good pilot. She can land on land or water or can skim the surface of the latter. The observer's seat in front gives an exceptionally fine uninterrupted view throughout the flight, and rolling or pitching is only experienced to any degree during rough weather. What more does one desire?

We proceeded at full speed as far as Sevenstones light vessel and after a 'confab' by semaphore with the lonely souls who inhabit it, started southerly in the direction of the Isles of Scilly. After gazing at the wonderful panorama they give to a beholder from the air, we turned back towards the Wolf lighthouse, that formidable guardian of the seas always having its base among a seething cauldron of angry foam. Then, taking a line direct to Poldhu Cove, the engine was set roaring again and, descending until the spray splashed into our eyes, we completed the last fifty odd miles skimming the surface and tore up over the sandy beach at Gunwalloe on to the Golf Links, startling the players and so to the base and the landing ground.

On 20 September [we had] spasmodic showers and heavy clouds, none too much sunshine and the wind inclined to be gusty gave none too good a promise for nice flying weather. Nevertheless, all ships had orders to prepare for patrol and Z15 was set down to ascend at 10.00am. Patrol orders were mapped out as needed at HQ Plymouth and sent through to the Intelligence Office Mullion to be handed to pilots. At first, when very little night flying was undertaken, it was the custom of those concerned to drop in this office first thing in the morning and scan the bill, but later on, when no definite line could be distinguished between day and night flying, orders were waited for by messenger and the crew curtly informed to prepare. It was a fascinating business for it was a positive fact one never knew where he would be during the next few hours night or day. On this occasion our orders were to patrol for mines between Black Head and Rame Head and to destroy any we came across. So at a few minutes to ten I walked out to the office, drew my codebooks and the issue of chocolate and Horlicks milk tablets for the three of us. The latter commodities are carried for emergency rations but I never heard yet of a case where they were ever intact on the airmen's return. Meanwhile Dicky James was hopping round the galley getting some sandwiches and filling our Thermos flasks with tea. The pilot was receiving final instructions from the commanding officer.

Then we took our seats, were hauled out of the shed to the open and ascended. It was none too cheerful a flight, that first patrol. Within five minutes of ascending the whole car, and our own hands and faces, were dripping water as we slid through the rain towards Falmouth Harbour. The harbour wore a particularly drab appearance, hills, town, shipping and sea all seeming to wear a melancholy countenance. Bright colours had all vanished and things looked grey. The sun tried desperately to break through a rift in the darkening clouds but had poor success, giving the sea a mottled green and black appearance, wherever its rays fell. We could see smoke drifting from the chimney tops of the houses, and it made us think of the bright fires within their walls and perhaps the family sitting round chatting, about every subject under the sun, you bet, except that of the uncomfortable Navy carrying on in cheerless weather. But very little shipping appeared to be out on the grey waste before us. A few trawlers here and there and a couple of fishing boats were all the shortened visibility would allow us to see. We slowed down our engine to between 15 and 20 knots and started in the direction of the nearest trawler. Upon interrogating her I found that she too was searching for mines, and so wishing her good luck we proceeded on up channel, keeping a good look out but seeing nothing much but white crests upon the water here and there.

By 11.30am we had zig-zagged roughly over 500 square miles of water and found ourselves lying in close to St Austell. Here we had lunch floating along at leisure and, long before twelve, had started at a fairly quick speed towards Plymouth. Here an enquiring destroyer asked our business and went her way, leaving us to turn our backs on Rame Head and zig-zag back towards the Lizard. Nothing was seen either by the trawlers or ourselves of any enemy's work and I finally picked up a message from the base telling us to return forthwith before the breaking of another storm. This we gladly did and landed soon after 1.00pm, cold and wet, and anxious to get near the fire.

Such was the first patrol of SSZ15. To the uninitiated it must appear to be a generally miserable, unnecessary flight, wasting public money and doing no good. In reality it proved to the Admiralty the fact that a few more miles of water surrounding our ports were clear of danger, and that the gallant merchant service boats who had reached thus far without destruction were sure of a safe voyage for the remainder of their journey, and so provide those people at home with a further stock of that necessary commodity – 'food'.

Next day brought entirely similar orders and we set out over the same waters to see if the enemy had been busy during the night. No signs of activity were visible and the same area was patrolled again and again until, being suddenly enveloped in heavy fog when off Plymouth harbour, we received order by wireless to land at an emergency station, which had just completed at Laira in that district. This we did, jumping thankfully and again wet through, to the ground some four and a half hours after leaving south Cornwall. Laira emergency landing ground, or sub-station as it was called, was a most conveniently situated aerodrome in all respects, being at that time at the eastern boundary of our patrol areas and also within a few minutes of Plymouth and incidentally headquarters. The station itself was totally different to Mullion, having for its landing ground a racecourse, with the personnel quarters consisting of two grandstands on one side and the offices etc. in a farmhouse on the other. It seemed funny to see the White Ensign of the Navy floating over a cow yard in which the cows continually ambled.

The airships on their descent here were to be towed into a harbour cut out in a wood alongside the farmhouse. Here it was hoped that, securely tied down, they would ride through gales, getting protection from the leafy trees. Z15 was towed there upon our arrival and we were then run round by car to the men's quarters at the opposite side of the racecourse. It was easy to see that a stay in this delightful spot would have boundless advantages over Mullion. There were only thirty officers and men here as compared with the several hundred at the base. In consequence of there being no proper accommodation and plenty of apparently rough things to put up with, discipline was greatly relaxed. Moreover, a few minutes away was the large seaport town of Plymouth and Devonport, giving promise of theatres and picture shows, cafes and a thousand other delights, in the place of what Mullion had to offer in her desolate moor and murky Helston. Before we had arrived ten minutes Dick and I agreed that this would be 'our' show if possible.

An interview with the CO during our report gave us to understand that we would have to make shift for bedding during the night until further arrangements were made. The two cooks in the galley welcomed us with open arms and filled us well up with goodly fare. From this very date until the end of the war nothing but praise was heard among the airmen for the splendid way in which we were always treated by the Laira cooks, and I may add that at times it is a hard task to please a dog-tired, cold and disconsolate airman after a hard day in the air. We were also made welcome at once into the Petty Officers' mess where ever after at Laira we had our meals. After we had fed, washed, warmed ourselves and generally got a feeling of life back into our blood we borrowed suitable clothes, having only our flying gear with us, and, accompanied by new chums, set off for Plymouth to explore its delights, from which city we returned about midnight, well satisfied and happy men, and made light of the somewhat hard beds which fell to our lot.

Next morning, to our dismay, we found orders awaiting us for patrol and return to Mullion, and with much mumbling at our luck and well wishes from our new friends an ascent was made, over the River Plym across the harbour and out to sea. Our orders were to search for submarines in the area east of Plymouth and so we turned up channel and approached Start Point. There were still signs of bad weather as we passed Start Point and Berry Head before cruising over the wide waters of Lyme Bay. As we left the coastline behind I was able for a few minutes to get a glimpse of Paignton lying snugly back in Tor Bay, and feeling joy at this sight of my home recompensed me for my return to the base. I was able later in the day to write a letter to mother to tell her of my close approach to her that morning, a fact I found she had already guessed upon seeing one of our ships out at sea We continued our patrol to Portland and Weymouth without incident, then orders were sent us to return to Mullion at once, and the craft was accordingly set down channel for the base where we arrived after five hours in the air and just before a storm broke in full fury over the aerodrome.

On 17 November we ascended at 10.00am to patrol Eddystone. Received SOS call from Norwegian steamer *Adolf Anderson* struck by torpedo some miles south of Falmouth. Sinking fast. Informed station we were proceeding to assistance. Distance from scene fifty miles. Reports from SS *Dence* indicate whole convoy in danger, also that *Adolf Anderson* sunk.

Airship C23A twenty miles from scene also closing convoy reports SS *Victory* ten miles north from her reports being hit by torpedo. Third ship in convoy, SS *Dence*, reports being hit at 3.00pm; submarine submerged. C23A reports *Victory* sunk before she reached her, and she is standing by Sailing Vessel *Abaris* herself disabled through picking up survivors. We arrived over SS *Dence* ten miles S.E. Dodman Point at 3.15 and learnt she was disabled but not sinking. Asked Falmouth for immediate assistance and meantime had to escort convoy towards Falmouth, leaving SS *Dence* to chance her luck. Met several trawlers out from Falmouth and advised them to proceed to tow *Dence*. We continued with remainder of convoy, seven vessels and got them safely to harbour by 4.30pm. Position then was *Adolf Anderson* and *Victory* sunk, *Dence* under tow by trawlers and escort. C23A was still asking for assistance to tow *Abaris*. We borrowed some of *Dence* escort for this purpose. *Abaris* safely under tow by 5.00pm. C23A and ourselves next search for subs. *Dence* safely in harbour by 5.30, closely followed by *Abaris*. Sighted periscope one mile east of wreck of SS *Victory* and bombed same in conjunction with C23A and destroyers. Good results. Landed at 8.00pm after eight hours of excitement. Supper at Genoni's and billiards later.

Part Three

Secret History

By Phillips William Norman St Clare
There are one or two items of secret history which occurred at Mullion which would rather surprise my chums should they ever read these notes. The first of them has to do with our wireless orderly, Goodwin by name, who was eventually allotted to us after others had proved failures. Goodwin was a particularly smart fellow, with quick alert eyes, sharp pointed features and a tall soldierly figure. He was very smart at signalling, which we heard he had learned in the Army before coming to us. In addition he took an awful interest in wireless. I'm afraid we were all a little fed up with his talk of what he had done or was going to do and we treated him rather coldly. He did not seem to mind, however, and no one could ever complain of his work; it was always thorough. He learnt the Morse code whilst with us and sometimes we let him use the set, laughing at the mistakes he made, but he was a sticker and got on well. Imagine my surprise one evening, when I discovered him in the cabin writing reams of German press news as he received it through the set. He laughed easily when I entered and said he was polishing up his German. I knew better, however, for it was a good operator who can write that quantity of wireless news without a mistake here or there. He left me soon after and I decided to keep my eyes open.

Another interesting figure who began to frequent the wireless cabin was a Lieutenant Bedard. What his job on the station was no one seemed to know; he was always coming and going without explanation. He took quite an interest in us lads and being a real good sort we readily welcomed his visits to the cabin, where he would talk on all sorts of subjects for hours. One evening we heard that Goodwin had been seen prowling around the woods at the far end of the camp and, on being questioned by us in the cabin next morning, he said he had been looking for spies. We laughed at the idea and so did Bedard who was present at the time. The latter officer, however, told us that several loafers had been seen round the camp and in the woods which was situated near the wireless cabin. That evening it was my turn to do the midnight watch and I was called from my bed by the quartermaster at 11.30pm. It was in the month of February and, the nights being chilly, I called into the galley on the way and got a pot of hot cocoa and some bread and butter to make some toast. It was a beautiful calm moonlight night and as I approached the cabin I could see someone sitting on an old rotten log near the woods. I went across to see who it was. It was Goodwin.

'Hello,' I said, 'waiting for spies?'

'Yes,' he laughed, and then asked me to stay and chat. There was plenty of time before the press news at that time so I sat down beside him and offered him some cocoa. After he had drunk I asked him what the game was.

'Very simple, Phil,' he replied. 'I'm not doing much use as an orderly as I'm trying my hand at this. You heard what Bedard said this morning about the loafers. Well I'm out to catch 'em.'

Somehow I felt he was genuine but, not being able to quite convince myself, I decided to watch him. I had no chance, however, for after I had entered the cabin and taken my coat, I looked through the window at the wood and saw that Goodwin had vanished.

There was a real spy scare next morning, for it was reported that I, on leaving the cabin at 2.00am, had seen someone running in the direction of the wood, that I had promptly given the alarm to the officers' quarters, but that search parties had found no one. I was a good deal chaffed about my night's work, but Goodwin stuck up for me against the other fellows saying I had only done what he would have done himself in my case. The incident was soon forgotten.

What really happened? The press news finished at 1.30am and it was a grand night, cloudless and blue with a myriad stars shining on that wonderful cushion. I was always a lover of 'the silent hours' and so now I decided to sit down for a few minutes and get the benefit of the fresh night air. I lit a cigarette and sat down on the step of the cabin. I don't know how long I sat there, but I was suddenly startled by the sound of breaking glass and, looking in the direction from which the noise came, could plainly see the huge shed silhouetted against the sky and the CO's office at its base. I could also see a figure running wildly down the road in my direction, towards the wood. Close behind him I recognised the figure of Goodwin endeavouring to catch up to the stranger. Suddenly, Goodwin tripped up and came down heavily on the road. The stranger looked like escaping so I dashed forward to intercept his path to safety. He saw me coming and veered to the left, but he was fagged and I was fresh and was soon running abreast. I tried to grab him but he threw me off. Next time I barged into him and he went down. I fell on top and struggled to get the scissors on him. Instead he got a punch on the chin which fairly staggered me. He was up and off before I realised what had happened, but Goodwin charged past me yelling to me to follow him into the wood.

Feeling very groggy, I got on my feet and followed. The wood had pretty thick undergrowth and the progress of the other two was slow, but following in their trail I soon caught up to Goodwin and the slower pace at which we progressed got me feeling okay again. As we ran and stumbled through the wood, Goodwin gave the orders.

'He's making for the Lizard Road,' he gasped, 'it's just down here. If he turns to the left, I'll follow. You nip along to the right and find Bedard at Cury Cross Lanes. Tell him to follow.'

I gasped a reply and followed close. The stranger was keeping his lead, fear evidently lending him wings and in another minute he had jumped the low wall bordering the woods and turned along the road to the left. Without another word Goodwin cleared the wall and followed him. After pausing for a moment to make sure of their direction I turned to the right and started off for Cury. I was feeling horribly fagged and could do little more than trot along the hard road. I had gone about three quarters of a mile before I sighted the Post Office which marked the cross lanes. They were silent and empty, but I called out 'Bedard' as loud as I could as I ran. A figure dressed in civilian clothes ran out of the shadow of an inn and down the road to meet me.

'Is that you Goodwin?. I recognised Bedard's voice.

'No, Sir!' I gasped as I drew up. 'It's Phillips. Goodwin is chasing a man down the Lizard Road. He wants you to follow.'

'Hell!' ejaculated Bedard. Dashing into the shadows again, he dragged a motorbike into the roadway and, admonishing me to jump on, started her up. I shall never forget that ride. We tore along the road at a rate I have never travelled on land before or since. Hedges and fields whizzed past and my eyes ran with tears. Down past the woods where I left Goodwin, on uphill the other side and out on to the moor we rushed. Once on the flat moonlit moor, we could see Goodwin and the stranger about half a mile ahead, still on the roadway. Bedard opened out still more as we approached and both men turned for a moment to see what was behind them. Then the front man swerved to one side of the road and the next second we were alongside Goodwin.

The suddenness with which we stopped threw me off into a gorse bush, but Bedard dropped the bike and yelled to Goodwin, who was completely fagged, to follow round the roadway. He ran after the stranger through the gorse. I followed as well I was able. The stranger could hardly get along now and it was an easy matter for Bedard to overhaul him. Suddenly he turned and brandished a revolver, but fell before he could use it and Bedard was on top. When I arrived the fellow had fainted and Bedard was transferring a bundle of papers from the man's pocket to his own. Then he glanced at me and said, 'They contain the details of new patrol orders to be adopted at Mullion shortly. It's a marvel how things leak out, Phillips!'

'Yes, Sir!' I replied and, stooping down, picked up the fallen revolver, which I handed to him. It was an extremely neat affair, small and would fold up to go in one's pocket. He tossed it back to me, telling me I could keep it as a memento. Meanwhile, Goodwin had arrived and after a cursory examination of the man's features turned him over and proceeded to bind his hands behind him with a handkerchief. Bedard rose to his feet and said, 'I'll get back to the station and fetch a car, Goodwin. Phillips had better stay here with you to see this man gives no trouble.'

With this he walked in the direction of the motorcycle and, having mounted it, was soon disappearing down the road. I looked curiously at Goodwin. There was no look of triumph on his face as I had expected to see, he was not even excited, while my own nerves were all of the jangle. We sat down beside the man and I remarked, 'Well Jack, you've got your spy at last. You will have the laugh on the other fellows now.'

'I don't think so, Phil!'

'But ...,' I exclaimed, 'how ...?'

'Look here Phil! I can't explain matters now, but probably Bedard will tell you to keep your mouth shut about this affair.'

Despite my questions I could get no further light on what he meant and when Bedard returned with a car he told me I was to return to camp and say no more than that I had seen a suspicious person about the camp, had roused the officers and that the search had found nothing. They dropped me again in the bottom of the wood and took their man on to Falmouth.

As I stated before, there was a spy scare when the camp went on duty next morning and I came in for a good deal of chaff. The fellows said I must be following Goodwin's footsteps. Considerably mystified, I waited for some explanation but I got none for several months. Then one day I had an interview with the CO and learnt for myself that Jack Goodwin's wireless orderly was none other than Captain Jack Goodwin, late of the Royal Engineers, at present attached to the RNAS for intelligence work.

Part Four

Western Front

ORDERS FOR DUNKERQUE

Aircraft Patrol

The object of this expedition is to establish an aerial control over an area within a radius of 100 miles from Dunkerque, with a view to attacking any German airships on the way to England, and preventing any temporary airship base being established within the area defined. The control will be established by means of an aerial reconnaissance, using Dunkerque as a main base, and will be supported by a force of armed and armoured motorcars, with the necessary personnel and stores to enable advanced subsidiary aeroplane basis to be established 30, 40 and 50 miles inland.

The whole of the area under control should be kept clear of all small raiding parties of the enemy, in order to secure any aeroplanes, which may have landed, from being captured etc. The force will consist of aeroplanes and armed motorcars, the necessary personnel and transport for the aeroplanes and an armed force of 200 Marines.

2. *Aeroplanes.* The aeroplanes will be made up of three squadrons, each squadron consisting eventually of 12 machines, when these are available. The aeroplane transport will be similarly divided up so as to work with its own squadron of aeroplanes.

3. *Armed Motor Cars.* 60 special motor cars will be armed with Maxims, and will be protected with armour plating. They will be manned by Marine crews and will be detailed to work with their respective squadrons.

4. *Commands.* The officer in command of the expedition will be Wing Commander C. R. Samson R. N.

The officers in command of the aeroplane squadrons will be:

No. 1 Squadron, Squadron Commander E. L. Gerrard.

No. 2 Squadron, Squadron Commander S. D. A. Grey.

No. 3 Squadron, Squadron Commander R. B. Davies.

Squadron Commander Risk will be in charge and will be responsible for the armed motor cars, and generally assist Major H. G. B. Armstrong in charge of the detachment of Marines.

Flight Commander T. G. Hetherington will act as assistant to Squadron Commander Risk as Transport Officer.

Squadron Commander E. F. Briggs will generally supervise all engineering work in connection with aircraft, motor vehicles and stores.

Mr Blundell, Gunner, will be in charge of the armament and of the supply of ammunition and explosives.

5. *Correspondence.* All despatches are to be sent direct to Director, Air Department, Admiralty. Any important information is to be telegraphed, for which purpose a code will be supplied. Despatches are to be forwarded at least twice a

week giving an account of all aerial Scouting carried out. All demands for stores, replacements etc are to be forwarded to Inspecting Captain of Aircraft.

6. *Communication with England*. Communication with England will be kept up between Dunkerque and Sheerness as requisite by HMS *Empress* or some other small ship.

7. Every care is to be taken to keep the French Authorities at Dunkerque informed of movements etc. and in all expeditions from Dunkerque French soldiers, if possible, should accompany the English so as to make up a Franco-English expedition. The greatest care is to be taken to avoid giving offence in any way to the French Authorities or to inhabitants of the country.

8. *Medical arrangements*. A small base hospital with personnel and equipment complete will be established at Dunkerque. Four motor ambulances will be supplied to work the outlying stations from the base hospital. Two medical officers will be appointed for duty at the base hospital, and four medical officers for work at the auxiliary station. As regards equipment, each outlying station will be provided with a field chest, surgical haversack and St John's Ambulance party.

9. *Commissariat*. An officer is to be detailed to be in charge of all of the victualling arrangements and for the accounting of expenditure of public money. A quartermaster-sergeant has been detailed to assist in the victualling arrangements.

A sufficient supply of provisions will be sent from Sheerness, and is to be maintained at Dunkerque. Special cases of rations for the crews of the motor vehicles and for outlying bases are being prepared. Further details will be issued as regards this. Receipts for all local purchases are to be obtained, and care to be taken to obtain competitive tenders wherever possible in making contracts or purchases.

10. *Attacks on Zeppelin sheds*. It is important to take any opportunity to attack the Zeppelin sheds at Dusseldorf and Cologne. Officers achieving this will render exceptional service.

11. Steps are to be taken as soon as possible after receiving these orders to establish the advanced bases mentioned in paragraph 1, and a report is to be forwarded as to arrangements carried out.

Air Department,
Admiralty,
12 September 1914

EARLY DAYS OF FLYING

Air Commodore E. L. Gerrard

The mechanic I took to Belgium in 1914 was one of Rolls Royce's best. He kept my machine, of de Havilland's design, perfectly; though it is true I had one engine failure and one near engine failure. In both cases I had narrow escapes of being captured by the Germans. In the first case the petrol pump broke down; I kept going for miles over Germany with the hand pump. Just as my shoulder was wearing out the hand pump wore out, and I had to land. Visibility was bad and I was not sure whether I was clear of Germany, so I took my pistol and hid near a path in a wood, and waited for someone to come along. Nothing happened for some time; at last an old woman appeared. She was very alarmed when I suddenly appeared from nowhere. I asked in German where she lived, and decided she was Belgian. She gave me an excellent meal – I had had nothing since the day before. Miraculously, she produced an air mechanic who was fleeing north from Liège. He said the Germans were five miles off, but stayed to fix the pump for me and help prepare a runway. I regretted having to leave him behind, but the run was too short to carry any extra weight.

Antwerp was being evacuated, and it was arranged that I would bring the King at the last moment. However, his ministers persuaded him to leave by train. I stayed on to the end as someone else might want to leave. All our men and stores had been despatched in good time. Bullets begin to zip all around when I took off. Immediately the engine began to vibrate. I was already over the Germans and there was no going back. I found that by continually wangling the throttle, the vibration can be kept within reasonable limits. I climbed carefully and painfully and soon, was clear of those *** Germans. The engine seemed to be sticking it, so I decided to carry on my proper destination: Dunkirk.

GUY LEATHER, WESTERN FRONT FIGHTER PILOT

Introduction and commentary by Guy Williams
Guy Leather joined the Eastchurch Flying School on 12 September 1915. Here he witnessed a mid-air collision between two training machines, resulting in the deaths of both trainees, who had only had about a couple of weeks flying instruction and were flying solo. His first experience of powered flight was on 13 September in the Caudron G.3, with his instructor Lieutenant Pizey. Leather must have been an apt pupil, because on the evening of the 15th he was told to go solo.

So after being shown the engine controls again I shut my eyes and said 'contact': thank goodness the engine did not start, there is still hope of seeing another dawn. However, it started next time and off I had to go, thank goodness, with great success. Once in the air things went much better and I really quite enjoyed a circuit of the aerodrome which was done with all necessary caution. Now for the landing, a difficult thing for a beginner – off goes the engine and down we come 'flattening out' when about eight feet off the ground – there! The wheels touch and we are safe once again. However, being so far away from the other machines I thought I would do another short flight towards them and land nearer – so off we went again, only, just as I was about to land, out taxis another machine so up I go again only just clearing it and the top of the sheds by about two feet, doing a horrible side slip outwards in my attempt to turn without any bank; it made my heart beat somewhat harder, but I stayed up until I felt normal again before landing.

For a ticket one makes two flights, the first making five figures of eight in the air and landing within fifty yards of a mark, the second making five more eighties and landing within seventy yards of a mark from 1,000 feet without using your engine.

I managed both these tests 'most satisfactorily' as Flight Commander Ogilvy (the CO) put it. Just think, I am now able to take up passengers and I have only been flying for a week. Heaven help the passengers if there ever are any; however my naval training is not half finished yet.

21 September: I went up on a trial flight on a new machine, a Maurice Farman Shorthorn, afterwards taking it up myself. I find it rather sluggish in the air and funny to fly as the engine is behind the pilot, while on a Caudron it is in the front. However, it is much quieter and not half as windy, in fact rather nice to fly.

24 September: In the evening listened to old Horace Short's yarns, which were truly wondrous, but some were hardly 'Drawing Room'. He is a wonderful old fellow and seems to have done nearly everything. He is the designer and owner of Short seaplanes which are our most successful machines and beautifully made.

On 25 September he went up with Lieutenant Pizey in a Graham White Box Kite, for fun it seems, 'contour chasing' he called it– or chasing cows around fields! The next day he went up in a Bristol two-seater and found it 'quite the nicest machine I have flown so far'.
It was quite cold up there but the view was lovely and I could see Westgate, Dover and Greenwich. Coming down to get out of the cold the engine went wrong at about 3,000 feet, so I had to land on the aerodrome. Afterwards I discovered that the old Gnome had three broken inlet valves.

20 October:Met Minifie and went down to Dover harbour and watched a 'Schneider' landing in a cloud of spray. I must say that I would far rather keep on land machines as it is a very cold and wet job to fly seaplanes.

8 November: I took up Morane Parasol myself and found it most pleasant to fly. This is the first fast machine that I have flown, made quite a good landing.

On 10 November he had his first crash – on take-off his BE2C was blown sideways by an unexpected gust of wind and fairly badly damaged. He was completely unhurt, luckily.

This is my first crash, and really the feeling of being involved in one is not so frightening as one thinks it ought to be.

On 17 November he heard that he would be allowed to go to Dunkerque with the squadron. On 26 November they changed into khaki war dress and preparations to leave were nearly complete. There was snow on the ground.

1 December. Off to France in the destroyer HMS *Greyhound*.I stayed on deck with Dallas but Minifie was very poorly and could hardly stagger on board the

monitor *Prince Eugene* when we got to Dunkerque – truly, these destroyers are little devils in a sea.

2 December: Went up in a double-engined Caudron for the first time – they are rather unwieldy but no doubt one gets used to most things in time. They are to be our service machines for the present.

On 5 December he got his own personal Caudron, N3295, with two 100 hp Anzani radial engines. He tied his mascot to it. On the 9th he took up a two-seat Nieuport for the first time. There were various trips during the month in the Caudrons and Nieuports and some coastal patrols between Nieuport town and Dixmunde. The odd wreck had to be patrolled and they thought they saw a submarine but the real thing was a planned bombing raid on Ostende. This raid, to be carried out in Caudron G4s, was eagerly anticipated and finally the day came.

30 December: We staggered down to the aerodrome at about 6am and were told that the Caudrons and Henrys were to start off first. Preberdy went first, then Dallas to whom I shouted 'good luck'. My turn came next, no time for more thoughts. I opened out both my engines and when just off the ground they both cut out dead, with the result the next thing was I struck something and found myself upside down in the machine surrounded by water and feeling rather 'tired'. People soon came on the scene with lamps and managed to haul me from the wreckage, unhurt again. Some mascots seem to work alright.

He had a half hour rest and in a spare machine went off again just as dawn was breaking and dropped bombs on Ostende harbour, just as everyone else was coming back.

My God, what hell for a quarter of an hour, every gun was on me and only me. To cut a long story short, everyone got back safely although all machines were hit. Norton had his prop cut nearly in two by a piece of HE, Peberdy's main spar was half severed (a very near thing).Petre had a desperate scrap with a Fokker who had put two bullets through his passenger's seat; luckily there was no passenger. I had a large piece of HE through my seat, luckily I do not cover much area when sitting or it might have found a billet.

It seems that the raid was judged to have been successful and the Germans admitted 'considerable damage'.

1916

9 January: Flew two patrols and on the second saw three Huns over Nieuport,

so stalked them from behind and managed to close with one. However, he flew away to fight another day.

10 January: Flew the Morane biplane for the first time just for 'fun'; she is really quite a nice bus and climbs well – but requires careful watching near the ground as she has warp wings.

14 January: By jove, it is my birthday today and I am 19 years of age – soon leaving the teens behind.

23 January: Now for something a bit special! Quite a nice day, so went for a fighting patrol to Dixmunde on a Nieuport Scout. Saw an LVG over the town and managed to side-slip under his tail, emptied a tray into him at very close range and he fell in Belgium all a 'fire – came back tremendously pleased with life as this is my first 'certain'.

In February they received three Nieuport Scouts and the CO asked Petre, Dallas and Leather to form a fighting flight.

4 February: No flying today, so went and patted my new machine; her number is N3981. I put my dear old mascot into her.

7 February: Did a patrol to Ypres on N3981; she is a topping little bus, and long may she last. Went to the seaplane base, spent a very instructive evening looking around their machines with Hodge, who is now a great pal of mine.

9 February: Every prospect of a good day, chasing wily Bosches. Sure enough one was reported over Calais at 09.25 so up and after him with Dallas as my companion. Arrived over Calais at 10,000 feet, a glorious sight, we could see dear old England stretched out almost at our feet; ominous white bursts appeared in the sky – denoting Hun. There he is 3,000 feet below us and going home – full out – after twenty minutes stern chase – just get within long range. Just beyond Dunkerque our AA made him do a sharp turn so now we are well on his tail. Dallasto port and self to starboard. He is also firing and one hears an occasional 'zip' of a bullet, but our blood is up and we are firing at him hard – as he got over Nieuport an ominous trail of smoke starts and he shut off his engine and commenced to glide towards the shore. Dallas close after him. He finally made a rotten landing at Middlekuke, his side of the line unfortunately. However it is a victory for us.

Leave came at last on 14 February 1916 and he took the destroyer HMS Tartar *to Dover. Then followed trips to his old school, Wellington College, and home to see his family.*

26 February: It's back to Victoria for the train to Dover and over to Dunkerque on *P11*, one of the new boats used for strafing the Hun submarine.

28 February: Went up on a 'scout' today, accompanying Minifie who was on a two-seater Clerget Nieuport, quite a new type of engine, it seems to be powerful but makes some comic noises.

2 March: Coastal reconnaissance. 'Daddy' Simms is my observer today. We took four bombs in paper bags in the bottom of our machine, which we propose to drop on Zeebrugge, feeling particularly full of hate. We are to have no escort as it is a 'special' and a crowd is easily seen. On our return journey we dropped our eggs from 8,000 feet on to or rather at the Mole. Here we were very heavily shelled and one particularly close one blew us right over on our back making us drop nearly 1,000 feet. We had a nasty time at Ostende, as there were three Huns waiting for our return; however, our orders were not to fight if possible, so we beat it for home as fast as we could, Daddy keeping them at bay with the rear gun.

We ran into a huge bank of clouds off Nieuport, this must have saved us as they lost us after that. About ten minutes later we fell out of the clouds at Malo – absolutely out of control and as far as I could judge spinning on our backs, but she soon righted herself and we came home. Both of us were badly frost-bitten, especially Daddy as his helmet had gone overboard while we were in the clouds. On examining the machine there were nine bullet holes in it, one of which had passed between Simms and myself – another close shave. It's the ones that hit that cause most interest!

There followed a period of bad weather until mid-March when the Bosche mounted a bombing raid on the aerodrome which severely shook the CO! Following this raid the whole Division set to to make an effective 'dug-out' which kept them busy when there was no flying.

18 March: Messages came through to the effect that a Hun had dropped bombs on Margate – so went up on the Morane Biplane with Hamlin. Naturally saw no sign of him, but it was a very pleasant trip all the same.

28 March: Mairax brought over a new type of machine, of Sopwith production, capable of enormous speed and climb. Great wonderings as to who will get it.

He was delighted to learn that he had been chosen to test the new machine, a Sopwith 1½ Strutter

29 March: Up in her at dawn with Furniss as observer and time keeper. She is a perfect beauty to handle and what speed! Furniss timed her doing 101.2mph and she climbed to 10,000 feet in fifteen minutes with full war load. Truly about as fast again as anything we have got.

1 April: We got off at two minute intervals. At first we saw nothing of each other as it was too dark, but as dawn began to break one could gradually pick up the silhouette of a machine here and there. It was a most glorious dawn and well worth the early rise.

A CONTEMPORARY HISTORY

It would be almost impossible to overrate the value of the naval airman to the work of that busy and also altogether remarkable section of the Navy, the 'Dover Patrol'. When the ships under the command of the late Rear Admiral Hood bombarded the German positions and trenches on the Belgian coast, observation for their gunlayers was arranged from the shore by means of naval balloons. Early in 1915 the naval aeroplanes were able to attack enemy strongholds in force in the region of Zeebrugge and Ostend. An operation of this kind was made by no fewer than thirty-four machines on 12 February 1915 and a still larger one by the French with forty-eight planes four days later. These were the forerunners of the constant attacks on the enemy positions in Belgium. Of the wealth of gallant achievements in this locality, a few may be mentioned as typical of many.

The first illustrates a high degree of technical skill of the RNAS pilots. On 26 August 1915 Squadron Commander Biggsworth destroyed single-handed a German submarine by bombs dropped from his plane. The U-boat was wrecked and sank off Ostend. It will be interesting to know when the information is divulged how many submarines owe their destruction to aircraft, for against the underwater craft of the enemy the RNAS have played an indispensable part. The work of the British naval airman on the Belgian coast has been many sided. One important activity was the protection of bombarding ships. Writing on 3 December 1915, Vice Admiral Sir Reginald Bacon recorded how, throughout the naval operations of that summer and winter, attacks had been made on his vessels by enemy aircraft, but latterly the vigilance of our Dunkirk aerodrome under Wing Commander Longmore has considerably curtailed their activity. There were many other stirring combats during this period, such as those recorded on 6 September 1915 in which Flight Sub Lieutenant R. S. Dallas took part. On one occasion he sighted at least twelve hostile machines which had been bombing Dunkirk. He attacked one at 7,000 feet and then another close to him. By this time his ammunition was spent, so we descended and reloaded and then climbed to 10,000 feet and attacked a large hostile two-seater off Westende. The machine took fire and nose-dived to seaward. Another enemy machine appeared and was promptly engaged and sent to shore but pursuit had to be abandoned as his ammunition was again exhausted. For this determination and on other occasions he was awarded the DSC on 6 September 1916. On the same date Flight Sub Lieutenants R. H. Collett and D. E. Harkness received the same decoration for bombing raids in Belgium. On 9 August 1916 these two pilots made an attack on the airship sheds at Evere and Berchem Ste Agathe. Sub Lieutenant Collett dropped all his bombs from 300 and 500 feet under heavy fire from all directions.

One very fine exhibition of daring was afforded during the operations of 11 July 1917. Whilst on patrol a flight of five machines of the RNAS met and engaged a formation of ten Albatros Scouts and three large two-seaters south west of Nieuport. Three of the enemy scouts were driven down out of control and two others attacked with the loss of only one British machine. Flight Sub Lieutenant James Farrar, whilst on patrol in November 1915 on the Belgian coast, sighted and attacked a hostile seaplane but found that he was not alone. Out of the clouds came three hostile aircraft, while a German destroyer on patrol duties opened fire from below. In spite of the odds against him, Farrar stuck to his first antagonist and eventually downed him, where he sank. He then went for the destroyer and only abandoned the attack after coming under heavy shellfire from the destroyer and the shore batteries at Westende. This gallant officer was awarded the DSO.

Such are a few fine stories of the work of the RNAS along the Flanders coast. Nor must it be forgotten that the first British airmen to destroy a Zeppelin in-flight was the late Sub Lieutenant Warneford, who was a naval pilot at Dunkirk.

AN ACTION REPORT

By Flight Sub Lt R. A. Warneford

No. 1 Naval Aeroplane
Squadron
5 June 1915

Wing Commander Longmore

Sir,
I have the honour to report as follows:

I left Furnes at 1 a.m. on June 7th, on Morane No 3253, under orders to proceed to look for Zeppelins and attack the Berchem Ste Agathe airship shed with six 20lb bombs. On arriving at Dixmude at 1a.m., I observed a Zeppelin apparently over Ostend and proceeded in chase of same.

I arrived at close quarters a few miles past Bruges at 1.50a.m. and the airship opened heavy Maxim fire, so I retreated to gain height and the airship turned and followed me. At 2.15 a.m. he seemed to stop following and I came behind but well above, height then 10,000 feet and switched off my engine to descend on top of him.

When close above him (at 7,000 feet) I dropped my bombs and while releasing the last, there was an explosion which lifted my machine and turned it over. The aeroplane was out of control for a short period, but went into a nosedive and control was regained.

I then saw that the Zeppelin was on the ground in flames, and also that there were pieces of something burning in the air all the way down. The joint of my petrol pipe and pump from the back tank was broken and about 2.40 a.m. I was forced to land and repair the pump. I had landed at the back of a forest, close to a farmhouse, the district is unknown on account of the fog and the continuous changing of course.

I made preparations to set the machine on fire, but apparently was not observed, so was able to effect a repair and continued at 3.15 a.m. in a south-westerly direction, after considerable difficulty in starting my engine single-handed. I tried several times to find my whereabouts by descending through the clouds, but was unable to do so. Eventually I landed and found out that it was Cap Gris Nez and took in some petrol. When the weather cleared I was able to proceed and arrived at the aerodrome about 10. 30 a.m.

As far as could be seen, the colour of the airship was green on top and yellow below and there was no machine or gun platform on top.

> I have the honour to be, Sir,
> Your obedient servant,
> R. A. Warneford
> Flight Sub Lieutenant

ACES IN DARK BLUE

By Graham Mottram

The organisation of the RNAS seems to have been designed to confuse. Originally it was organised in wings and, if these had sub-units, they were usually called squadrons, identified by a letter. For instance, 1, 4, and 5 Wings, based on the airfields around Dunkirk, each had A, B and C Squadrons. In the autumn of 1916 the RNAS re-organised its scout or fighter units and most of these were derived from the earlier formations. The new fighter units were squadrons with numerical designations. On amalgamation into the RAF on 1 April 1918, RFC squadron numbers were unchanged, but 200 was added to the RNAS numbers

At Furnes in Belgium, A Squadron, which had been responsible for testing prototype scouts in addition to giving fighter protection to the Channel ports, became 1 (Naval). At St Pol, C Squadron became 3(N); at Couderkerque, A Squadron of 5 Wing became 4(N); 6(N) formed out of the Dover Defence Flight and then moved to Petit Synthe; and finally 8(N) formed at St Pol from a pool of personnel and equipment drawn from 1, 4 and 5 Wings.

Naval Eight was the first to be attached to help the RFC on the Western Front, moving to Vert Galant in October 1916. By the end of the year the unit had replaced its miscellaneous equipment with Sopwith Pups and had scored twenty victories before it was relieved by 3(N) in January 1917. In the following month 1(N) also moved to the Western Front, adding a second squadron of naval Pups to support the hard pressed RFC. When the world's first strategic bombing unit, 3 Wing RNAS, was disbanded due to political pressure in early 1917, the aircrew were absorbed into the existing fighter squadrons and also into some new ones, the most notable being the largely Canadian unit, 10(N).

Because the RNAS was not so firmly tied to the mud-bound carnage of the land battles, it did not suffer the dreadful wastage of ill-trained young men which characterised much of the RFC's operations. A young naval pilot was usually posted to a comparatively quiet sector such as the Coastal Defence flights, or to one of the bomber/reconnaissance wings, where he had a reasonable chance of building up his hours and air awareness at low risk.

The RNAS also enjoyed a good supply line for its aircraft. For much of the war, naval fighter pilots were equipped with the latest Sopwith fighters, first the Pup, then Triplane and finally Camel. When he was eventually posted to a fighter squadron a pilot would be hardened and confident and mounted on an efficient aeroplane. It is hardly surprising that this background produced a number of deadly naval fighter pilots.

The first of these was 'Red' Mulock. He had served in the Canadian Artillery before transferring to the RNAS in 1915. Flying with 1 Wing from Dunkirk he was credited with five victories by May 1916, being both the first RNAS ace and the first Canadian to achieve that status. He was awarded the DSO in June 1916 for what were probably inconclusive combats, but his experience was put to good use when he commanded 3(N) later in the war, where he was a highly respected CO. One of his pilots was another Canadian, J.J. Malone, who had flown with 3 Wing before joining 3(N). In March he was one of the British forces' top scorers, gaining four victories, as did a 3(N) Flight Commander, B.C. Bell. After scoring ten victories in a little over two months and being awarded the DSO, Malone was shot down and killed on 10 April 1917, the first victory of Lieutenant Billik of Jasta 12, who went on to be a high-scoring German ace.

By this time the Sopwith Triplane was in service, notably with 10(N) whose all-Canadian B Flight under Raymond Collishaw was probably the most successful fighter formation of all time. Collishaw himself shot down thirty opponents in the two months of June and July, heading the list of scorers in both months. Altogether the Flight accounted for eighty-seven enemy aircraft in that short time.

A member of Collishaw's flight was E.V. Reid, who scored nineteen victories in the same period, seventeen of them in one aircraft, Sopwith Triplane N5483. Reid was killed by flak on 28 July, and never lived to wear his DSC. Although several more leading aces such as Robert Little, C.D. Booker, Bill Jordan and Roderick Dallas accumulated high scores on the Triplane, Collishaw was the top scorer on this uniquely naval fighter, with thirty-three. The type's operational career was short, the Camel coming into service even whilst the 'Tripehound' was dominating the combat scene of summer 1917. The last Triplane victory was scored by H.V. Rowley of 1(N) on November 1917, and on the following day the squadron left the Western Front for the Channel coast to re-equip with Camels.

GUY LEATHER
A visit from Admiral Bacon:

23 April: At twelve noon the great god arrived (in a Rolls, of course). Capt Lambe, Lt Evill and self met him and escorted him round everywhere (except where things were not tidy, etc.) He examined the machines. The old sea dog suggested we should build dug-outs for all our machines so that the Hun bombs would not damage them. (He was looking at a Breguet whilst speaking. Heaven help the working party that has to bury that, it has a span of 80 feet.) The great man cleared off after about 1½ hours having completely disorganized the work on the station, and having talked rot the whole time. Bless our gilded popinjays – they are what makes England what it is.

A raid on Ostende and Zebrugge. Escort duty at short notice:

24 April: Dallas and I slipped our flying coats over our pyjamas and hurried down to our machines. Over Dunkerque there sure enough was old man Hun, just a little above us. We manoeuvred to cut him off about la Panne. Dallas got right under his tail and managed to shoot him down just the other side of the lines – good for Dallas. Flossy Simms and Furniss managed to bag a Hun off Zeebrugge. He was a seaplane, they shot the pilot and the observer jumped out before the machine hit the water. A good day's work for the flight!

More routine patrols and gun spotting for Monitors along the coast as usual – it seems they were responsible for keeping an eye on the coastal area for about fifty miles. They also had Zeppelin alerts from time to time and had to respond to urgent early calls, but they always seem to be in the wrong place and various 'Hun' raids on their home area were rarely intercepted mostly because they couldn't climb to the height of the attackers in time.

G.L.'s appreciation of the view from high altitude and at dawn led him to take his little Nieuport Scout to 14,000 feet on 27 April which he claims was the height record for any 'Baby Nieuport'.

4 May: Heard that poor old Green-Smith is missing – I hope he is alright as we are great pals, this is his first trip over too, such bad luck.

5 May: Great news this morning. Heard that Green-Smith is alright and got over into Holland, although he landed in Belgium, however only about 500 yards from the frontier so he managed to slip over. A signal has just come through saying that Simms and Mullins have been shot down off Ostende and undoubtedly they were drowned.

This news badly affected G.L. who felt somehow responsible for 'his' pilots. However,

Went up again in the evening to try and get something - and luckily found a Hun over Dixmunde, he was for a fight and got it as I thought of old Simms and saw red, he crashed right into our second line trenches and he was a two-seater L V G.

When not flying these lads had quite a lot of fun and visited local farms to enjoy the French cuisine. One activity was sand yachting, quite an exciting sport. They also visited ships in the harbour and even went for a little cruise in a submarine – C: 17 to be precise. They also went fishing and duck shooting so life was not too tedious or stressful all the time.

Thursday 16 May has a very full entry all about the work of the wing. It seems that the whole of the coast for forty-eight miles had to be photographed once a week with Ostende and Zebrugge being their principal concern. The German front line was not far up the coast and constant vigilance was called for.

There was some excitement on this day too:

16 May: A Hun came over Dunkerque. I made straight for Nieuport, climbing hard the whole way, managing to arrive there at 9,000 feet after about 15 minutes. I saw the old man Bosche coming home, quite low down, so waited until he was almost directly underneath, then switched off my engine and dived plumb, firing both guns hard, pulling out just as I felt like hitting him. Oh joy, away he went in a spin, but then I lost sight of him under my wing and never saw him again. Very unlucky!

He went out again later to cover a destroyer action in the channel to no real effect. He had done five and a half hours flying that day. The squadron had shot down fourteen Huns in four and a half months.

23 May: On leave. A lovely hot day so took a comfortable chair into the garden and slept all day – only waking at meal times – gad, I do feel tired. The time here is one hour ahead of France – this is the new Summer Time stunt – quite a good idea – as the evenings seem longer.

26 May: Shot a black rabbit in the evening, am going to cure the skin and make it into a flying helmet.

Leave is over but getting back to France was difficult as the destroyers were chasing submarines. However, at Dover aerodrome there was some business.

4 June: Cheers, there was a Sopwith Pup, and I am booked for it. Dashed up to the aerodrome as it was fine and found all ready. A few good stunts to oblige the station before I started across – showed them all I know and one or two others and then buzzed off for Dunkerque. Landed about 5.30pm.with two chickens, 1 lb. of butter and some soap in the fuselage of the machine – luckily they were still separate on landing in spite of the stunts. Heard that No. 1 Squadron are to move to Furnes, about four and a half miles from Nieuport,

so went to look at the place by car – it is just a field – also it is too d... d near the lines, we are in for a warm time.

5 June: Given charge of the new station and told to make it ready.

10 June: Half the squadron flew over to Furnes to take up their abode.

12 June: The 'Dug-out King' (Haskins) rolled up this morning to take over the station. He is not a bad sort, if only he would fly. He was upset to find no dug-out so all set to make one after lunch!

14 June: Painted name on my machine which is a new streamlined model Nieuport, I called it *Discovan* after a Belgian pub near here

21 June: Arrived back in time for lunch and found Prince Alexander of Teck sitting in front of the mess room. He is really a most charming person; he will come and see us more often. He likes to get away from his staff for a bit.

22 June: Did a two and a half hour patrol after breakfast. In the evening a Sopwith Triplane arrived from England. This is the first of its kind and most interesting to this squadron as it is the outcome of our own ideas, sent to T.O.M. Sopwith at his request. It is almost half as fast again as the Nieuport and climbs twice as fast. We shall hope to do great things with it.

25 June: Dallas, Minifie and self went up for a long patrol in the evening all on our own account without orders – we got one Hun each over Ghisbelles, came back and reported same. CO was not quite sure whether to strafe or look pleased. Boulanger, a French pilot, kindly went out to photograph our victims before it got too late. Many congratulatory telegrams, dinner developed into a rather noisy affair.

2 July: Dallas, Minifie and self went up several times during the day – once in the evening after Huns bombing Dunkerque, we had a long range running fight all the way back along the coast but we were not fast enough to overhaul the enemy. Certainly their two-seaters are wonderful for speed. I had a bullet in my tail skid, which collapsed on landing.

7 July: B Flight (Petre, Dallas, Minifie and self) did a sweep after our old friends the Bosche. We went up the coast to Blankenburg and struck into near Binges. Coming back about fifteen miles south of Ostende we flushed a covey of Hun single seaters, four in number, so honours were even – until Dallas put one neatly down at long range – he certainly is a fine shot – Minifie and I closed in on one of many colours and chased him away towards Ghistelles – we managed to bag him before he had gone very far – the machine went down spinning with the pilot hanging out over the top plane, so there was not much doubt.

9 July: Irving met a Fokker and shot it down but was shot down himself half a minute later, he had to land half a mile our side of the lines and bolted for shelter in a trench – the Bosche shelled his machine to pieces; he was luckily unscathed. Dallas brought down two Fokkers, one of which he downed right on to their aerodrome. Gerard also shot down a Hun two-seater, Quincey drove off single-handed five Hun machines, damned good!

My job was standing by with our new machine, the Sopwith Triplane, to render aid where it was most needed. I had five calls in the morning alone and bagged two Huns over Ostende; they simply cannot look at this machine for speed or manoeuvring capacity. I got another Hun in the afternoon, making three in all, a lucky day's work. After tea I took up a Nieuport to escort a French spotting machine– but got shot down myself by a nasty Bosche single-seater, the result being that I landed two miles out to sea off Nieuport piers and had a good two hours swim for it. Divesting myself of all clothing – it just about did for me. Dallas put in nine hours between dawn and dark and he and I have come to the conclusion that we are both about beat.

10 July: Lots and lots of congratulatory signals. Prince Alexander of Teck came personally down to the mess to congratulate me on my good swim yesterday …all too tired to celebrate our victories.

22 July: Heard that Dallas and Gerard, our flight commanders, have been given the Croix de Guerre. So glad Dallas has got something at last as he has got at least twelve machines to his credit.

24 July: Croix de Guerre given out, great show, Prince A. of Teck and many big bugs were there.

29 July: Promotions out this evening, Dallas, Clayton, Minifie and self all confirmed flight commanders – this is good news.

4th August: The second year of the war is now over – how much longer will it last? Things look like a deadlock on the front, so perhaps the end will come internally and not on the battle fields.

C. HIBBERD

No. 1 Squadron, RNAS

Stationed at Furnes from June 1916 to February 1917, during this period we carried out over 1000 patrols. There were forty-eight combats, nine decisive, also one kite balloon destroyed in sight of the aerodrome; during this period we were working with the French and Belgian aviation Corps and for the good work done by the squadron we were awarded the Croix de Guerre. Whilst at this aerodrome, which was situated on the Furnes-Coxyde Road, we were on one occasion shelved by a 6-inch gun, 120 shells falling in two hours and a half, all bar three of our eighteen machines were sent away to Dunkirk that evening at dusk, eight machines that were out of action having been made flyable in the space of one hour; we were also bombed on every fine moonlit night.

The Belgians' aviation garage was burnt out one night, and on another occasion a mess of ours which had been evacuated three hours previously was totally wrecked by an aerial torpedo which fell outside it. We eventually shifted to Chipilly-sur-Somme in February 1917, where we were working under the RFC. The squadrons on the same aerodrome being 22, 24 and 34, we were standing in reserve here for seven weeks, consequently did not do much war flying. While we were there, however, all hands had a trip to see the 'war' and quite an interesting afternoon was spent by some in tramping the battlefields around Pozières, la Boisselle and Courcelette Wood, the famous sugar refinery at Pozières being closely inspected, a number of tanks *hors de combat* were seen and also visited. The squadron eventually shifted to la Bellevue on the Arras-Doullens road in May 1917.

Returning to our time in Chipilly, just before leaving there one of my machines crashed in the French disused lines near Roye. I went with an officer and about nine men to recover what we could. On arriving there we found to our dismay that, after tramping about three miles over the trenches and barbed wire, a valley and river was between us and the machine, which by the way had been lifted on its nose by the wind during the night. We returned to our lorry and tried to reach Roye that night but unfortunately the lorry went into a shell hole and broke its steering. So we all (officer included) tried to sleep in the lorry that night, being as we were, about eight miles from any living soul. Most of the fellows got up at 3.00am as it was so cold and lit a roaring fire and sat by that until dawn, and then we started out once more with our pockets stuffed with rations to try and recover our wreck. After splitting up into two parties we tried to find the shortest route to cross the river; eventually one party reached it after about three hours march and we then found the wind had put the bus on its back. We dismantled the bus and burnt the planes and started off to find a passable road to wheel the machine on.

I sent the party with the machine to try to reach a village and the officer and myself set out to re-cross the river and battlefield to find out how the drivers and the lorry were faring. (During the whole of this time we only had spring water to drink out of cigarette tins.) Officer and myself found the lorry about two miles away from the place at which we had left it and we were then right exhausted. The driver gave us cocoa and managed to take lorry slowly to Roye, where we met our fellow who had been sent over to telephone for another car, he having been on his knees eight hours trying to get through to our squadron via Amiens. Arrived at Roye and got a decent billet at the French Telephone HQ, which was owned by an old lady, who before the war was very well-to-do but, at the time of our visiting, the Germans had only evacuated the town three weeks previous, having been there since 1914. The lady was, at the time of writing, living with her gardener and was dependent on the French Government for her food ration. She made us very comfortable with what beds and blankets they had left her and the officer and I slept on a bed that had been used by a Hun colonel. They had even gone so far as to leave a grenade detonator up the chimney, but happily the French electricians found it. We stayed there three days, an AM2 and myself doing the cooking, which consisted of our bacon rations we had with us and eggs we managed to buy in the town. We had in all fifty-four eggs in three days for five of us.

A car arrived in the evening of the third day and on the morning of the fourth we started out to try and find the remainder of the party, whom we had sent on with the machine. Well, after working with the map about three hours we traced them through chalk arrows which they had put on trees along all by-roads leading from the main road to the village they were at. We came across them looking extra clean and well, except for a shave, and found they had put the machine in a stable and had slept in the one whole house that remained of a deserted and shell-racked village named la Boissière. They had managed to get food from a French working party who were clearing up the battlefield. After that everything was plain sailing and we arrived at Chipilly that afternoon to find that the squadron had shifted to Bellevue. We stayed at Chipilly two nights and thank goodness arrived in Bellevue next day only to find all the good bunks were occupied.

At Bellevue we had extremely good luck as we fetched a large number of Huns down and only lost two of our pilots. I had one or two breakdowns very close to Arras but nothing exciting occurred. On one occasion an aircraft of my flight came down at Essars (in front of Béthune) with a broken connecting rod. I started out at 6.30am with a tender, one spare engine and one engineer, one driver and two carpenters. We went via Doullens, St Pol, Béthune, arriving at the machine at 10.30am. The machine was only about a mile behind our heavy artillery. By luck it was very hazy, otherwise the troops around there said we should have been shelled. There were Huns over all day long but they evidently didn't spot us. We changed the engine and then while the carpenters were repairing the wires that were broken, had dinner with the Sub Lieutenant of an ASC [Army Service Corps] Park. The machine was ready for flight at 1.30pm. The pilot turned up at 4.00pm and got away. We packed up the engine and tools and recommenced our journey back, arrived at St Pol and stopped for tea, then at Doullens and stopped for a drink, eventually arrived at Bellevue at 8.30pm. I was congratulated by the CO for my smart piece of work getting the machine back so soon. Bow wow!

On one occasion, three of our machines started out on a roving commission (Mr Dallas, Mr Cullen and Mr Carr) they met fourteen Huns of the famous Richthofen Circus. Mr Carr gave up the scrap with engine trouble. But Mr D. and Mr Cullen made good by going at it like hell and Mr D. brought down two and Mr C. one. They received respectively a Bar to DSC and the DSC. On one occasion Flight Commander Gerard came back with a bullet lodged in his bus and it had passed through his coat, flying boot and socks but not a scratch.

After a very successful career at Bellevue, we shifted to Bailleul (behind Messines) in June 1917. At this place we did some very good work, including a lot of low flying over the trenches and enemy aerodromes but, worse luck, we lost quite a number of very good pilots. My flight broke a record by bringing down five machines on one patrol, 'some stuff'. After another good record here we moved again but back to our old comrades the RNAS at Bray Dunes and here I am sorry to say we sent back the good old Triplane and had a new outfit complete, namely 150hp Camels or Sopwith Fighter F1 type.

A Contemporary History

Of important military notice were the raids by naval airmen into Germany. These began quite early in the war when aeroplanes were stationed at Antwerp. On 22 September 1914 the first raiding flight took place on a Zeppelin shed at Düsseldorf, carried out by the late Flight Commander Collett DSO. Flying a Sopwith tractor biplane, this gallant officer, who was the first RNAS pilot to 'loop the loop', made a successful flight across the Rhine to Düsseldorf and was very quick to mark his object. He glided down from 6,000 feet, the last 1,500 feet was very misty, and he finally sighted the shed at 400 feet a quarter of a mile away. This took the Germans completely by surprise and they had another shock when Lieutenant Marix flew to Düsseldorf on 8 October 1914 and from 600 feet dropped two bombs on the shed. Flames 500 feet high appeared within thirty seconds. The roof also collapsed. On the same afternoon Squadron Commander Spencer Grey, who was in charge of a squadron at Antwerp, penetrated as far as Cologne during a three-and-three-quarter-hour flight and successfully discharged his bombs. Another remarkable feat in the early days was the attack on the Zeppelin factory at Friedrichshafen on 21 November 1914 by Messrs Briggs, Babington and Sippe. Leaving at three-minute intervals, these airmen kept in sight of one another as far as Schaffhausen, where Flight Commander Briggs was lost in the fog. All three successfully attacked the sheds and a factory causing a panic amongst the workmen. Unfortunately, Briggs had his machine damaged and was obliged to descend and was made prisoner by the Germans. He has since escaped and is carrying on with the same determination and grit.

In the summer of 1916 No. 3 Wing was lent to the French in response to a request from them. These machines raided Mülheim and other places from 30 July onwards and the French Government expressed great satisfaction with their performance. In March 1917 Field Marshal Sir Douglas Haig expressed his appreciation of the good services rendered by No. 8 Wing, which was attached to his armies. It then had to its credit fourteen hostile aircraft destroyed and thirteen driven down, some of which were certainly destroyed.

Graham Mottram

Although the Sopwith Triplane's era was over, the type's superiority in that one high summer prompted the Germans to order their own. The Sopwith and the Fokker never met in combat, although both are assured of their place in aviation history. If the two triplanes never fought one another, their two 'descendants', the Camel and the Fokker Dr1, most certainly did. In May 1917, 4(N) became the first unit to operate the Camel. A few weeks later, another Canadian, A. MacD Shook, who had served his apprenticeship with 5 Wing on 1½ Strutters and then on Pups with 4(N), scored the Camel's first victories. On the evening of 5 June, flying N6347, Shook shot down an Albatros DIII into the sea off Ostend, and also claimed a two-seater 'out of control'. Shook ended the war with twelve victories and the DSO, DSC, AFC and Croix de Guerre.

N. M. Macgregor had scored four victories on Camels with 6(N) before transferring to 10(N), flying the same fighter, in September 1917. In the late afternoon of 15 September Macgregor's flight clashed with a number of German fighters from Jasta 11, part of Richthofen's JG1. The German leader was Kurt Wolff, the Staffelführer and personal friend of the Rittmeister, flying one of the few brand-new Fokker Triplanes to reach the front. Wolff had thirty-three victories to his name but he was to score no more. Macgregor's claim was confirmed as having spun down and exploded on impact, the first Dr1 to be lost in combat. A luckier pilot was Leutnant Steinbrecher of Jasta 46. He came off worst in a fight over Warfusee with E.B. Drake, late of 9(N) and now (on 27 June 1918) flying a Camel of 209 Squadron RAF. Steinbrecher's Pfalz DIII became uncontrollable but the pilot survived by making the world's first successful operational escape by parachute.

Naval pilots continued to make good use of the Camel. In September 1917 and January 1918, British top scorers were Joe Fall of 9 (N) with eleven and Bill Jordan of 8(N) with nine respectively. Bill Jordan became Mitsubishi's test pilot in the early 1920s and was tragically killed in a road accident near Guildford around 1926. Another post-war test pilot was Howard Saint. He had been a CPO in RNAS armoured cars, but was commissioned and trained as a pilot in 1916. He flew operationally with 5 Wing before joining 10(N) in July 1917, where he scored seven victories, became a flight commander and was awarded the DSC. In peacetime he became Chief Test Pilot for Glosters.

Probably the most unusual and tragic personal story associated with RNAS aces is that of H.A. Patey. He joined the Royal Naval Division at sixteen, by lying about his age, served in Egypt and then Gallipoli, from whence he was invalided home with dysentery. His true age was discovered and he was demobilised in November 1915. Remarkably he received his call-up papers in March 1917, and his request for a commission in the RNAS was granted. He trained as a pilot and joined 10(N), scoring eleven victories and becoming a flight commander with a DFC. He survived being shot down and became a PoW but the internment was debilitating and, shortly after his repatriation, he contracted influenza in the epidemic of 1919 and died in February of that year.

Fortunately for aviation historians of today, some of these remarkable men did live long enough for us to meet them and to listen to their wonderful stories of what must really have been a stressful time. 'Empty chairs in the Mess' is not a phrase dreamed up by a Hollywood scriptwriter; it is a graphic description of a daily event in the lives of men barely, and in many cases not even, out of their teens. The friend with whom one played pat ball cricket in a French orchard two hours ago now lay one knew not where. Yet I have only heard one veteran talk of his flying years with bitterness.

One who did not and whom I was honoured to call a friend was among the greatest and at the same time the smallest of this valiant band, L. H. Rochford (known universally as 'Tich'). He cannot have been much more than five feet tall and how he ever saw out of the cockpit of a Pup or a Camel I will never know. I found it almost unbelievable to hear him tell of drinking in the bar at Eastchurch with the Short Brothers, or being caught short on patrol at 15,000 feet with nowhere 'to go' and hoping that the wet trousers did not freeze solid to the legs. Here was a man who had stayed with a front-line squadron, 3(N), from January 1917 until the Armistice. There can be very few others with such a record, but more than that, he was the squadron's highest scorer with twenty-nine victories, a DSC and Bar, and DFC.

He inherited the aeroplane from a Canadian ace, Lloyd Breadner, who in April 1917, whilst flying Pups with 3(N), had shot down a Gotha GIII, the first one of these large German bombers brought down over the Western Front by a British fighter. Breadner liked the ladies and, in the fashion of the time, named his aeroplane after then. 'Them' is the operative word in this case, because Breadner had a fiancée and a girlfriend. On each side of his aeroplane he had one girl's name painted. He was then able to send photographs of himself with his machine to both women, and both believed the aircraft was named after them. Breadner survived the war, but one wonders if he survived his love life.

GUY LEATHER

12 August: Went up after a Hun reported at Bruges, just south of Dunkerque nearly ran into old man Bosche, who was coming back. Turned after him quickly and opened up both guns on to him; at first nothing happened – and then he began to send out smoke and dived steeply earthwards – when he was lost in the mist they sent a car out and found him down near Adinkeike – this is another Hun.

Grouse shooting starts on 12 August!

18 August: Dallas and Haskins returned from leave. The latter, our CO, much improved by the change. There is no doubt that one does get a bit on edge after a time.

24 August: Went to Dunkerque in the afternoon to see about 3981 (his Nieuport Scout) which is being recovered – and high time too – the old bus has seen some service already but it is still the best machine. Our 3lb AA gun (anti-aircraft) arrived this evening.

There followed some windy weather which held up the flying but various social engagements and duties filled the time. The French squadron on the airfield had some pilots who became good friends. It seems the French flew photo-reconnaissance sorties and sometimes the RNAS 'fighters', as Dallas, Petre, Minifie and Leather termed themselves, flew as escorts. G.L. now had a wooden hut type cabin to replace his tent and he found time to paper the walls and make it dry and comfortable. He also kept pets including two (or more, eventually) Belgian hares and a mongrel puppy called 'Joffre'. His friend Dallas had become smitten with a nurse, Miss Stevenson, at la Pauvre Hospital. G.L. comments: 'Hope nothing serious happens – though she is a very nice girl.'

On 2 September G.L. is getting worried for Dallas! 'Things look serious and I shall have to talk to him, the war is no time for cupid, one wants all one's energy on the one job.'

The weather allowed some flying of patrols but no serious encounters with the enemy. There was some concern about the enemy observation balloons and they had been practising with 'Le Prieur Rockets'; these are attached to the struts between the wings and fired electrically, hopefully to ignite the enemy balloon.

7 September: MacKenzie shot down the Westende Kite balloon – a very fine show indeed as the AA round there is very hot. He is a Dunkerque pilot so our CO was rather fed up as we have been practising with our rockets for this very stunt.

13 September: This is the anniversary of my first flight at Eastchurch. I have done 264 hours 31 minutes flying to date – not so bad for one's first year.

22 September: First fighter today. Did two long patrols feeling full of hate. Had a brush with three Huns but they would not fight. Got splashed with AA coming back. Several holes in my machine. Hear that my turn for leave has been confirmed.

23 September: At 10 a.m. saw Hun coming from Nieuport, so Minifie, Gooderham and self went up after it and managed to cut him off. We all three got within range and pooped off a tray a piece. We went down in a very steep dive, but could not see what happened though we followed down to 3,000 feet over Middlekuke. Heavily shelled by Westende during our return journey. A very busy hour.

28 September: On Leave. Caught the 10am destroyer, the 3.30 from Dover, arrived London at 7.00. What a funny world. Fighting humans and trying to kill – within less than twenty-four hours here I am in London – dining with F.S.L. Culling – who is joining our squadron in a few days and then we are going to see the 'Big Boys'. All a very relaxed time for a week or so.

5 October: Went to the Admiralty about flying new Triplane over, nothing definite yet but told to wait.

7 October: Told to go and fly Triplane at Chingford. Arrived there to find machine not ready.

8 October: Saw Haskins (CO) at the Admiralty – he told me to wait and fly something back. Met all the boys (Dallas, Bell, Mullock & H.)at the York Hotel; they are all over for a few days to attend the investiture at Buckingham Palace.

16 October: After a frustrating wait for the Triplane or anything – at last I

am moving – went down to Brooklands at 3.30pm and flew a Pup to Dover – very foggy all the way, landed at dusk. Weather thickening.

G.L. flew across to Dunkerque depot in the Pup and by the next day he was in the thick of it all again doing rocket practice as they hoped to get the Ostende balloon.

20 October: Accompanied Norton who is going to have a try at the Ostende balloon. It is a fine hazy day. My job is to fly low and attract the AA etc. – nice job!! We arrived over Ostende at 3,000 feet and I dived vertically over the harbour to about 2,000 feet and began to stunt about – this being the best way to avoid bullets. Then I suddenly saw an enormous Hun seaplane about half a mile to seaward of me and about 500 feet lower. Had no time to manoeuvre so just went bald-headed at him. I gave him a burst of about twenty rounds from fifty yards range and had the satisfaction of seeing his observer sit down in the bottom of the machine. I passed over him about twenty feet up – did an Immelmann turn and emptied another twenty rounds well forward – this killed the pilot as the machine went into a vertical dive and he fell out. The machine hit the sea an awful bump from about 1,200 feet and was entirely wrecked.

This is quite a new type of seaplane, it had two engines and two very long floats. I went home out to sea about 50 feet up. In the meantime, Norton was successful in getting the balloon, and had come home overland at about 200 feet up. He had an awful amount of stuff fired at him, but was not touched.

21 October: Took Triplane up for first trip this morning, nice up but very cold. General of French division came and congratulated us this morning. Petre managed to get a Hun over Perryse, very good effort. Went for a patrol in the afternoon, it was wonderfully clear up but very cold. The English Nurses at la Panne came to tea and we had a sing-song afterwards. Congratulations kept on coming through all day. Don't know why everyone is making such a fuss. I had a far better day last July – perhaps they are going to give me a DSC – it is my ninth Hun.

22 October: Had another trip in the Triplane this morning. Beautifully clear so went up to 20,000 feet. This is the highest I have ever been yet. Terrific cold up at that height, 70° of frost. It is freezing on the ground. Had a forced landing from that height, it took forty-five minutes to come down at a slow glide.

23 October: Petre and I delivered two Nieuports to Petit Synthe. This is a new aerodrome and their quarters are really most comfortable.

25 October: It poured with rain. A French general came and presented Norton and self with a Croix de Guerre avec Gold Star, not too bad. A most amusing show with kisses. Norton kept on making funny remarks under his breath, and it was all that I could do to keep a straight face.

1 November: A fine day early in the morning so went up on patrol in the

Triplane. Always an enjoyable machine to fly as one feels so safe – being a good deal superior to anything else in the aeroplane line at the moment.

12 November: My old friend Slade from Portsmouth days landed and crashed here on a Sopwith 1½ Strutter. He was one of the raiders (of an attack on Ostende). Heard that Malet, one of our star seaplane pilots was killed whilst stunting off Dunkerque in a Schneider.

13 November: Huns were bombing Dunkerque, I went up on the Triplane. Managed to pick up four of them just off Nieuport – but they dived to the shore so was unable to come up with them.

17 November: Managed to get a two-and-a-half-hour patrol in the new 130hp Clerget Sopwith Triplane. She is a lovely bus and so fast. Met a Hun off Zuycoote, started to engage him, but my gun jammed so had to break away to clear it. He did not wait for me and I don't blame him. I must have been 30mph faster. Norton was given his DSC today for his kite balloon effort at Ostende.

On the 23rd Dallas returned from leave in another Triplane and Petre came in later with the fourth.

Soon we shall have a flight of them.

28 November: A disastrous and sorrowful day. I was up about noon on the Triplane N504 when I experienced complete engine failure. Managed to reach the aerodrome but under judged, so had to land in the field. It was muddy and soft so the machine turned over breaking the upper plane and the tail. In the evening a fog came up very quickly – Riley and Fraines were up on patrol. The former managed to land. Poor Fraines must have lost himself. Later we heard that he had hit a house flying at full speed. The lower plane and undercarriage were completely removed. One machine gun was thirty yards from the machine. Some of the cylinders had been wrenched right off and piston rings lying about. Fraines was terribly mutilated and died on the way to the hospital. This all happened at Odinkerke not far from here.

1 December: I have been out exactly a year today. Quite a crowded year too. It will be just a matter of time before they do me in. I am getting stale.

4 December: Dallas and I are heartily sick of this inactivity so decided to do a stunt on our own. Took our two Nieuports and flying low at about 500 feet, in the clouds, made for the German aerodrome of Chistelles. Arrived there to find a few machines out on the tarmac but nothing doing. Quite a lot of people about though. Dallas flying low over the hangars threw a football out. Self following after could see the scared faces of the Huns as they saw this large 'bomb' coming their way. It was most amusing to see their faces react when the 'bomb' bounced harmlessly across the aerodrome. When they recovered from their fright they got nasty so we proceeded to shoot them up – having a wild and giddy time for a few minutes. We ended up by landing on

their aerodrome and taking off again. Headquarters were 'not amused' when they got our report on this morning's effort.

18 December: Weather not too good, however decided to have a go at the world height record on Triplane N504. Reached 20,908 feet in thirty-five minutes. This is a record without oxygen – in fact I think it is the record. Fearfully cold up there.

22nd December: Self to St Pol, headquarters, to get orders. Saw the CO; he will be in hospital for some time, I think. Minifie's brother arrived while I was there, he is joining the squadron. It is funny to think that, at nineteen, I am in charge of this station. Such a responsibility – but everyone is very nice, the aircraft mechanics – orderlies and all.

They had been erecting some more substantial 'Bessoneau' hangars, but strong winds caused trouble and they had to call out the watch to lash down the anchor ropes. At this time also Leather was having some trouble with his ears – no doubt due to his high flying adventures – he had taken his Baby Nieuport 3981 up to 14,000 feet in April and was fascinated by the ability of the new Triplane to climb to great heights. He actually claimed the world altitude record of 22,400 feet in N504 on 21 October 1916. Of course this was unofficial but very significant. At this time he had no oxygen or heated clothing.

25 December: A dud day for flying.

26 December: The younger Minifie crashed rather badly on a Nieuport Scout, and cut his face. This puts both brothers out of action. A big loss for the squadron.

29 December: A most disastrous day. One of my new pilots, Carr, crashed his Nieuport but was not badly hurt. Unfortunately his gun went off and hit a Frenchman in the neck. This will mean a lot of 'Entente Cordiale'. Hardly a minute after this than Culling had an awful crash in a Triplane, but miraculously did not damage himself. By this time I had got the 'jitters' so took a flight up on patrol. Chased after a couple of Bosche but diving hurts my ears very much now. Could not hear when I landed and had quite a lot of pain during the night. Heard that Minifie is OK except for cuts about the face.

1917
On 1 January the CO returned from hospital and G.L. was glad to see him as he had had enough of office work!

2 January: The Young Huns, as we call the new pilots, crashed around in a two-seater Nieuport under instruction from older pilots. They do not seem to have had enough experience before coming out. It would be suicide to take them over the lines. Dallas came back from sick leave.

4 January: Goodenshaw got blown over on his back whilst landing, so another Triplane is out of action.

5 January: (*Ear trouble now quite serious so G.L. was sent to the specialist.*) Saw Cooper who sent me to Jacobs who has stopped my flying for a month at least. He is arranging leave and hopes that my ears may be temporarily damaged only – so do I.

This effectively ended G.L.'s active service but fortunately not his flying career. After a month's sick leave he was eventually passed for low altitude flying and appointed flying instructor at the new flying school at Eastbourne.

Here Murphy was our CO, Fowles second in command and self third. We were a very happy crowd. Had a very bad crash here on 17 August – landing amongst some houses – breaking my ankles and nose. The rest of the year passed uneventfully.

1918

Still the war drags on. On 18 January I went to the school of special flying for instructors at Gosport – and was there until 30 January. This was a school of highly specialised stunt flying etc., and I gained a lot of knowledge there. Managed to obtain the much coveted A.1 certificate. This is about the highest award for proficiency in flying obtainable these days.

On 1 April, 1918 the RNAS and the RFC were amalgamated to form the RAF. This will be the end of RNAS officers. I had been offered a squadron of DH 9s but was out of the running as soon as this happened. I left Eastbourne on 18 August and joined an active service squadron of armoured Snipes, 'Salamanders' they were called.

However there was no call to France before the Armistice on 11 November and G.L. was demobilized in January 1919 at Catterick in Yorkshire.
In his summary at the end of this diary he notes the following:

APPOINTMENTS
   1. Flight Sub Lieut. 14 August 1915.
   2. Flight Lieut 30 June 1916.
   3. Flight Commander 30 June 1917.
   4. Captain, RAF 1 April 1918.
   5. Acting Squadron Commander 1 August 1918.

HEIGHT RECORD FOR WORLD –22,400 feet, Sopwith Triplane, 21 October 1916. INSTRUCTOR – Taught 134 pupils to fly.

His flying of varied types has appeared in the diary. Of note are as follows: total flying time 2,506 hours, 38 minutes, of which 488 hours were in the Nieuport Scout, 128 hours 42 minutes in the Triplane and 1402 hours in the Avro 504 (trainer).

Types Flown: 36
Among these types, those not previously mentioned are as follows:

Type	Hours	Minutes
Morane Parasol	7	47
Blériot Parasol	3	24
Bristol Fighter	2	
Sopwith Schneider	1	8
Morane Monocoque	5	39
Spad	15	12
REP Monoplane	1	8
Sopwith Dolphin	8	15
Sopwith Camel	28	
DH 4	5	27
DH 9	44	27
SE5a	3	9
Sopwith Snipe	4	40
Sopwith Salamander	17	28

Unfortunately, his log books were stolen in 1920, so we are fortunate to have this diary as a record of a very full five years.

Part Five

Mediterranean and Middle East

A CONTEMPORARY HISTORY

On more than one occasion, Constantinople has sounded to the detonation of our bombs whilst at the same time the armoured cars have been doing splendid service on the Eastern front with the Russian armies and also in the Caucasus. When there was a call for aerial forces to fight submarines in the Mediterranean, it was quickly responded to. When the operation of digging out the *Königsberg* from its hiding place in an African river needed similar assistance, a vessel and a seaplane section were soon on the spot. And when the question of prolonging the resistance of Kut-al-Amara was exercising the minds of those in charge in Mesopotamia, the Navy were able to bring up aeroplanes to drop provisions into the beleaguered city. It has been the same in Egypt, in Syria and elsewhere – the RNAS in three years has succeeded in building up a reputation for itself which many another service has been a century in building up. As a recent official writer has said, 'the Navy that flies is quickly building up its own peculiar and imperishable traditions'.

THE MAXIM BATTERY ARMOURED CAR FORCE

By AM1 Stammers

1917

October 6: Parade at 10.00am. Waterloo station on Monday 8 October. Will now write as things of interest actually occur.

Mother and Belle accompany me to Waterloo and said goodbye, as train left at 11. 05am. CPO Whiteley in charge of draft of ninety-nine men of the RNAS for Malta, Port Said, Otranto etc. Accompanied on train by the Northumberland Fusiliers and the Naval draft and a party of Royal Marines. A bag and a mug, plates, spoon, knife and fork served out to each man. Eight days' ration consisting of ham sandwiches, bread and cheese, a pork pie and a rock cake. Non-stop run to Southampton dockyard, arrived about 2.00pm. Unloaded kit bags and hammock and stowed in compound. No boat tonight, so march up to Rest Camp on the Common. Army and American Troops encamped and in huts here. We are put in bare huts. Fall in for dinner; unexpected but the food was terrible, two pieces of gristle and some fatty water and Army biscuits. Cannot help but throw it away.

6.30pm. We drift down to the Cowherds Inn, a cosy little place on the common. We have a nice time in front of fire until nine o'clock when we return to the camp and draw two blankets each and pipe down on the floor. We managed to make our tea of rations supplied. Pouring with rain.

9: Awoke about 6.00am very stiff but slept well. Fall in for breakfast. After waiting about for three quarters of an hour, we each get a small piece of good bacon. Hang about all morning. Dinner same as yesterday. Visit YMCA in afternoon and visited the town for a short while. Fall in and leave for the boat

A Sopwith 1½ Strutter takes off above the massive 15-inch barrels of B turret of HMS *Renown*. A two-seat biplane powered by an 80hp (60kW) Gnome rotary engine, the aircraft entered service with the RNAS in April 1916. In the shipboard role, it was known as the Ship Strutter. *Renown* entered service in 1917 and the picture probably dates from early 1918, when flying-off platforms were fitted.

The control car of a Coastal-class airship, with the crew (from the front) as follows: wireless (W/T) operator, pilot, co-pilot, observer and engineer. These airships undertook long patrols; the exposure of the crew to the elements, and their cramped conditions, can clearly be seen.

HMS *Argus* in late 1918. Visiting French officers show varying degrees of interest. The aircraft is a Sopwith 1½ Strutter. Note the longitudinal wires on the deck – an early attempt to reduce the risk of an aircraft being blown over the side on landing. This system was soon replaced by the more familiar athwart-wise wires and aircraft arrestor hooks still in use today.

HMS *Ark Royal* at the Dardanelles. The second RN vessel to bear the name, the ship was purpose–built on a merchant hull and commissioned in December 1914. *Ark Royal* was a valuable component in the RN's early experiences of the deployment of naval air power.

The rugged Short 184, of which Horace Short's company built nearly 1,000. Widely-used for reconnaissance and anti-submarine patrols, this is the type of aircraft flown by 'Rutland of Jutland' at the eponymous battle, also the first aircraft used to sink a ship (at the Dardanelles) by air-launched torpedo.

HMS *Ben-my-Chree* hoists a Short 184 out of the water off the Dardanelles in November 1915. The vessel was a converted Isle of Man packet steamer. Another important aircraft support vessel in the Gallipoli campaign, she had a short but eventful life, being sunk by Turkish gunfire in early 1917.

A Coastal-class airship at RNAS Kingsnorth, Kent, in 1915. Note the size of the ground handling party needed to manoeuvre these unwieldy balloons. Specifically designed for anti-submarine warfare, the Coastals had long endurance, undertaking patrols of up to twenty hours.

HMS *Ark Royal* deploys a Short seaplane. The aircraft has been swung outboard from its stowage on deck and is in the process of being lowered into the water. On completion of its sortie, the aircraft would be recovered the same way. The process needed relatively calm water, so stormy weather and high seas could prevent aircraft operations.

The French company Borel produced several monoplane seaplane designs before the war. The RN procured this one, calling it the 'Admiralty mono-hydroplane' and using it for various trials, although the type did not enter operational service. Note the temporary canvas hangar.

Flight Lieutenant Roderick Dallas, an Australian pilot of extraordinary skill, stands before a Sopwith Triplane. Promoted to major in June 1918 in the amalgamation of the RNAS into the RAF, Dallas was lost, probably shot down in combat with three Fokker Triplanes, shortly afterwards.

HMS *Ark Royal*, seaplane carrier, off the Dardanelles in 1915. The illustration shows the two steam-driven cranes, used to lift seaplanes into and out of the water. Well-equipped to support and maintain aircraft, she could carry five seaplanes and two to four wheeled aircraft

HMS *Campania*, a seaplane tender converted from an old liner. The picture shows the ship after the downward-sloping flight deck had been extended to enable floatplanes such as the Short 184 to take off from a wheeled trolley. Although the ship was present with the Grand Fleet in May 1916, she missed the signal to deploy for what became the Battle of Jutland, and so saw no active service.

The forward flying-off deck of HMS *Furious,* pictured at an intermediate stage in that vessel's conversion to a true aircraft carrier. The aircraft are Sopwith Camels and the vertical planks are wind-breaks, providing some protection for the fragile aircraft.

An early RNAS armoured car, probably deployed at a temporary base in northern France judging by the tents in the background. The original caption says only: 'Samson's dog'.

Sopwith Baby seaplane, often known as the Sopwith Schneider because of the pre-war involvement of that type in the Trophy races. The pilot is releasing a carrier-pigeon in this posed photograph. Note the single bomb on its carrier under the fuselage.

Sopwith 1½ Strutter takes off over the 12-inch guns of the wing turret of HMS *New Zealand*. The ship is an Indefatigable-class battlecruiser and was paid for by the people of New Zealand. The ship in the background is HMS *Australia*.

Nieuport 10, twin-seat fighter widely used by the RNAS. The design is known as a sesquiplane (one and a half planes) as the lower wing is significantly smaller than the upper.

A typical certificate, given to naval officers on completing a posting and universally known as a 'flimsy'. In those days commanding officers were required to comment on an officer's sobriety! The officers named played a significant pioneering role in the RNAS. In 1912, Schwann became the Deputy to Murray Sueter, Director of the Air Department at the Admiralty. He transferred to the Royal Air Force in 1918, in which service he rose to the rank of air vice marshal.

No. A/6

Dated ___26 January___ 1912

THIS IS TO CERTIFY, that Mr. ___Oliver Schwann___

has served as ___Commander___ on board H.M.S. ___Hermione___

under my command, from the ___twenty-ninth___ day of ___September 1910___

to the ___twenty-fifth___ day of ___January 1912___, during which period

he has conducted himself * *with Sobriety and to my entire Satisfaction. Commander Schwann is a capable and hard working executive officer and very able in experimental work. He has ably assisted me in all the experiments connected with the first Naval airship and has carried out valuable aerohydroplane experiments.*

Murray F. Sueter

{ Captain,
  H.M.S. *Hermione*
  Inspecting Captain of airships

* Here the Captain is to insert in his own handwriting the conduct of the Officer, including the fact of his Sobriety, if deserving of it.

London : Printed for H.M. Stationery Office by Waterlow & Sons Limited.

Sopwith Camel mounted on a seaplane lighter. This was the initial trial, with the aircraft fitted with skis in place of the normal wheels. The trial was unsatisfactory and the only successful operational sortie from a lighter was with a wheeled aircraft. The lighters were designed by Thorneycroft, who used their experience in building high-speed launches with planing hulls.

A much-published photograph of Samson taking off from HMS *Hibernia* while the ship was underway, the first time this feat had been achieved. The generally-accepted date for this flight is 9 May 1912, although a letter printed in this book makes an unsubstantiated claim for a slightly earlier date.

A Sopwith Camel takes off from an unspecified warship. The aircraft has already lifted well clear of the end of the short platform. The picture illustrates to perfection the potent nature of this successful fighter, the pilot sitting close behind two machine guns, with an almost unobstructed field of vision.

The Sopwith Aviation Company, Kingston-on-Thames, in the process of delivering two of its famous aircraft - Sopwith Schneiders – on one of the company's Daimler lorries and trailers.

A Sopwith Baby seaplane taxying in calm waters. The size of the pilot shows the diminutive scale of this aircraft, which was procured in large numbers by the RNAS for use in reconnaissance (and, occasionally, bombing!) as well as for tracking German fleet movements.

A Submarine Scout (SS) airship, developed quickly in 1915 and the forerunner of the most numerous classes of these invaluable submarine-hunting craft. The picture clearly shows the glued patches on the side of the envelope, from which the car was suspended.

The control car of Submarine Scout SSZ 15. Note the air scoop behind the propeller, used to deliver airflow to keep the internal ballonets inflated. A bomb is carried on the port bomb rack.

An excellent view of Sopwith Triplane 'Peggy' in front of a Bessoneau hangar. The three narrow-chord wings, of fairly short span, gave a light but rigid structure with an unmatched roll rate. The staggered wing design gave the pilot good all-round vision and for a few months in 1917 the aircraft was unbeatable in the hands (exclusively) of RNAS pilots.

A column of RNAS armoured cars in northern France in 1914. These are Talbots, improved under Samson's instructions by the addition of armoured plating with sloping sides to protect the crew. They have been given ship names to commemorate various skirmishes in which RNAS armoured cars were involved in the opening stages of the war.

at 2.15, marched down to docks with the Tommies and rest of draft. We hung about the docks until 6.30 then boarded the SS *Antrim*, a Midland Railway boat now a troopship. Left dockyard at 8.15, very dark, picked up pilot at 8.45pm and proceeded down Solent. Got into Channel, can see nothing whatever except a light in the distance, sea fairly calm with a silent swell on.

Serve out tea and bread and cheese rations issued earlier in the day. We only see the tea and cheese. I stop on forecastle till it gets too cold and go below deck for a sleep. We get between two cabins, return on deck about 10.00pm, two destroyers escorted across, can just see them that's all. Speed about 20 knots, no rain very cloudy and dark. Well out to sea and feeling it too. Go below again to sleep in same place. We ship a sea and it rattles and thumps on the iron deck. The Maltese stewards in the cabin get the wind up and rush out scared to the wide thinking we are torpedoed, nearly smothering poor old Hargreaves who was asleep on the floor. Get to sleep again.

10: Woke up at 3.30am. Have just arrived outside Cherbourg harbour. Just been hailing and a very cold. Lots of seasickness about, chiefly down in the hold amongst the Tommies, quite all right myself. No landing for some time yet so we go below again and I pipe down from some more sleep for we are dead tired, on the lower deck at the foot of the saloon staircase and sleep like a top in full rig, water bottle and overcoat, etc. When I awoke again we had pulled up alongside the quay or Gare Maritime at 6.30am. We landed at 8.00am. The town very quiet, my first step on French soil and first view of a French town. First impression the neatness and cleanliness of the streets and houses. A few French soldiers and fishermen about. We hang about till everyone is ready and march up through the cobbled streets and narrow gauge tramway lines to the rest camp on the hills in the estate of le Château de Tourlaville. The château is at present a Red Cross hospital for officers and was for sale. Camp situated on the slope, under canvas with Nissen huts for mess rooms. Plenty of mud, no roads in camp, Nissen patent hut is constructed with a semicircle of corrugated iron which forms the roof and walls. They have a wood floor and wood lining. Our kitbags and hammocks are left in the train. The original contingent is intact. No rations arrived, so no breakfast. Grumbles everywhere. The army managed to scrape up some dinner for us. Stew with a suspicion of meat and a biscuit each, no afters. We find a washroom. Walker has a towel and soap, all my stuff is in kitbag. Fifty-three hours without one, so you can guess our condition after the passage and train journey. Feeling very hungry we visit the Expeditionary Force canteen and get some biscuits (not army ones). Gold Flake etc. 10 for 2½d [1p] no duty. The French people will do anything to obtain an English cigarette, the duty is so high that the price is above very poor. Rations arrive with luggage of officers on lorry, should have been served up this morning before leaving ship. Served out with two army biscuits and a tin of bully at 8.00pm. The tea we should have had at breakfast we have now at suppertime. Draw two blankets and pipe down, twelve in tent. Raining still, more mud, slippery chalky stuff.

11: Rose at 6.30am, night under canvas spent fairly well but cold. Breakfast extraordinary well, some fat ham, good stuff and bread and tea. Wrote some postcards. Dinner, Army stew, more meat and better stuff too, rice and jam afters. No more rations supplied. Did some washing and watched a football match in progress, Army versus Navy. Have absolutely no gear so have to use handkerchiefs as plate wipers, some mess too. Let's hope we get our kitbags soon. Have tea and fall in preparing to march to Gare Maritime; arrived 7.30pm, passing labour battalion camps on the way down. Here we entrained in French carriages, worse than an old third class Northern Railway carriage, all wood rattling draughty contrivance, six men in compartment. Train starts with many grunts and jerks at 8.00pm. Twenty-nine carriages, all the contingent aboard, wonder where we are bound for, some say Paris, I wonder?

Journey carried on through the night; slept sitting up on seat, very cold and miserable. Woke up at 1.50am to find that we arrived at Caen; we got out amidst the bustle and bang of the French goods trains and stamped about to warm ourselves. Returned to carriages at 2.10am Friday and tried to sleep again.

Arrived at Lyons Bretteaux at 3.45pm. French Red Cross nurses gave us little flags, must have been a flag day here. Stick to our carriages. Sunday tea, bread, jam and cheese. Rumours of tea being served by French people at 5.00pm. More stoppages on sidelines. 7.30pm, no tea yet, give it up and admit we have been had. Hurrah! We reached a station at 9.30 all in darkness. Numerous cups and mugs found and a general din made to let people know we have arrived. Cold coffee served out; no wonder it's cold, has been waiting for us since 5. Everyone gone, we might have had some reception. We pass through St Michael–St Praz. Again we stop somewhere in the most deserted hole and darkness all around, far from civilisation or any sound at all.

MY SERVICE IN HMS *BEN-MY-CHREE*

By Flight Lieutenant George Bentley Dacre

July 1915

19th: Up at 4.00am. Prepared to hoist out Edmonds off Turkish coast but propeller went dud. My machine had to be got in readiness to go off, but at 6.30 I got another attack of half vision and had to lie up. We cruised off the coast all day, but Edmonds' engine continually went wrong so we returned to our base at 4.30. Edmonds is hoisted out to go from base to another objective but engine and propeller still dud so he lands after fifteen minutes.

I then get my machine ready but find starting gear has been used on

Edmonds' machine and it would be too late to go when the starting gear has been fixed up in my machine, so the stunt is postponed until tomorrow morning, and I am glad as I am feeling far from fit after this morning.

20th: Get up at 4.15am. Went off with Mid [shipman] Nichols as observer to Aivali Bay to look for a motor boat, submarines and entrenchments with six bombs. Went around at 4,000 feet but was not fired on this time. Observed an object sunk in the channel entrance to harbour, possibly a sub, so eased off one bomb at it and returned to base. In the afternoon Bank-Price went off in the Schneider with bombs to some place and came back to say the sunken object had gone, but dropped bombs on an olive factory used as a barracks. Wright tried to do a test flight but had engine trouble during afternoon.

21st: Excitement at lunch when a motor patrol boat was reported on fire in the harbour. Other boats went off as quick as could be expected with hoses etc., but the blaze had got too great a hold and the boat had been run aground. When the oil and petrol caught there was a joint flare-up and the magazine went off in a series of pops. The wreck subsided completely burnt out in about one hour. Did an hour's test flight in afternoon in extremely bumpy weather round the harbour.

22nd: Went ashore to base a machine in our land air station. When we were returning we received orders to immediately pack up the station, taxi off the machine as we're going to change our base. Strong wind blowing. I taxied one machine off and one float was full of water, also engine gummed up and had to drift and take down pipes before we could proceed, also machine was rapidly sinking and almost unsteerable. However, got all our gear aboard and left Port Tero Mytilene at 7.00pm. Arrived at an island about 500 yards long and five miles south of the Dardanelles entrance at 4.30am. Guns were booming and we could see our shots hitting the water and some hitting the shore at Kum Kale. A French transport full of troops was alongside us and a tramp was on the rocks. A weird monitor with 14-inch guns came up and anchored alongside. Guns are going off most of the day and land aeroplanes fly directly over us on the way back and forward from Tenedos to Gallipoli peninsula.

24th: Test flight during morning for wireless gear. Afternoon, went aboard the monitor HMS *Roberts* to get all details for spotting for them. The *Roberts*, hidden behind the island, was to fire on concealed battery a few miles south of Kum Kale. At 4.10 went off in 40mph wind and after circling over batteries at 2,500 feet observed the effect of the shots and wirelessed back. R.N. Snooty Sissmore as observer. We were fired on by machine guns but not hit. The shells made a lot of damage and we could see hundreds of Turks running both ways along the road like hares. The shells ploughed up the earth alright. Wireless broke down so we had to return after one hour and thirty-five minutes. After landing I found that the propeller shaft was all wobbly, a ball race having gone. *Ben-my-Chree* was just astern of the *Roberts* and they took photos of the latter as she fired. Very bumpy up, making one's arms ache and machine would not climb. Bathed in the evening but found it icy cold compared with Mytilene.

25th: Worked all night getting a new engine in my machine, also all day. Hands who could be spared held service, being Sunday, which was punctuated by the booms of shells. In afternoon Edmonds spotted for the *Roberts* which bombarded concealed batteries near Kum Kale. Several monitors made a heavy bombardment of the Kum Kale shore. From the masthead of the *Ben-my-Chree* I watched the *Roberts* drop shells on the batteries or rather near them. War is too scientific nowadays. Firing a weight of half a hundredweight onto objects seven miles away which the guns can't see, and being seen by aeroplane which wirelesses back the results. Very interesting, being today at the ship watching the shooting, and yesterday spotting for them.

Six machines of No. 3 Squadron RNAS passed over from Tenedos to Gallipoli on a bomb exhibition and passed back again about 6.30pm.

26th: Fearfully tired, have been up two nights getting my new engine in my machine and will have to stay up again tonight. Spent much thought in devising and apparatus for strafing flies in my cabin. Edmonds out spotting for the firing of the *Roberts* in the afternoon.

27th: One of the Huns' aeroplanes dropped forty bombs during the night, so our land machines are out on the strafe. Very busy all day, but thank goodness I am getting to bed at normal time tonight. Hurray, after three nights following. Hear that a submarine is ashore up the Dardanelles, so stand by with torpedoes on our machine. The *Roberts* eased off the 14-inch in afternoon without warning and gave us a jump. Another comic battleship arrives like a small destroyer with a large 9.2-inch gun in the bow. Now we call the *Roberts* 'Big Willy' and the new comic 'Little Willy'. The latter belched flames from her funnel and looked to be on fire. Her wireless was burnt down and we sounded fire stations, but no further conflagration took place.

28th: Busy with my new engine all day. Edmonds spotted for gunboat *M-19* (Little Willy) with her 9.2-inch guns. Very good shooting at concealed batteries on the Asiatic shore. I watched the shots from the rigging of the *Ben-my-Chree*.

29th: Went out to test my new engine. It emitted a vast quantity of oil all over me and my passenger, so came back. A Frenchman on a Morane got chased by an Aviatik and he and his passenger both got wounded but returned safely. The flying Huns have got busy again, so we must dunt them. Collier alongside giving us water. Got some war trophies in the shape of a Turkish rifle and ammunition. Heavy shelling tonight on the peninsula.

30th: Tested new engine again in 40mph wind but quite steady up. Vice

Admiral came aboard and watched the *Roberts* bombarding. Edmonds was spotting but had to come down between here and Cape Helles with a broken pinion in engine. He was towed back here by a patrol trawler. We watched a very heavy bombardment of Achi Baba in the afternoon and could see shells bursting in great quantities all over the mountain, which was enveloped in a cloud from the bursts

31st: Calm and hot. Did a test flight in morning. Afternoon spotted for *Roberts* on Asiatic batteries. Flew up Dardanelles nearly up to Narrows. Saw all British, Turkish, French and the division between them, also field batteries bombarding Achi Baba. Went over the Asiatic batteries in the east of the few Archies [anti-aircraft guns] at us but none came very clear. Flew up and down Dardanelles spotting the shots of the *Roberts'* 14-inch. A Voisin land machine of our side chased us and when very near discovered who we were and flew off again. We flew down the Asiatic shore to look for gun emplacements and I eased off my revolver and Sissmore his rifle at the village of Yena Shear, afterwards casting down empties and my empty glass water bottle at them. A real fine hate! Turks were observed on the run below. Discovered gun emplacements and new trenches, thence back to *Ben-my-Chree*. While bathing in the evening, five land machines of Allies were flying above. A Hun on a seaplane was sighted and chased in the morning.

August

1st: Store ship arrived with parts of another Short machine. Got a sudden attack of half vision after breakfast. In afternoon I was suddenly aroused out of my bed of sickness to go aboard the *Roberts* with my gear, machine and stores, also three air mechanics. This was done in ten minutes. I don't know how long I shall be in the *Roberts*, but *Ben-my-Chree* was ordered away from here and left directly after I cleared out. Of course some things left behind – just my luck being sick on such an occasion – the air bottle for starting the engine was missing, which made the skipper of the *Roberts* furious, so we wirelessed the *Ben-my-Chree* to stop and send off the necessary. Got the machine fixed up on deck and obtained a cabin in the upper deck between the tripod mast; 'very airy'. Sissmore also came aboard as observer. The Number One or First Lieutenant aboard named Vernon is a great pal of Burney's. All fellows aboard very cheery.

2nd: Busy teeing up my machine most of the day. Discovered that one lieutenant aboard named Hoskyns is a first cousin of the Hoskyns we used to visit so frequently at Nairn in northern Scotland while I was at Fort George.

3rd: Vice Admiral de Robeck in command of the Allied ships in the Dardanelles came on board from the destroyer from Mudros. He looks worried by the heavy responsibilities, but is very pleasant. He took a great interest in the machine and asked me how long I had been flying and if I was still keen.

Afternoon, my machine was hoisted out spread on the water. The ship's side, which flattens out in the form of a bulge, is very convenient for wading so as to spread wings and for bathing. Went up to 5,000 feet to spot for ship and gunboat *M-19* on concealed batteries. Did not get fired on this time to the best of our knowledge. After circling round over our trenches got chased again by Allied aeroplanes which we had not seen before. Thought it was a Hun and got distinctly cold feet to see a machine making straight for us. They evidently discovered we were not a Hun and knocked off. Coming back we did our usual local hate on the Turkish town with a rifle, revolver, to empty bottles and cartridge cases. Hear that *Ben-my-Chree* will be back here on the 6th. Today completes one year of strife and strafing.

FLIGHT SUB LIEUTENANT R. S. W. DICKINSON

February 1916

6th: Arrived at Kephalo at 4.30. Very cold dark and miserable! Again unexpected. Taken to Mess and given another person's cabin with Belton.

7th: Reported to CO after a v. cold night. Hun reported off Helles. Nieuport, Bristol and BE off. Returned after lunch. Over to HQ after lunch. Played soccer with engineers and carpenters: excellent game, won 3-1.

8th: Much better night. Missed breakfast again. Lecture wireless to thirty. Reid and Kinkhead off to Gallipoli. Twin Caudron ready afternoon. Walk towards Kephalo point after tea. Admiral Freemantle visited aerodrome.

9th: Sunny and hot. Biscoe crashed Bristol in morning. Up in the BE for eighteen minutes in afternoon. Fairly satisfactory.

10th: Very windy. Unpacked Nieuports in the morning. Walked to Panaghia in afternoon, arriving 5.00pm. Tea in a Highlife Hotel. Excellent omelettes. Hacked home late, arriving 8.45. How those little devils kept their foothold and found their way along a very rough and steep path I don't know, especially in the dark as the moon wasn't very bright. Very amusing. Panaghia quite a pretty place but very dirty.

11th: Sunny and warm. Team came for hockey from HMS *Russell*; most amusing game. Went over to dine on board with Thorold, Reid, S.P., Bosley, Savory, Littleton. Great fun.

12th: Rainstorms occasionally. Kinkhead smashed Nieuport on landing. Concussion. Soccer match versus servants. Won 2-0.

13th:Up at 6.00am. Fire in cooks' galley. Outed it. Windy. Bad diarrhoea all day.

14th: Still unwell. Parade at 8.00am to hear new warning signals explained by SP. Two submarines actually reported at 11.00am. General panic. Hockey match versus HMS *Russell*. Lost 3-2.Improving.

15th: Decided to go to sick and have done with it. Castor-oiled and put to bed. CO and Scarlett looked in during evening.

16th: Better. Up by 10. Soccer match versus A Flight. Lost 3-1. Healths to Littleton and Smiley leaving. Drunk, sick and ashamed. Not again.

17th: Feel as if had had a very bad passage yesterday! Calm and sunny. Hockey versus *Agamemnon* afternoon. In early.

19th: Bad night. Much colder. Up late. Sky gradually cleared until it turned out a lovely afternoon though very cold.

20th: Still no mail. Raining hard all morning and at times later. Out with Thorold and gun. No shot.

24th: Bush and Simpson went home on leave. Up in BD at 10.25 for thirty minutes during afternoon. Landed downwind as the smoke in harbour was blowing south and on aerodrome was blowing north. Collected shells with Thorold in evening on beach between Salt Lake and harbour. Beautiful sunset and evening, sunny but very cold air though wind coming from the south.

25th: Dunston left. Bought his gun and ammunition. Up in Henry Farmer [Henri Farman aircraft] for short flight. Not a movement in the air. Enjoyed it immensely. Played A Flight *Agamemnon* and won 6-1. Most amusing as ground was still soaking and very slippery.

27th: Windy and wet. Letters during morning. Walk with Thorold to Bluff in afternoon. Rowdy singsong by Belton, Thorold, Hooper, Kinkhead and Burnaby while I wrote letters.

28th: Sunny but cold with strong north wind. Up late and had boiled eggs in cabin. Received £8 pay.Walked out to Kephalo point with Thorold between 4.30 and 7.15. A long way but very nice though; especially the cup of tea and homemade dough cake at the Lighthouse. More and worse singsong.

March 1916

1st: Up 7.00am. Dull afternoon with south wind and wet evening.Watched Captain Carver of Repington fame salving stranded lighter. Signs of coming southerly gale.

2nd: Squally and wet. In bed till 12 feeling very ill. Very sick when I got up. Walk by myself along hills to south west. Terrible night. Roofs blown off. Everything flooded. Terrific lightning and thunder. Our cabin only leaked slightly in a few places. Poor Belton had to get up twice to see that Bessoneaus were still intact. Personally, slept very well.

3rd: Glorious morning. Sun shining brightly. Wind still fairly high from South. Aerodrome one large lake. Feeling better. Walk with Fitzherbert around Salt Lake after tea. Very young!

4th: Another glorious day, sun very hot. Strong south wind. Stood by at 8.00am for bombing, but nothing reported in the Straits. Took up H-F [Henri Farman] 3994 for forty-five minutes at 10.30am. Went over to Helles and along the coast of peninsula to Suvla, then home. Glorious view all along the coast to Mount Athos. Went on board HMS *Agamemnon* for concert from 2 till 5. Extraordinarily good.

5th: Sunny but a very windy from south. Went aboard *Agamemnon* at 2.00pm where with Thorold I procured a glorious hot bath, after which we had tea with Lieutenant Commander Murray. Left at 5.30. Went to see Reverend Bloggs up at Field Ambulance Unit. Attended 6.00pm service. Very nice, quite simple but perfectly sincere and obviously convinced. One of the most affecting services I have ever attended.

6th: Glorious day, very hot with gentle southerly breeze. First service flight in afternoon. Spotting for *M-17*'s fire on batteries on Hunter-Weston Hill. Out for two hours twenty minutes between Fusiliers'Bluff and Kum Kale. Fairly satisfactory. High explosive being fired at us from Helles and Fusiliers' Bluff not badly, but Kum Kale's shrapnel very far in front and below so that I took it to be shells from the *Edgar* bursting high over the town. Feet got very cold: otherwise most interesting and even enjoyable. Turned in early, being tired.

7th: Cloudy during morning but cleared up in afternoon, the evening was glorious just like summer. Played cricket against HMS *Russell* and won by one wicket. Brisley made a marvellous 45 in about ten minutes. I got four wickets including a very hot return to my right hand which I somehow got out to and held. Only made three! Very good coconut matting, but outfield a bit rough. They are making three tennis courts which look extremely good. Longing for a game. Came back to find an order from CO forbidding the consumption of alcohol owing to officers disobeying previous orders re wine bills. General fury, especially from Savory, Harvey, Bettington and Brisley. Of course it's SP's doing and seems a bit thick, though some do drink a good deal too much. However, it doesn't affect me. Slingsby moved over to HQ to take Jones' place as intelligence officer, so I am now alone in my cabin.

8th: Called at 06.15 for reconnaissance of Straits with orders to bomb ships on Chanak. Very nice up, but cloud between 2,000 and 3,000 feet. Took Portal and three 65lb bombs. Climbing steadily, reaching 5,000 when over Anzac and 8,000 when over Chanak. Went due east from Anzac to Kilia Liman, then due south to Chanak where Portal dropped the bombs. One fell just short in the Straits, second about 100 yards from wharf edge and third in the main street a little further. Pray to God that they didn't kill any women and children, or men for that matter. It's very unpleasant to think that we may have killed harmless individuals, especially kids. I hope not, and it all seemed so like a game waiting for the right moment and then watching the clouds of black and brown smoke that resulted in a few seconds. If this is war, I don't think much of it and I feel something like a murderer or at least an accessory after the fact. Of course, it was too exciting to let me think that at the moment: but it came afterwards. The contrast in sensation as we glided back quite slowly over the most glorious fleecy clouds, through which we could catch glimpses of the sea and the Peninsula to the right and below and Imbros occasionally in front while only the peaks of Samothrace emerge from the clouds in the distance.

It was very lovely and that made it all the worse. I should think that under brutal circumstances in callous surroundings, we must grow callous if not brutal. But everything is so lovely up above, even the shells exploding, which are meant to bring you down, that the sin of injuring or killing others seems greatly intensified and the horror of causing pain increased an hundredfold. It is too peaceful and beautiful to give one the least desire to do anything but to enjoy the peace and beauty of it and let others do the same. I can't help thinking, as Carlyle puts it in *Sartor Resartus*: 'Ach nein Werther, I am above you all, I sit alone with the stars', and whenever I looked down from above on a glorious beauty of the earth and sea, which passes all description, I have a great sensation of benevolent superiority. I can't imagine anyone entertaining feelings of real malevolence for the poor mortals underneath. I don't think that if Tennyson had ever flown above 8,000 feet above the Earth with a veil of fleecy clouds below him, only allowing occasional glimpses of the land, and glorious sunshine everywhere with a clear blue sky overhead, he would ever have written of hostile:

Gods sitting with their nectar
And their bolts are hurled
Far beneath them in the Valley
And the clouds are lightly curled
Round their golden houses girdled
With the gleaming world.

I don't think he would have conceived it possible to hunt for the joy of hunting from such a seat of vantage. Only charity could spring from such a place full of such divine beauty, and it makes one feel ever so much more powerfully, how infinitely greater must be the charity, the benevolence of a deity whose gaze is not limited by even an horizon 100 miles distant, but he sees not only everything but every individual and further still the mind and soul of every individual. It seems a sacrifice of the worst kind to have committed deeds of hate from a place whence only deeds of love and charity should come, but this is war and I can only pray for forgiveness for those poor creatures whom I may have unwittingly and unwillingly injured.

I have written a lot of what some may call 'rot' and some 'sentiment' but my only defence is that this struck me very forcibly and I am not ashamed of what I have said. Is it 'rot' or 'sentiment'? Or is it the result to a certain degree of the artistic temperament? Or is it once more because I do love humanity, especially the children? Anyhow, I feel it all terribly and I hope it may not occur again that I have to bomb any place without an immediate and obvious military reason. Though under the circumstances I console myself by the thought that even this may hasten the Turks' desire for peace and so save further slaughter. They have been busy blowing up their mines in the Straits, so it looks as if they intend opening them preparing to let the *Goeben* out before making peace. Let us hope so.

Getting my cabin into order all the afternoon. Too hot to do anything else. After tea went and bathed with Thorold off the far side of the Bluff. Coldish but very enjoyable to get even a short swim. One letter from Mother, a bill from Gieves and my commission from the Admiralty.

9th: Cloudy and dull. Much colder and glass going down. 'Battle practice' at 10 o'clock consisting of rushing all machines to edge of Salt Lake, fitting them with guns and Lewis bombs and putting 'em away again. Jaw from CO. Began to rain at lunchtime and continued to pelt all evening and is still coming down in torrents.

10th: One inch of rain fell last night. Submarine reported off Helles at 10.30. Went to beach with Belton and Kinkhead after tea and bought some stuff at the canteen. Turks evidently hard at work exploding the mines in the Straits and we are expecting the *Goeben* and *Breslau* at almost any moment. Barnato and Oxley hit Menders Bridge this morning with a 65lb.

11th: Finished indexing the gramophone records during the morning. Out for two hours with Davey looking for mines. Very unpleasant as I had to keep under 2,000 feet and most of the time was between 1,000 and 1,500 feet. Too much wind on the surface to see anything. Bloggs came to dinner with the others, but I had to go to the *Russell*. Excellent dinner and two rubbers, both of which I won! Result 3/7d [18p] in pocket. Oh monstrous! Came back about

11.00pm to find half the station in dug-outs as the sentry had sounded the klaxon on hearing a submarine in the harbour charging her batteries (we think) thinking it was hostile aircraft! Arrived to find everyone just returning to bed very bored. So funny!

12th: Lovely day though north wind still quite cold. Spent the morning mending two pairs of shoes greatly to the detriment of my fingers. Went to tea with Bloggs, watched the *Abercrombie* fire two shots at Helles from the harbour, stayed to service, back to dinner at 7.30. Big strafe at Helles about 9.00pm. Most interesting watching tremendous flashes as the gun is fired and then a much duller and slower flash of the explosion.

13th: Was going to do evening reconnaissance to Gallipoli but wind was too strong so played soccer, officers versus the Wing and won one nil. For the second time deserted Bloggs and Dr Adams whom I had asked to tea. However, they looked around and we had some tea after the game and then went to HQ to see Helles as seen from above, to the doctor's intense delight as he was on the peninsula from July 6 to the end and was fearfully pleased to be able to pick out all the trenches, his dug-out, and a hundred other places which I suppose he will never forget. Bath and cooked some duck and green peas for dinner as I was too late for that meal. Very good and piping hot.

14th: Much colder, still blowing from the north. Bettington came back late last night from his submarine trip having spent an hour and a half with the hydroplanes jammed by a mine rope just as she dived off Helles going up to inspect the net! Played dominoes and lost 17/6d [77.5p] after lunch: very little amusement. I don't think gambling appeals to me. Off on evening reconnaissance up to Gallipoli in HF 3904, sky having cleared. Unfortunately all north of Gallipoli was cloud covered – a glorious white feather bed stretching as far as we could see. Curious, this cloudbank: it was laid clean cut and as straight as an arrow between Enos and Imbros where it came to a point like a wedge, the other side running back just of Suvla and the east side of the Gulf of Saros, though less evenly, and spreading out into the great mass of cloud that he hid all the Sea of Marmara and everything north of Gallipoli. As there was a strong northerly wind I was rather afraid that all this would drift over Imbros and make coming down difficult, but on return we found only a few clouds round Imbros and nothing between about Eski Tugla and the island. The whole cloudbank had disappeared. After missing a ship off at Ach Bahi Liman by many yards we rose to 10,200 feet over Helles and, when clear of the peninsula, I shut off my engine hoping to make the aerodrome without using it again. As the sea seemed calmer, I thought the wind must have gone down so crossed the sand spit at 1,000 only to find that I could only get about halfway across the salt lake, so was disappointed and had to use a little engine to get in. Up 100 minutes. Played three quick rubbers of bridge with Barrington, Sassoon and Reid as Sassoon leaves probably tomorrow and they couldn't find a fourth. Won 3d! [1p]

15th: Fine but strong north wind still blowing. HF 8904 with Besscoe, Oxley and Sassoon, HF 3909 with Maitland-Herriott, Adams and Bettington in Bluebird. Left for Mitylene at 14.15, with stray hats, boots and paper bundles hanging about everywhere. Everyone down to see them off. Most entertaining. Took eight photographs which I hope will come out well. Very late in.

16th: Hauled out to do rounds at 9.15. Wrote a long letter to mother and a few more to catch the mail. Nicholson and Portal came back from evening reconnaissance after being attacked by a Fokker which got a dozen bullets through planes, struts and carburettor! Thorold the escort had lost sight of the Henry and so failed to attack.

MAROONED IN THE MALDIVES

By Ian Burns

Rudyard Kipling used some of the elements of this tale in a short story *A Flight of Fact*, published in 1918, hiding the true purpose of the eventful flight. My tale is told in part using the words of the principal actor, Flight Sub Lieutenant Guy Duncan Smith RNAS.

During the First World War, the Maldive Islands were a long way from any active fighting front. Were it not for the German practice of using disguised merchant ships as commerce raiders they might have been completely undisturbed. One of these raiders was SMS *Wolf* (formerly the freighter *Wachtfels*) which in early 1917 was operating in the Indian Ocean. Over fifty Allied warships were employed in the search for the raider, including a single seaplane carrier, HMS *Raven*, with several Short 184 floatplanes and a single Sopwith Baby floatplane. *Wolf* eluded *Raven*, her floatplanes and every other searcher, to return safely to Germany at the end of February 1918, having accounted for fourteen ships totalling nearly 40,000 tons. They may not have found the raider, but the crew of one of *Raven*'s Shorts had an extraordinary adventure, the subject of this tale.

Guy Duncan Smith was born in England on 21 October 1894 and he accompanied his family in his mid-teens when the family moved to California. On the outbreak of war Guy, with many other young expatriates, sought to join up and 'do his bit'. He travelled to British Columbia where the family had relatives and once there he wrote to the Canadian Department of Naval Service in Ottawa applying to join the Royal Naval Air Service. The RNAS recruiting procedure in Canada required applicants to appear for an interview and medical examination. If the applicant was judged suitable he was accepted as a probationary flight sub lieutenant and, provided he had first obtained a pilot certificate from a flight school in either Canada or the USA, sent on to the UK for service training. The cost of obtaining the certificate fell on the applicant, but partial reimbursement would be made following commissioning as a temporary flight sub lieutenant.

Smith was accepted as an RNAS candidate on 2 July 1915 and returned to California, signing up at the Christofferson Flying School at Ocean Beach, San Francisco. By 18 September he was sworn in as Probationary Flight Sub-Lieutenant Smith, RNAS, and he sailed for England by the month's end. Once in England, Guy learned to fly again, the military way, at the Central Flying School at Upavon, then on to the Isle of Grain to convert to floatplanes. On completion of training, his commission as temporary Flight Sub Lieutenant was approved and he was posted to join the East Indies and Egypt Seaplane Squadron at Port Said, Egypt, arriving in June 1916. At this time the Squadron comprised four seaplane carriers, HM Ships *Ben-my-Chree*, *Empress*, *Anne* and *Raven*. The first two were fully-converted passenger ferries, equipped with hangars, workshops and defensive armament. The two latter were German prizes, which had received austere conversions in Egypt and had been given a token armament. Their aircraft were maintained in the open, or under canvas shelters on the hold covers. *Empress* was based in the Aegean, a part of the fleet keeping watch on the Dardanelles. The remaining carriers operated out of Port Said, where the squadron had a base on an island in the harbour. From Port Said the ships ranged throughout the Eastern Mediterranean, primarily along the Palestine coast, and through the Suez Canal into the Red Sea and Aden.

Aircrew and maintainers were based at the island and assigned to ships as required. The pilots were all RNAS personnel, but the observers were a mix of army and naval officers. *Ben-my-Chree* could support up to three large, folding-wing Short 184s and a couple of Sopwith Baby single-seaters, *Anne* rarely had more than two Shorts and the larger *Raven* three or four Shorts and Sopwiths. Guy was soon put to work. During July and early August he was aboard *Raven* flying a Short on bombing and reconnaissance missions along the Palestine coast. On 25 August, still based on *Raven*, he took part in the squadron's raid on the inland railway junction at El Afuleh. Six Shorts and four Sopwiths took part, a maximum effort by all three seaplane carriers. After a brief rest at Port Said he joined Anne for an extended period of operations in the Red Sea and returned just in time to join *Ben-my-Chree* and a raid on the railway bridge at Chicaldere, about thirty miles from the coast of the Gulf of Alexandretta.

The 1917 New Year started badly for the squadron. *Ben-my-Chree* was lost to gunfire on 9 January whilst at Castellorizo, a small island just off the Turkish south coast. *Empress* was recalled from the Aegean but required a refit before she could rejoin the squadron, so *Raven*, loaded with several Short floatplanes and a single Sopwith, was sent to search for SMS *Wolf*. Raven sailed from Port Said on 10 March, bound initially for Aden, then the Indian Ocean to fly searches in the Laccadive Island and Maldive Island chains. On 21 April, Guy and his observer Lieutenant W. C. A. Meade were hoisted out on Short 8018 to conduct a reconnaissance flight of Ari Atoll, located in the west of the Maldives archipelago. When they failed to return, *Raven* searched for two days before continuing the hunt for the raider. Smith and Meade, however, were not lost, merely marooned. The story of their adventures is told in letters Guy wrote to his father.

I suppose the Admiralty will have cabled you, which is a nuisance, as it will have caused you a lot of unnecessary worry. Of course there is no doubt of it, but that my observer and I were missing. We are quite safe now. We started for flight about 4.15pm and I missed the ship on returning. The visibility was very bad. The clouds were thick and black and I don't think my compass was correct. My observer kept on pointing to things which he thought was the ship and as he had the glasses I followed his directions. We flew until it was dark and I managed to land alright. Then in the dark we taxied right on to a coral reef as we were trying to get on an island. We tried to get the machine off but failed so I fitted up a wireless station and sent our signals.

About 10.30 we floated off with the tide into deep water. I started up the engine and we taxied over to some other island, but kept on getting on to coral so we went up and down firing signal lights to see the reefs, and finally got on the beach of an uninhabited island. It rained all night and we had no sleep. It rained up to 3.30 the next afternoon. I made three ineffectual attempts to start up the engine, and had only one more start in my air bottle so I overhauled everything thoroughly, and started up. The machine did her full amount of revolutions. If it hadn't we would have been in a fix as we only had a few biscuits and a little water left. I climbed a palm tree and got a few coconuts. The natives from the other islands would not come near as they hadn't seen many whites before and never an aeroplane and so they were scared to death.

Well, we flew for about an hour and a half trying to find the ship, and then my petrol ran out, and I landed near an inhabited island but my engine had stopped so I could not taxi up to it, and the wind blew us slowly away from it, so we tried to swim ashore without avail. Then we blew on to a coral reef again so we took the emergency flotation balloon out of the tail and swam to the island having first hailed a dhow which was too afraid to come up. Also, the people on the island hid themselves. It was about a mile to the island and took us about an hour to swim through shark-infested waters. When we got ashore we were all in, and after resting we had a look around, but although everything bore signs of life, and fires were alight, we could not find anybody, so we went to sleep in one of the huts. All we had was our shirts, and I had brought a water bottle. In the night I was awakened by hearing some natives talking right in the entrance of our hut, and as I thought I had better say something in case they came in and trod on us, I said the only word I knew of their language, 'Salaam', and they jumped about three feet in the air and were off in the bushes in a second.

In the morning we got up and had a bathe, and each put on a native loin-cloth and had coconuts to eat, and then we went around the island to find the natives, but they had evidently been watching us, for as we went around one side of the island they went around the other, and took the only boat there and rowed away in it. We came back and found it gone, and were rather worried as we were feeling pretty rotten, and none of the natives on the dhows would come near, so we ransacked the huts for food. There was plenty of water, also coconuts and some chickens, so I killed a chicken with a stick, plucked and trussed it, and then boiled it.

In the meantime the observer had been hailing fishing dhows that were passing the island, but they paid no attention, and I then went out and joined him. After waving our shirts for about two hours, one came close in and we swam out to it. This time I had only my shirt on, and my observer had none at all! As soon as we went on board they seemed to lose their fear, and gave us loin-cloths and stuff to eat, and betel nuts to chew. I then directed them to go to the seaplane, which had drifted out to sea, and after much talking and waste of time, eleven dhows lined up and took it to an inhabited island close by. When we reached the island there was a lot more talking, and we were taken to the village. After having some food we came out and had them haul the machine up on the beach.

We lived for several days there, sleeping in a shed with about fifty natives, and every evening we would have a concert, and one old fellow would sing a song, and then I would sing one. They made me sing at all times of the day and night. I nearly taught them to sing 'Hello, Hello, Who's Your Lady Friend?' We used to go swimming twice a day, but we always had a guard of from twenty to fifty. One morning when all the men and women had collected around, and we had been singing and giving them electric shocks from the wireless out of the machine, I told my observer to show them his false teeth. So he took them out, and they all ran away! I also made some dice to pass the time away. It was very awkward not knowing a word of the language, and whenever I tried to go near the machine I was forcibly removed. Finally the head [man] of the atoll arrived, and we were taken in a dhow to Male (capital of the Maldives) where we now are. They are treating us awfully well, giving us everything we can possibly need, and either tomorrow or the next day we leave for Colombo in a sailing vessel.

[The following is from a further letter, written after they had landed at Colombo on 6 May.]

We arrived at Colombo Sunday noon in a dhow from Male, dressed in gorgeous red uniforms and fezzes of officers of the Maldivian Army. We both had short beards, and as we walked up the gangway of the *Raven* and saluted at the top, nobody recognised us, and we nearly got to our cabins before someone finally did, and then we did have some reception. The Commanding

Officer (Commander C. R. Samson) was awfully pleased. They had given up all hope of us.

Raven collected the Short from one of the islands in the Male atoll later in May, finally returning to Port Said on 12 June.

Flight Lieutenant George Bentley Dacre

4th: Nothing doing. Saw the *Ben-my-Chree* on the horizon go to Tenedos. Swam ashore in evening and stepped on a cactus. Much cursing.

5th: 1.00am. General Quarters sounded and everyone turned out. I went up in the control top, while two rounds were fired by 14-inch guns at the Asiatic batteries. A huge flame shows at night and the explosion of the shell seven miles away is very visible. The row and concussion up in the control top is terrific.

5. 30. Hoisted out in a hurry to spot for *M-19* on Asiatic batteries. One petrol pipe was stopped up which delayed matters an hour. Started at 6.35pm and after half an hour light began to fail. A Morane, looking just like a Hun, came out of the clouds about 2,000 feet above us when we were out 4,000 feet – another of our French Maurices took us for a Hun and dived down to within fifty feet of the water flying away at that height. Saw the *Ben-my-Chree* in the distance going off to Imbros.

6th: 3.00pm. From the control top we watch with field-glasses the opening of a terrific battle for Achi Baba. The roar of the guns for hours is almost continuous. Our fellows are pouring shells into the Turkish trenches. The smoke from these shells forms a thick brown fog, which drifts towards the Straits. How men can live in such an inferno beats me. We give the Asiatic batteries a few 14-inch pills to keep them quiet, which has the desired effect. The other Monitors off W Beach send shells which burst with terrific clouds of smoke on the enemy's observation post at the summit of Achi Baba. While we were firing, I went in the turrets to see how the 'wheels go around'. The shock and noise is not half so great inside the tower as outside. The Yankee gear is nothing like so simple as ours.

At 7.00pm our shelling on land falls off and quite a lot of white Turkish shrapnel is falling amongst our lines. The incessant roar and continual flashes go on through the night. From 3.00pm the ship's company are at General Quarters and will remain so, at their quarters to silence the Asiatic batteries when necessary. As I have no General Quarters station, I turn in, but my cabin is only a few yards off the muzzles of our 14-inch guns. If the guns go off while I am asleep I shan't probably wake again as the concussion is terrific. I have arranged with the quartermaster to call me just before firing and *Gott Strafe* the quartermaster if he forgets; if not I will.

Tonight 30,000 new troops will land and I expect that *Ben-my-Chree* is taking some over from Imbros to W Beach.

7th: No strafing by the ship during the night, thank goodness. News says that the Colonials have captured 500 Turks and six machine guns, also the French are doing well. The general infantry advance is timed at 9.00am. We hear the landing of 30,000 troops took place just north of the Australians at Gaba Tepe. The Asiatic batteries started to give the Frenchman a hot time, so most of the time we strafe them at a range of twelve miles. One shell is observed to knock out one of the Asiatic guns, and the Frenchmen cheer us from the trenches. No news has come through regarding the operations, but heavy firing goes on or around Achi Baba incessantly.

8th: News comes through that the *E-11* has sunk the Turkish battleship *Barbarousse Hairedane* six miles east of Gallipoli. The ship with its 11-inch guns has been worrying our men considerably. Also the *E-11* has sunk a gunboat transport, while the *E-14* on the surface bombarded Gallipoli town. Cheerio for them.

The land forces are doing well while our men in the south of the peninsula are giving the Turks all they want and keeping them busy. At the same time the new landings north of Achi Baba are getting several miles inland. They have captured several hundred prisoners and some machine guns. We did some strafing at 7.30pm. Gave him a couple of 14-inch high explosive to shut up the Asiatic batteries. Incessant firing goes on all day on the peninsula.

9th: News comes through that the northern forces have captured the high ridge north of Achi Baba. This ridge is the next highest on the peninsula and commands a narrow neck of land adjacent with the narrows. Strafing has being going all day. We have done nothing.

10th: Not very much strafing today. What was done was bad shooting. Swam ashore and back in evening. *Ben-my-Chree* returned at 9.00pm.

11th: Left *Roberts* in the forenoon with my machine. Wright takes my place with number 841 as I'm wanted for a torpedo stunt. Left the Rabbit Island at 12 noon and, after passing near Cape Helles, put in to anchor off the bay where the northern landing took place. The whole place is stiff with transport and battleships mostly of the antique type. A large net surrounds all of us. We are only 300 yards from the shore, which is thick with our troops. Shelling is very near and the rifle firing upon the near hill is very plain. A monitor nearby is being shelled and clears out. With my glasses I can see everything that is going on ashore and our fellows advancing in the distance, while near ashore they are digging trenches hastily in the heat. Several Red Cross bases with their flags dotted about and boats come off with wounded to the three hospital ships. Our ships give the enemy an occasional shelling and trench mortars can be easily distinguished from guns. Stores and food supplies constantly keep going ashore in cutters and special low barges. Quite a lot of horses are galloping about.

We stay there about two hours and then push off to the Gulf of Saros where Bank Price is sent off in a Schneider across the lines to see what ships there are in the Sea of Marmara off Gallipoli town for us to torpedo tomorrow. He returns with a favourable account of a large ship off the coast north of Gallipoli at anchor. This we shall attempt to torpedo tomorrow if whether it is all right, etc.

12th: Got up at 2.45am. Edmonds on a new Sunbeam Short and myself on my old machine were hoisted out at 4.30, after two or three things being done on my machine which were found necessary at the last moment. Edmonds rose well with this torpedo, but I took twenty minutes trying to persuade my old bus to lift. After twenty minutes, by violent piloting and determination I got off, which gave me much delight. However, my delight was short lived for after ten minutes the engine spluttered out and I had to land. After a quick look around nothing seemed wrong, so I made another attempt and after twelve minutes the same happened, so just as Edmonds was returning I was obliged to give it up. I was bitterly disappointed not to have been able to be the first to actually torpedo an enemy ship.

Bank Price went up also to have a look at the ship after Edmonds had got away. Edmonds returned and reported that he had hit the ship with his torpedo and returned unmolested across the Sea of Marmara, over the narrow neck of the peninsula to the Gulf of Saros where the *Ben-my-Chree* was resting. During the flight the *Ben-my-Chree* bombarded a Turkish village with its 3-pounders, and a destroyer was bombarding some Turkish positions which were replying to the destroyer. I could see while I was up, shells falling short of the destroyer. In order to get height enough to turn while getting off with a torpedo I was obliged to go at 200 feet or so over hostile country where they fired at me but with no result.

Bank Price came back to say he could not tell whether the torpedoed ship was sinking or not. The *E-11* and the *E-15* were told to keep a lookout for us in the Sea of Marmara. In the forenoon we returned to Imbros to coal, passing the northern landing on our way where heavy shelling was going on.

13th: Coaling all day. Bank Price tested a new machine, a Schneider, and went over to the land squadron to show them how we could fly seaplanes. The translated Turkish wireless says, 'hostile water aeroplane coming across the peninsula attacked an abandoned ship with bombs. The machine, which was under heavy musketry fire, was brought down and disappeared rapidly in the sea.' Hurray!

14th: Went ashore in afternoon to see No. 3 Squadron RNAS (Samson's crowd). They were encamped on the hill with about three land machines pegged down and out in the open. Everybody there was very gallant in spite of the swarms of flies, heat and sand dust. Two more RNAS squadrons are arriving. The ground is small and bumpy. An airship shed is in course of erection, the work being performed by Greeks. A band of Turkish prisoners do quite a lot of useful work. They seem very happy and are very, very civil. We have tea in a tent with tin mugs and tin plates. Bread and jam, tea and tinned milk. Met Collett, Newton Close and Bromet from the *Ark Royal* which is just alongside us now. The headquarters staff is just adjacent with No. 3 Squadron. The submarines again appear on the scene after a long absence and ease off a torpedo at a transport without effect. A new Sunbeam Short is taken aboard from a collier.

15th: Sunday. Busy in the morning getting a new Short erected. Heavy swell running. Colonel Sykes of the RFC came aboard to inspect machines and equipment.

16th: Busy all day getting machines ready for torpedo run tomorrow.

17th: Got up at 2.30, feeling very sleepy. Hands fell in at 2.45. Tried our engines and looked around to see everything was correct. I was hoisted out at 4.00am in the Gulf of Saros and Edmonds just after me on a new machine, mine being the original No. 184. Edmonds got up quickly, but I took a quarter of an hour struggling to get off with my torpedo, the safety pin of which was now out. After twenty minutes I struggled the machine up to 1,200 feet around the Gulf, thence passing over the narrow neck of the peninsula. It is only three miles across here and about 200 to 300 feet high. It, however, looks mighty wide when you're lowdown over it and have your life hanging on your engine. In the semi-dark several flashes from individual rifles were firing at me, but no goals were scored. Having got across into the Sea of Marmara, I glided down to 300 feet and eased my engine a little. At this height it is very hard to be seen with the mountains as a background in this, the semi-light. I passed down the centre of the Straits, past Gallipoli town, several small vessels and a lot of sailing ships. Six or seven miles further down I could see a hospital ship coming up and in the distance Edmonds alone, returning from his objective, which were several large ships in the Bay about three miles north of the narrows. Just then my engine started to make terrible noises and die out so I was obliged to land. This I had to do across the wind as my height was not sufficient to turn into the wind. A heavy landing resulted but no damage. The hospital ship was quite near and altered course towards me. I thought this must be the finish, either the numerous batteries would sink me or I should be captured and made a prisoner. I had left my usual spare clothes behind this time to save weight. These I carry in case of capture so that during my stay in the country at the enemy's expense I should not be without clothes and money. I thought this was a proper fix to be in, taxiing slowly in the middle of the Straits and absolutely fed up with the engine failing me the second time. I was determined to make the best of it in consequence.

Now, if I dropped my torpedo it would hit the bank and wake up everything, so I thought a ruse might work. The hospital ship was only 300 yards off now, so I came close up to it and waved my hand; all the wounded on board waved back at me and the ship passed on up the Straits. Everyone must have taken me for a friendly craft as boats were dodging around taking very little notice. I let the hospital ship pass up and half a mile up I can see two ships in a little bay. One a large old wooden sailing ship which hardly looked sinkable, and a large tug alongside a new wooden pier. I taxied up to within 500 yards of it and let go my torpedo, turning round directly after up the Straits. A terrific explosion followed and as I looked over my shoulder I could see spray descending and the target giving a huge lurch. Then, all of a sudden, rifle shots pattered in the water beside me, and my first idea was to get out of it, being in a desperate funk. By a miracle nothing hit me and, inspired by the thought of a bullet in my back, I coaxed the engine up slightly and after taxiing two or three miles got off again, then again in touch and off again to my great joy. Just after getting off I noticed some way back an aerodrome right opposite the scene of action. All five sheds were closed. I pushed the machine up to 1,800 feet, the engine making a fearful row. Passing Gallipoli town I made for the narrowest part of the peninsula, and when halfway over worse noises occurred and a compression tap came open. I was then only able to make a long glide, passing very low over the last part of land and finally with great relief reached the ship. Here I hoisted my little skull and crossbones flag which I kept on the machine, but it unfortunately blew off with a propeller draught.

I learned that Edmonds had hit a large transport with his torpedo. Colonel Sykes, Aeronautical Commander at the Dardanelles, together with a reporter to the Admiralty, were aboard *B-M-C* at the time and were fearfully pleased with the effort. Banks Price went up immediately afterwards and successfully set two large ships on fire with bombs on the narrow peninsula. So altogether we've won the war today all right. Vice Admiral de Robeck sent a signal congratulating us.

We returned to Imbros and in the evening the Vice Admiral sent for the skipper, Edmonds and myself. He congratulated us and said 'A very fine piece of work'. We related our stories to him and he was altogether very pleased indeed and said we now have a new weapon which must be seriously reckoned with. Everybody aboard was also pleased, and the ship's company of *Ben-my-Chree* showed they were pleased by holding a noisy concert in the evening.

Flight Sub Lieutenant R. S. W. Dickinson

17th: Stood by between 6.00am and 8. After yesterday's performance Thorold and Portal on Gunbus and Hooper as escort took evening patrol hoping to bring down Fokker. Returned with Thorold badly hit in the back, Portal with two bullets in wrist and leg and four other slight wounds, Hooper with engine hit and half a dozen other places too. Thorold did a glorious landing and it's a positive marvel how he got back, being quite unable to move. Pray he may be all right. Spent the evening packing all his stuff except foods etc., which I snaffled. This Hun must be some pilot and it has shaken as all up a bit. Of course, what it all comes to is that these Huns are very highly trained fighting pilots with any amount of experience who go from place to place as necessity arises, flying a very high-powered machine with a very quick climb and able to turn in its own length, so that he can pass the machine and turn back before he is 100 yards behind with his sights on. Only a very highly trained pilot, and a specialist in this machine at that, could do this; whereas we send out *quirks* who have only just learned to do a gentle turn! It's rather piteous. In very late.

18th: Very windy from north. Thorold and Portal to be moved to hospital ship, so their gear went off at eight. Bettington arrived back from Mytilene. Portal had just been moved off to the hospital ship, but Thorold were still at FAU [First Aid Unit] so after buying some things at the canteen we went over there and find him quite cheerful despite great discomfort. Talked to him for some time and the surgeon told us that it was a piece of metal and not a bullet and that it had been found wrapped around his kidney and about 1/8th of an inch off it! It had made a large hole in the muscle which would leave him very stiff for a long time. And finally, thank God, that he was doing very well. Returned and wrote a letter giving a few details to his mother which will, I hope, encourage her. Went over again to tea with Hooper and Belton and found him worse – a slight relapse – only just looked in. Hope he will be better tomorrow. Looked in at Deputy Naval Transport Officer at K Beach and played with his motor bicycle. Kept up late by Reid!

19th: Nothing during morning. Got a shock when the surgeon at hospital wanted to speak to me on the phone. Thought Thorold must be worse, but he only wanted my eau de cologne. So went off with it and stayed to tea. Did not see Thorold as he was dozing, but told he was much better after a good night. Greatly relieved to hear it. Cabled to Dads via CO for six bullet-proof waistcoats yesterday. Who should turn up in the evening but old Blandy with a Flight Lieutenant Jacob. Awfully glad to see him. In earlier, but we have now got into a very bad habit of holding a little reception after dinner and old Reid will not go. Monstrous! Very cold all day.

20th: Lovely day but north wind still very cold. Nothing doing during morning. After lunch went and did some work on the tennis court for an hour. After tea played stump cricket with S.P., Bosley, Barnato, Belton, Burnaby. Most amusing but got very hot.

21st: Woke at 1.10am to hear klaxon sounding a long blast. After deciding to stay in bed was got out by Brisley yelling through the window. Put on dressing gown and coat and shoes and roused Belton and we went and waited but heard nothing. Decided to go up the hill rather than into dug-out. After a few minutes heard very faintly sound of engine and the klaxon went off again. So found a safe spot and lay down to wait. After a little while, sound of engine became much clearer but we couldn't see the machine. Then four bombs exploded in quick succession in the Salt Lake on the other side of the aerodrome. Anti-aircraft fire from HA and the ships in the harbour for a short time then all quieted down and we went back to bed. Looked into Savory and told him what had been on. 'I thought something had been happening,' was his very sleepy reply!

Woke with a stiff neck. Glorious day with a slight north wind. Tested HF 3914; found her tail heavy. Fearfully bumpy; at one time thought I was going to be sick, and could not come down. Overshot mark three times and the fourth left ground again after landing! Grim display. Lay in the sun and read during the afternoon; very hot. After tea we played rounders until we saw Fitzherbert come in very low and land on No.2. He had come back from Suvla with only 800 revs. Kinkhead did one of his stunt landings on the Scout and Reid a fine one on the Gunbus. Kinkhead had had a fight with one Fokker and seen a second above him. Wasn't hit and I think he hit the Hun. Hope so. Late again. In fact I see no hope of getting to bed early until Belton moves. Suggested it.

22nd: At last the wind has gone round to the south again and is blowing fairly hard. Wrote a long letter to Dads with an account of all last week's happenings. After tea went over to see Thorold and found him very cheery and much better. Stayed with Slazenger till 7.15 hoping to see nurses on their arrival but were disappointed. Lent some of Barnato's records for the occasion. Very late again. Reid gets more immovable every night!

Flight Lieutenant George Bentley Dacre

August 1915

18th: The ship's cat has taken a liking to my new machine and has been wandering about on the tail and sleeping on the radiator all day. I saw a lad smash up one of the land machines of No. 3 Squadron RNAS on shore. Hope no one was hurt.

19th: Rained for the second time since we've been out here. Very rough.

Another machine of the land squadron crashed to earth today and caught on fire directly afterwards.

20th: Heard that in the smash recorded yesterday, Collett, who won a DSO by bombing a Zeppelin shed at Cologne last year, was burnt to death. Awfully bad luck, seeing what a good pilot he was. His passenger broke his leg but got clear. The machine stalled, due to engine failure just after getting off, and crashed to the ground on fire. The smash before was Newton Close, who was turned over by the wind just before landing. He got off with a slight bruising. The actual dangers of war in the air are small compared with the aviation accidents. Tested my machine in a harbour of Imbros and found several adjustments necessary.

21st: Tested new machine today with Sub Lieutenant Christopher as passenger to take experimental photographs. Kilner DSO from the *Ark Royal* came over for dinner.

23rd: Left Imbros in the night and arrived at dawn at Saros Island, an island in the north of the Gulf of Saros, about fifty acres in area. Our landing parties go ashore armed to the teeth and after crawling on their stomachs along the ground for several hundred yards, someone suggests that they are making fools of themselves and all got up and advanced. Finding the island deserted, they hoist the Union Jack, having captured the entire place including an old hut and dry well. A very fine victory.

During the morning Edmonds goes out to spot for *M-21*, but returns with engine failure. I go out at 2.00pm with Childers[1] to do some spotting in very windy weather. The machine was almost uncontrollable and it was really hard work keeping right way up. While over the land near a village, just at the spot where we crossed to do our torpedo stunt, and at 3,500 feet, we got it hot from anti-aircraft. One burst d*** near just underneath. The *M-21* put lots of shells into the middle of the village, which must have done terrific damage.

We're supposed to be here for a week or so to carry out a programme of photographic survey spotting, bomb dropping etc., but a sudden signal from the VA [vice admiral] tells us to go immediately to Port Tero, Mytilene as a submarine has been reported near there. We are thither wandering at present.

24th: Hoisted out at 5.00am a few miles off Aviali. Bank Price on the Schneider; Edmonds with Flight Lieutenant Maskell as passenger and myself with Childers. We flew around Aviali Bay, where a submarine was reported. The bottom could be easily seen everywhere. No 'Fritz' was sighted so we all

---

1. *This was Erskine Childers, author of* The Riddle of the Sands, *who subsequently became involved in Irish nationalist politics. He was executed by the government of the new Irish Free State in 1922. His son later became President of the Republic of Ireland.*

proceeded to blow up an olive oil factory, now used as a barracks, with our bombs. Also a saline factory reported used as a store. I did my usual hate over Aviali town with empty bottles. A very good strafe, which we quite enjoyed as the weather was calm and we met with no opposition. We are all picked up by *Ben-my-Chree* in Mytilene, our old resting place. Once more oppressive heat, altogether different to elsewhere.

25th: Very hot. Remained in Port Tero all day and left for a submarine 'makee looksee' in Smyrna harbour with Childers tomorrow morning.

26th: I was hoisted out at 5.45am with Childers as observer several miles north of Fuges. Rising gradually we arrived over Smyrna harbour at 5,000 feet. Here we had a good look round for Fritz while 'Archies' were firing tons of shrapnel at us from the hill behind Smyrna town. They all were a long way off.

We were just starting to blow up ships in a slipway and several [gas holders]when the engine dropped 200 revs suddenly, so we had to turn round and hope the engine would last out as we had thirty-odd miles to go to get out of hostile waters. However, with a prolonged glide from 5,000 feet and the engine as it was, we reached the *Ben-my-Chree* and broke a propeller coming alongside, partly my fault and partly the ship's fault. The damaged engine, when it failed, was a broken tappet rocker and very similar to the engine failure I had on the last torpedo stunt. We got several photos of value.

In forenoon Edmonds and Maskell went off again to Aviali Bay to once more look for Fritz, without result. We returned to Port Tero in afternoon as started to coal at 7 pm, which will continue all night.

27th: Did a test flight on No. 184 before breakfast in exceeding lumpy conditions. Compelled to land after twelve minutes as the muscular effort required to keep the machine right side up is too great. Finished: at 12.00 and left Port Tero at 2.00pm. After a stormy passage we arrived at Mudros harbour, Lemnos Island at 7.00pm and found the place stiff with ships and others.

28th: Collier came alongside with three new Schneiders which we got aboard. We dumped two old Schneiders on to the collier, having no further use for them. Mail arrived.

29th: Erecting Schneider machines all day.

30th: Hospital ship came and anchored just alongside us, full of pretty nurses. All field glasses were trained on them as we had not seen a female (other than Greek refugees) for three months. Everyone had violent pains in the hope of getting put aboard, but nothing going. However, we noticed Surgeon Hall has pressing business over there.

31st: B. P. went out to test new Schneider and got up to 10,000 feet. I tested my repaired engine. Hear that Chitty is in the hospital ship alongside.

September

1st: Very windy, and rain for a change. Nothing doing.

2nd: Left Mudros about 9.00am and, when just outside, an SOS was received from the troopship *Southland*. She had been torpedoed by a submarine and was in a sinking condition about fifty-eight miles away. We raced full speed (26 knots) to the scene and on arrival two hours later found the ship down by the bows and with a considerable list on. A hospital ship was nearby. The see all around was dotted with boats, cutters and collapsibles full of troops. We got to the nearest, hoisted out our motorboats and cutters and towed in, one by one, the survivors. The first boat was half full of water and the men in it only half clad; some had practically nothing on. Several casualties were amongst them, including broken limbs. We had a very busy three hours getting all these boatloads aboard. The sea was fairly rough, which made matters more difficult, and injured men were with great difficulty brought aboard. The troops consisting of the 21st Australian Headquarters, Signal Corps and the RFA [Royal Field Artillery]. It was wonderful how cheerful they all were. Nothing seems to upset the colonial fellows. Several were suffering from severe shock, some were seasick and others could not move, being cramped by being in the water so long.

We got twenty officers, 680 men and 120 of the ship's crew. Amongst these were 200 casualties. We gave them what we could of food, clothes and cigarettes and they were all most grateful. Some said 'Thank God for the British Navy'. Others as they came alongside sang 'Here we are, here we are, here we are again'. There was no panic and no one was hysterical. We picked up two boats and abandoned the rest. Several men in the water were picked up by our motorboats. Some boats were barely floating, while some contained over sixty men.

The *Southland* was torpedoed, according to survivors, at [9.55] and several of the ship's seamen and stewards panicked. One was shot. The injuries were caused by the boats upsetting due to careless lowering. Also someone had cut the boats' falls and so the ropes were useless for lowering the collapsibles. The brigadier general was injured by an upsetting boat and died in a French destroyer after being picked up. £30,000 in money was aboard, but they hope to be able to beach the ship and recover it and the total equipment.

We returned to Mudros in the evening and the Flagship played us in while all the ships in the harbour cheered lustily as we passed up, including the French ships. We went alongside the *Transylvania* and got all the troops off into her. Later we went aboard and spent the evening with the surviving officers who are just as cheery as if nothing ever had happened.

3rd: Left Mudros at seven and arrived at Imbros. Soon after our arrival the *E*

11 came in and was cheered heartily by all ships. She has sunk about eight large ships, including the battleship, and lots of small ones and was just returning from the Dardanelles.

4th: Went aboard the monitor *Havelock* with Wright to look over her make a report on suitability of stowing seaplanes in her. Dined aboard *Ark Royal* and spent the evening there. Commander Clark Hall, Kilner, Garnet and Dunning were aboard; also Strane, the lively Scottish observer.

5th: Went ashore with Low, Wright and Maskell to K Beach. Walked through the Indian camp, Egyptian sappers' camp and passed all sorts of general war equipment: through the camp of the 4th Worcesters and 10th Royal Scots. We then went up to the camp and aerodrome of No. 2 Squadron RNAS and saw Squadron Commander Fawcett, Ian Davies, Adams, Mills DSC, all in khaki, looking fit but suffering from dysentery. After a drink there we walked round the lake of Imbros to the Seaplane Base Station.

HMS *HECTOR* – NO. 3 KITE BALLOON SECTION, DARDANELLES

By Henry Preston, RNR
Balloon length eighty-six feet, width twenty-six feet, cubic capacity 28,000 cubic feet of hydrogen.

Left Birkenhead 2 June 1915.

8th: Arrived Gibraltar after uneventful run, feeling a little anxious about submarines, having no guns on board. Left Gibraltar, arriving Malta on 12 June, leaving the same day for Lemnos, arriving there [on the]15th.

Lay at Lemnos making several practice ascents, but did no active service until 2 July.

3rd: Arrived north end of Gulf of Saros. Balloon ascended to observe for HMS *Venerable*. *Venerable* fired several shots into the town of Gallipoli, also set docks on fire. I think balloon is going to prove very useful, as it would be impossible for battleships to find the range unless the balloon was up.

9.30 a.m. Off Escomile. Balloon up spotting all the time. Receive our baptism of fire, several shots fired at balloon and ship but no damage done. Rather an eerie feeling being under fire for the first time.

12th: Went to Imbros, making it our base. Went with *Agamemnon* and *Talbot* to bombard at Gaba Tepe, destroying 350 yards of Turkish trenches. *Hector* and balloon being heavily shelled by shore batteries. No damage done.

13th: Went with *Prince George* who bombarded Achi Baba for about two hours.

14th: Left with monitor HMS *Abercrombie* bombarding Krithia with 14-inch guns, doing great damage and enabling our troops to advance.

16th: Spotting for *Chatham* off Achi Baba. Shelling was uneventful, batteries opened fire on us but all shots fell short

19th: Got a rude awakening at 6.30am. While lying quietly at anchor, a hostile aeroplane came over us and are dropped two highly explosive bombs, one close to our starboard quarter, the other close to our port bow. These threw tons of water in the air and over *Hector* but doing no damage. Although there are several battleships as well as other fighting craft in the harbour, they singled us out as their objective, which makes us quite proud of the old ship for annoying them so much.

20th: Spotting for *Endymion*, monitor *Roberts* and *Theseus*. *Roberts* fired over the peninsula with 14-inch guns at Chanak. *Theseus* and *Endymion* firing on the shore batteries around Achi Baba.

29th: Turkish batteries opened fire on us with shrapnel, several falling only a few feet away from us. Balloon hauled down and we steamed further out. Put balloon up again, when we were again fired on with high explosive shells; several burst close to us but no damage done. (I think the old ship has a charmed life.) Hostile aeroplane appeared overhead just after we had hauled down balloon, steer zig-zag course back to harbour.

2 August: Spotting for *Theseus*. Batteries clearly visible from the balloon and *Theseus* quickly on target, her salvos falling on and in between the batteries, believed to have put all their guns out of action. Have been informed on two different occasions by army lieutenants that when the soldiers in the trenches see the *Hector* coming along they send up a rousing cheer and when the balloon commences ascent they send up three cheers, so *Hector* must be proving herself very useful.

4th: At base. One of our aeroplanes came over this morning, performing tricks which consisted of looping the loop, descending in spirals and rapid ascent. Aircraft, hostile or friendly, are by now nothing new to us, but this morning's performance was distinctly clever. (Rumour says it was Commander Samson.) Submarine *E-11* came in today and Lieutenant Brown came on board and gave us a very interesting account of their work. Lieutenant Brown is an old Blue Funnel officer.

6th: Left in the company of thirty-three warships. Looks like being a big day today. Achi Baba bombarded from land and sea. I cannot describe the unearthly din; anyone who has not seen warfare needs to read Dante's *Inferno* to give any idea what it has been like today. Shrapnel and high explosive shells bursting all over the place; after a while nothing could be seen but the flashes of the guns owing to the thick smoke and sand in the air.

7th: getting plenty of work to do now, I think we are earning our corn. Merchant Service life will seem very dull for us for some time when we get back to it again.

15th: Went out early again to spot off Suvla Bay. Sun was too strong for spotting so balloon was sent up with two dummies to represent men; the idea of the ruse was to stop enemy's guns firing on our troops for fear of being located. We could see fighting going on, with troops quite early ashore, with the naked eye. In the evening left-flank wireless station reported German Taube flying in our direction; shortly after a message was received that he was sighted. We opened fire on him with our AA guns, hauled down as soon as possible as he was making directly for us, we steered a zig-zag course. He dropped three bombs all very close to the ship. (No damage.)

11th: Again off Suvla Bay spotting. About 8.00am a submarine fired a torpedo at us; he was sighted before firing only a few feet away from us which was our salvation. The torpedo passed close under us amidships. Our light draft and him being too close was the cause of his missing. I think there must be a reward out for the ship, probably the Iron Cross. Certainly balloon ships are their pet aversion.

Submarines are christened 'Underground Bills', aeroplanes 'Percy the pigeon'.

Flight Sub Lieutenant R. S. W. Dickinson

23rd: Very hot sun. Oxley returned to replace Portal. In the afternoon took up Davey for thirty minutes in 3911 to practise bomb-dropping, and as she would not throttle down and I switched off too soon, nearly landed on the football field, but Davey luckily reminded me to switch on again. Went with Hooper to see Thorold and to arrange for a working party for the tennis lawns. Late again. This is awful. I shall have a collapse soon!

24th: Strong south wind. Still very hot. More bomb dropping practice with Davey for forty minutes. Much pleasanter than yesterday. Went to K Beach with Blandy to get roller. I am now talking with Barney, Belton and of course Reid at 10.00pm and it almost looks as if I might get to bed before tomorrow. Cheerio!

25th: A prophecy alas has proved incorrect. Moved into Thorold's cabin and think I shall be a good deal more comfortable. Savory had a scrap with a Hun which nose-dived towards Chanak. Fearfully bitten by some fiend; probably a flea.

26th: Still very hot. Duty officer. Nothing doing. Dr Slazenger came to dinner and met S.P., on whom, with Lane, he had operated two years ago. Went with Reid back to hospital as Thorold is off tomorrow morning early.

27th: Cloudless and hot. Took Davey up for bomb dropping again.Lovely between 1,000 and 5,000 but very rough above that. Fairly good I think, but Barrington most offensive. Up one hour ten minutes. Went down to beach after lunch to get the roller and went over with Halliwell to No. 3 where he bathed.

28th: Working on the tennis court all the morning with working party. Up with Davey for an hour bomb-dropping again. Three Henris and three escorts to bomb seaplane station at 5.45 tomorrow. In early accordingly.

29th: Up at 5.00am but clouds very low so went back again to bed. Clouds cleared off before lunch before a strong north wind. Sun beautifully hot, so went round and bathed in the sea. Water coldish but very pleasant. Up at 4.45 tomorrow. Poor old Fitz needed a tonic which I provided.

30th: Up at 4.45. Started at 5.00 in 3911 to bomb seaplane shed. Understood Brisley to say that if Barnato with three 100lb bombs seemed unable to climb I was to go off without him, which I did. Archie was extremely good, right height and quite near. Rev counter broke before leaving the island. Sun rose out of cloud bank just before six. Carburettor began to freeze and engine to get tired before we reached Chanak. Lost height accordingly. Clouds hid all north of Chanak. Dropped our bombs off Kephez and staggered back down Straits losing 3,000 feet before we reached Kum Kale. Prepared to ditch, seeing convenient destroyers in front of us and told Davey so. But after closing the throttle for a minute she picked up again on reopening and we got back all right only to be severely strafed for leaving Barney who meanwhile had been attacked by a Fokker which Hooper had driven off. S.P. told me that I had ***** the whole show and that I should have bloody well have been responsible for Barney's death if he had been shot down. Awfully upset thereby, especially as my finger was hurting me. Finished with difficulty a letter to mother and slept all the rest of the day. I feel very wicked only writing this one letter since Sunday but I can't sit and write when it's so hot, as it has been. I don't know what will happen when it gets really hot. In early after finishing the *Knave of Diamonds* by E. M. Dell which I thought awfully good. Lucas reminded me of Dads.

31st: Glorious day with moderate north wind. Up again with Davey in 3911 for aerial manoeuvres, which were moderately successful for one hour thirty minutes. Finger better. I'm getting irritable and easily worried. Must pull myself together. Cannot understand Brisley. He was awfully nice to me until quite lately and now he never sees me without scowling. What wouldn't I give for a couple of days at home! Perhaps I'll get them in another four months or so.

April 1916

1st: Very strong north wind blowing. Much cooler. Read *The Way of an Eagle* by E. M. Dell during the morning. Nurses came over to tea quite unexpectedly; all quite nice though elderly. Went over to a concert of the Hawke Battalion during the evening. Most amusing. Back late.

2nd: Northerly gale still blowing hard, very cold though the sun was bright and the sky clear. Walked down to K Beach and saw a mail coming in. Very little for us and we think that some of it must've been lost or sunk but I was lucky getting a parcel.

3rd: Northerly gale still blowing. Letters most the day. In early.

6th: Cloudy with strong north wind. Duty officer. The most adventurous day in my life. HF 3911, 3914, 3902, three escorts, Fitzherbert, Hooper, Jacob and the Gunbus started at 16.30 to bomb seaplane shed at Kusa Burnu. Went off against a strong wind west of Suvla. Then turned across peninsula keeping 3902 on my right bow, with 3914 to the left and rear. Went over Asia as far as Bergaz, then turned and dropped our bombs; quite good shots but fifty yards short. Then we went straight on towards home, keeping about halfway between Anzac and Fusiliers' Bluff. When about halfway across suddenly we got a terrific dunt and I thought an Archie must have burst just under my tail, but a second after Davey shouted 'Hun!' and my engine started sputtering. Down went the nose and I threw the old Henri all over the place. Evidently, he got another bead and the engine stopped dead. A piece in the corner of the windscreen suddenly disappeared and I remember putting my finger through the hole to see if it was only my imagination. Meanwhile Davey had unshipped the gun. As I looked around I saw the Fokker, a monoplane of a brownish colour, turned from us with a Nieuport turning after him and on top of him and Davey got a good target from underneath. Meanwhile we were doing the strangest of stunts and I thought I had lost control, for we were nose-diving with the right wing vertical underneath us. But I pulled her straight and then looked around to see if I could see any damage. There were several holes in the petrol tank, three wires in the inner section of the right wing and one in the inner section of the left were curled up; and the upper aileron control was severed at the right extremity. Davey thought he was hit in the elbow and his nose was bleeding owing to the rapidity of our descent. Still, so far so good. We left the peninsula at about 5,000 feet and before us lay the ditch. It was about 5.30pm. Between us and Kephalo lay a trawler, and two destroyers were just leaving the harbour for their patrol. At this point it is about fourteen miles between Gaba Tepe and Kephalo. The destroyers were about a mile from Kephalo and the trawler three miles nearer. Realising that we would be out of range from the peninsula it was obvious that the only thing to do was to get as near the destroyers as possible, turn and stand dead slow into the wind, which I accordingly did. I suppose we glided about six miles from the coast, turned when we were about 300 feet and just pancaked quite gently and perpendicularly from some ten feet. I only got slightly splashed, but the nacelle began to fill very quickly and the right wing began to get slowly lower. So we stood on our own seats and blew up our Perrins, which luckily worked perfectly. The machine continued to sink rapidly by the right wing, while the left kept out of the water. So we scrambled along the left extremity and then that began to go down. So seeing that the weight of two would soon sink it, I went off into the water while Davey hung on. Of course at this time I expected a TBD [torpedo-boat destroyer] to arrive in a very short time. I suppose we hit the water at about 5.40 and my watch stopped at 5.58 and Davey finally left the plane just about 6.00. She continued to float with a left wing arising perpendicularly out of the water for perhaps ten 10 minutes longer. It was pretty cold but we are very cheerful as we could see the smoke of a destroyer coming up over are very limited horizon. It never occurred to us that they would fail to find is very quickly.

I gave Davey some of my brandy and had some myself and after we had been in about half an hour we were just beginning to feel that we had had enough. I said that it was pretty cold and that is not an exaggeration. I saw a destroyer coming up and passing about 300 yards off nearer the peninsula. Still it never occurred to me that we were such minute marks that they could fail to pick us up and every moment I was expecting to see them turn and come towards us when Davey, who had all the time been floating about with his back to the wind (he can't swim a stroke) shouted 'Here's another'. And there came a second hell for leather only about 100 yards off, and we yelled and yelled and then I suddenly realised that only a colossal piece of good luck would save us, for obviously we wouldn't be noticed unless a destroyer came within fifty yards or less of us. Both of them passed us going towards Suvla and I will make no attempt to record my feelings as they disappeared into the distance. I will only say that the light was rapidly falling and the rising sea was making it every moment more difficult for me to keep sight of the ships and for them to catch sight of us. Davey was absolutely comatose by this time and I was getting decidedly chilly too. We watched three of the machines flying quite low towards Suvla and we heard the Turks firing at the destroyers which were underneath them. Disappointments were frequent as one of the machines came over us continually, but always failed to see us. Had I been alone I would have pushed off towards the land or at least the trawler; but as I have said Davey couldn't swim and he kept on saying 'For God's sake don't leave me'. So there was no alternative but to stay where I was and go on swimming around him. We must have been in the water about an hour and a quarter when suddenly back came one of the destroyers and before I had realised she was passing us despite our rather feeble yells. She was past actually and I thought it would only be a repetition of what had happened half an hour earlier, when she suddenly turned and made at us. Then she sheared off, passed us again, and came to a stop to windward.

I wonder if I should ever forget the stupendous relief of that moment. The boat was quickly lowered and came towards me, as I was some twenty yards nearer the destroyer than Davey. So, knowing he was in a worse condition than I was, I shouted to them to pick him up first, which they did, and a long time they seemed to take over it too. At long last they hauled him in and came towards me and with some difficulty, as I was of course quite incapable of helping, got me in too and I fell down on top of Davey, who was lying as stiff as a poker across the thwart. Then we got up to the destroyer and were slung up and a dear fat little snotty helped me along to the wardroom hatch where, by the way, we met a dear little black cat, and down I went into the wardroom where they rubbed me with towels and laid me in a blanket on the settee and gave me some brandy, which I couldn't drink as it made me feel very ill. And then I began to shiver and all the time that dear little snotty, on whose head let fall all blessings, was rubbing. I shivered and shivered till the whole place shook and I thought I would never cease shivering. All the time I was jawing hard, although every third word I failed to bring out except as a prolonged shiver.

Meanwhile Davey was doing the same on the settee at the other end, being ministered to by two splendid warrant officers and the coxswain; but he was in very much worse condition than I was, and when at last we arrived at Kephalo I summoned up enough energy to go over, still shivering, and speak to him. He was lying like a log and didn't say anything. Slowly we returned to life and after drinking some splendidly hot and excellent soup, which certainly warmed me, they dressed us up in a medley of clothes and we got into the *Russell*'s boat to go ashore with our wet gear. After going alongside the *Russell* we got ashore, went to HQ, wrote a report, spoke to the CO, and finally got back to some dinner about 9.00pm. Great had been the excitement here. Hooper had dashed back after seeing us go down and then landed after a sharp turn, cutting off two other machines which were just landing, and jumped out before she stopped. Savory then went out and Jacob also, after re-fuelling, and the former met Fitzherbert who, after chasing the Fokker to Chanak, had by a near fluke seen us on the water. He then flew to the destroyers and back to the Henri a few times until the Henri sank, leaving only some oil to show where it had sunk, and he couldn't see us! So when Savory arrived he beckoned to the place he thought we were and then went home after being out two and a half hours. They thought he was lost too, and when he appeared all A Flight started to cheer like mad. Undoubtedly he saved us, first by driving off the Fokker when our own escort failed, and then by attracting the destroyers, though the other machines did mislead them in the end. Poor old Fitz had then got back with a face a yard long and reported that we were drowned, thinking all the time of the terrible job before him, writing to tell mother! Jacob had then returned and reported that they had failed to find us and finally Savory landed about 7.15pm, having seen a destroyer put out a boat but not knowing whether they had picked this up. So we arrived to find everyone in a highly electric condition all very curious to hear about our 'show'. Poor old Hooper was rather upset at having failed to keep him off us, but he did drive him away the first time he attacked and so really there was nothing to worry him. I shan't forget quickly what I owe Fitzherbert. Nor shall I forget looking after that destroyer as it passed us and disappeared. Altogether it was an experience which is not likely – I sincerely hope at all events – to be repeated. But all's well that ends well and the finale came in the form of a great big mail from my family and others in which Dads was afraid I was having a very dull time and Molly accused me of leading the life of the idle rich!

AM 1 Stammers

15th: Managed to sleep, awoke frozen, find ourselves in a deep valley close to mountains. Dawn just broken. Dark sombre mountains both sides, snow on caps and stars still shining faintly above part of the French Alps. Two engines coming up to rear of train. Travel through valleys and beside mountains, very pretty little cottages and neat gardens, mountain springs etc. Grand sight in this early morning. Arrived Modane at 6.30am high up amongst the cold, nearly frozen through being crammed in carriages. Here we change on to the Italian railway, and discover we have to continue our journey in horseboxes. Never mind, it might be worse. We get fixed and tea served out by George; did we not need it? We have plenty of time to look around and see things. Italian guns on trucks painted all colours. Frontier post higher on top of precipice, communication by wire rope. Left at 8.45am. Here we go in and out of tunnels and across streams coming down from the snows. Passed through the tunnel of Frejus at 10.50am. Here we first noticed the Westinghouse Electric Railway. Current obtained by plant driven by mountain streams led down long pipes miles long to powerhouse down in the valley. Arrived Chiamonte at 2.15; here we get the chance to wash and air ourselves. Getting much warmer. Passed through more than thirty tunnels. Arrived at Alessandria at 8.00pm. A large station full of trucks. Beggars crowd around, the usual cry of 'cigarette' and 'beef'. Italians go crazy for 'bully'. Here ten of the sailor draft leave us for HMS *Liverpool* in Greece. Cheer them off and piped down again, for we were asleep when we arrived.

16th: Awoke sitting up in trucks 5.00am. No more sleep, much too bumpy and draughty. Arrived at Faenza at 9.00am. A Rest Camp, and are we not glad. Fifteen minutes from the station uphill road to right on the town ground. The best situated of the lot. Large, well drained and planned. Buy postcards and grub, maize and rice bread very good. No rain and warm, only going to stop for a short while. Tents. General clean and get some sleep in between meals. Cloudy, more rain seems to have followed us. Tea at 4.00pm, a real good blowout for the conditions. Fall in and depart under cover of darkness at 7.00pm. Raining cats and dogs. Very muddy now. Arrangements made for us to get our hammocks and sling in trucks. Cheers but rather late to think of things now. Left station at 8.45pm. Sling hammocks, everyone much happier in anticipation of a good night. Supper and songs. Songs, mark you on a pouring wet night, thirty boys on wood benches round a single candle and all wet. Hammocks A1. Happy dreams.

17th: Awoke very fresh and warm. Glorious night. Fancy we slept all night amid the bumps and crashes. Sea on our left, the shores of the Adriatic Sea. Much warmer air. We stop some while here 7.30am. Arrive Castellamare at 9.15. Shunted on to siding for a halt, one day's rations served out; these we promptly put away for breakfast at 10.00am. Fruit bought very cheap. Grapes three pounds for a penny, green figs and pomegranates. Mounted guns still about, gunners standing. Probable air raid from Turkey. Wash etc. Last night's rest did us any amount of good, made us feel new again. First dose of quinine, 10 grams. Left at 1.30. Sun glorious, we sunned ourselves. No rain about here for ten weeks. Our travels still continue along the coast. The sea looked glorious, in fact everything is grand. The houses are very weird, all built out of a kind of hard chalk, built in the middle of the field, similar to a block with a quarter cut out; sometimes a quarter stands alone in the field. Irrigation troughs, all dry, soil cracked. Thousands of dwarf fig trees. Tourigo di Sangro at 2.55pm. This is built practically on the seashore as are many of the stations of our long journey, right down the coast to Brindisi. It is here where one notices the difference between the French and Italian railways. They are tidier altogether. The stations are all compact square buildings built of the same stone and the line itself is kept in very good order, a proper embankment and gullies. The guards signal by means of a horn, not as the French do by a blaring of whistles constantly. There is not a large sign of fishing as one would expect to see on such a length of coastline; in fact not a vessel of any sort to be seen about for several days. Piped down in hammocks at 8.00pm, no tea. Awoke at Foggia at 9.00pm. Tea we should have had waiting for us here. Two and half hours late. No one allowed out so we miss our wash and airing, left at 11.50pm. Got to sleep at midnight.

18th: Awoke at 8.20am. Splendid night, nice and warm in hammocks. The door of our truck was left partly open and in passing through some of the wayside stations, or stopping as it is a single line, a thief helped himself to a pair of boots and a handbag, not mine thank goodness. Boots are a terrible price. People go barefoot. Around this district, as much as we can see from the line, the soil seems to suffer very much in the dry season. The soil appears to be about a foot deep and when the rain does come it washes most of it away; consequently in the dry season it cracks right through to the rock bottom, so that when it rains again the water pours in the cracks and undermines it and washes more away. To prevent this, the land is laid out in a series of steps and a concrete ditch at the bottom to drain off the water. At present all the ditches are dry and the riverbeds, which are rushing torrents with the snow from the mountains, which we can see in the distance, are mere dribbles. We saw nothing growing except pumpkins and figs, all trees are very short and look years and years old, very thick foliage.

Arrived at Brindisi at 1.00pm. The sun is out in a big expanse of light blue sky making everything very hot. The sea is a lovely colour of blue, only describable as Mediterranean blue. Several signs of aircraft FBA flying boats about, first signs of any flying yet seen. There is a washing place erected here in the vineyard of some sort and beneath the shade of the creeping vines, which are trained over the stonework and trellis, we perform our ablutions. Away in the distance we can see shipping of sorts, presumed to be the docks. Nothing else worthy of mention can be seen. Departed at 3.30pm. This place appears to be the residence of the better class as the houses are built with domes as in pictures of the east. Another forty miles or so and we arrive at Taranto. Arrived at Grottaglie at 5.40pm. Twilight set in. One can just see part of the town on a hill and the square white houses and domes with the large similarly built churches make you realise we are in Italy.

Flight Lieutenant George Bentley Dacre

21st: Although blowing very hard, we left Kephalo in the morning after putting one machine aboard *Ark Royal* and arrived off the Bulgarian[2] coast opposite Dedeagach. Here in a young gale I was hoisted out with Childers and got off easier than expected and with difficulty flew along coast about three miles out, up to 2,000 feet. Above were clouds, so I made inshore where the bumps were worse, and turning by Dedeagach returned past the barracks at Micro along the coast. As the bumps were so uncontrollable, made for the ship then landed, folded and taxied with difficulty to avoid being overturned on the water up to the ship.

---

2. *At that time, Bulgaria's southern borders included a stretch of the northern Aegean coastline. Dedeagach is now the Greek town of Alexandropolis.*

We saw lots of rolling stock on the sidings at Dedeagach and men in parties digging trenches along the coast. In the meanwhile, our fleet consisting of HM Ships *Theseus*, *Doris*, *Hussar*, four destroyers, three monitors, trawlers and a patrol vessel, had arrived on the scene and started a fair strafe. We saw the first shell burst near the barracks and every man and horse scattering away. The barracks are fairly riddled and will be pretty drafty to sleep in tonight, gaping holes and half roofs. The best strafing to watch was on the carriage and trucks on the railway. A destroyer got an engine 'plunk' and a great green explosion took place followed by clouds of steam. The railway bridge was strafed and a great concentration on the small harbour destroyed the breakwater and most the caiques which were packed inside. A lovely big-fronted factory, presenting an excellent target, was blazed at and points on the railway destroyed.

It was a horribly one-sided affair as no opposition was made, but a real fine sight to watch. The Vice Admiral came up in the *Triad* after one hour's strafing and, after watching the bombardment for three hours, we were sent back to Kephalo as the wind had increased.

22nd: Nothing doing. Very windy. The rat in my cabin, which has been quite friendly for the last three weeks, started to bag my food so I declared war. After four desperate encounters with the aid of two flight lieutenants, and after breaking the electric light and generally turning the cabin into an ash pit, we were victorious by our combined efforts. The rat measured twelve inches exactly. Some sport in these monotonous days.

23rd: Nothing doing at all. Maskell gave a lecture on bombs and warheads and the Lewis gun.

25th: Left Kephalo midday for Bulgarian coast. No wind. Found that Dedeagach was now a smoking ruin. Edmonds with Childers went off on a reconnaissance and took some very good photos. They also found the coast was heavily entrenched. Banks Price and Wright on Schneider went off with explosive and incendiary bombs to strafe anything left of the railway and town. We watched from a mile out to sea.

Returned to Kephalo in evening and Paymaster from *Roberts* came aboard, bringing a piece of the shell which had hit them this morning at Rabbit Island. He says directly a shell burst aboard the men rush out for souvenir fragments. The shells are made by an American firm – the same firm that made the *Roberts*'s guns.

26th: Left Kephalo at 4.00am and arrived at Dedeagach at 7.00pm. At 9.00am I went up with Childers to spot for the two monitors on the railway junction six miles inland north of Dedeagach, called Bodoma station. We went over the town about 600 feet and saw well into it. The front part facing the sea is still burning well. The railway bridge just outside is damaged, trucks are lying about damaged. The large factory is gutted and so are all the walls. Caiques in the harbour half sunk. No sign of life about, but the coast is heavily entrenched from the beach backwards to the hills. A train and fifteen carriages and trucks left the junction as we approach. If we only had had some bombs we could have chased it. Clouds were thick above 4,000 so we had to spot from below. A strong wind above keeps us from flying very far inland. An engine failure would mean landing on the land with consequent exit to everything. The monitors got on the junction on the fourth shot and I can see the ticket collector shouting 'all change here for Dedeagach, excursion train number four platform' run away and drop his tickets (I don't think).

After being up two and a half hours with plenty of work to do, the oil pressure suddenly went down, so I returned over the *Ben-my-Chree*, cut out the engine and landed with a dead motor. Propeller stopped. Edmonds went up later to spot for same and returned after one and a half hours. Ten shots were hit, one shell burst in the gun and went to pieces halfway from the ship to the shore. HMS *Doris* strafed the rails near in. We returned to Kephalo in afternoon.

28th: Went ashore with Wright with our guns in afternoon and wandered up the stream running down a fertile valley. Very similar to the Doon Valley, except where there are oak trees in the latter there are olives and fig trees in this place. Blackberries were plentiful, and sloes. I shot a large sparrow hawk, but it didn't see any partridges. I blew a small yellowthroat to bits at short range and just lost a lovely big squirrel. It was quite like old England with the rushing bouldered stream and I expect there are plenty of fish there when there is more water.

Returning, we came across a Greek outside his hut and by signs we asked him if he had any honey and eggs for sale, but no good. We then with great difficulty made him understand we would like to shoot his hens for payment. He would not, but he would kill them himself for us. We thought a chicken or two would be a very nice luxury for the mess, so we told him to carry on and slay two. He enticed them into a pigsty with seed. And then we bargained hard with him: Two shillings each? No, we said. Two shillings and one shilling for both? No! Finally one and six and one shilling did it and he proceeded to slay them with my pocket knife. We got plenty of chafe on our return to the ship with a gun and a hen apiece!

Cependant!

29th: Coaling hard all day and night.

30th. Left Kephalo at 10.30am for Bulgarian coast. A dummy Dreadnought came in before we left. A comic ship, disguised as a battle-cruiser.

Arrived off Dedeagach at noon. Edmonds and Childers went off on reconnaissance, Wright with Smith and two 100lb bombs went off to Dedeagach, but had to return. B. P. went off with six bombs and dropped them over the town. Later I went up with Childers and found it very bumpy in parts. We went on reconnaissance of coast up to Port Lagos. We had to dodge several rainstorms and went in over the coast to start with at 800 feet, circling round and gradually working our way to Port Lagos. Here we had to put up with the rain. Port Lagos is a mass of lagoons, which we circled round. We found a three-masted schooner at anchor so I came down to 200 feet and Childers blazed away at it with his rifle, I with my revolver. No one was on deck. We thought we might come down and board the ship, tie up the seaplane astern and sail the ship away. Unfortunately, a strong wind was blowing inshore, which would make it difficult to get aboard and difficult to beat out once the anchor was up and the sails set, so we gave up the idea.

We next went down near a hut onshore and started to strafe it, but a volley of rifle fire greeted us from the trenches nearby and we got out of it. It proved that armed forces were in the trenches along the shore, which from high up look lifeless everywhere. Our reconnaissance revealed that the large camp at the Duma junction had packed up altogether after the strafe of 26th. Also this was the first time seaplanes had engaged the enemy in trenches with rifles and revolvers.

31st. Fairly slack day. All ships cheered in the submarine *H-4*, which had just come down the Dardanelles having sunk, amongst other things, a transport laden with munitions.

November

1st: *Ark Royal* after about six months continual lying at Kephalo left this morning from Mytilene. We have to take over her work besides our own.

3rd: Went ashore in evening in dinghy and paid a visit to No. 3 Squadron RNAS. They had a fire here two days ago, which burnt their workshop, destroyed fourteen engines, stores, workshop equipment, cartridge stores, three bombs and gas cylinders. A fine flare-up. The officers' cabins are fine, an aeroplane packing case divided into two, with green canvas outside and inside. Fly-proof window. Two 100lb bomb cases make an excellent wardrobe. Petrol cans suitably biffed make excellent washing utensils. The whole is raised a foot on logs with a step down. Electric lighting. Some luxury! We went down the weird bombproof dug-outs where all the Turkish prisoners flee to when a Taube comes over and have to be cleared out.

They told me a good story about the last nocturnal visit of a Hun. They heard he was coming over so Marix and the Commander went up and were only in the air two minutes before the Hun arrived. When they got over the

Turkish aerodrome, the Turks, thinking their pal was coming back, lit flares for him to land, which gave our friends the spot so they came down quite low and dropped their bombs right on the runway and next day our machines dropped twenty-four bombs on the aerodrome, so they haven't paid us a visit since.

5th: Went ashore and afternoon to visit the field dentist. He gave me about twenty minutes as he was very busy and during this time he revved up his drilling machine at top speed and fairly buzzed around the old tooth of mine. The whole show was not exactly the latest American outfit. Afterwards I went along to No. 2 Squadron RNAS where I found Gaskell, Bass, two or three other old acquaintances, and Teesdale of School House, Clifton, whom I haven't seen for about seven years. He was sick with dysentery, however, but quite cheery. Here they also live in luxurious packing cases full of pictures from weekly periodicals.

6th: Went up to Gulf of Saros in afternoon, but we found that the weather conditions too bad for spotting so we returned to Kephalo.

7th: Very busy all day from 6.00am until 11.30 pm, preparing machines for a bombing expedition tomorrow.

8th: Put to sea at 7.00am and went to the Bulgarian coast near Dedeagach. Here Edmonds and I were hoisted out with two 112lb bombs each. We both got away, but I had to land again as my engine was 60 revs short. Edmonds went on, I had my trouble remedied and started away again. Our objective was to attack a very important bridge over the Maritsa river over which the main line from Adrianople to Constantinople runs. This bridge lies seventy miles inland, up a very narrow winding river, so winding that if you went up it you see yourself coming back in places. There were very few places on this river where it would be possible to land in the seaplane, and with our unreliable Sunbeam engines, on which we have to entirely depend for our life, it was some stunt. I had with me food, tools, instruments etc., so that if a landing could be effected safely, it might be possible to walk over the mountains 100 miles to Greece.

The valley winds up between high mountains, down which come plenty of gusts. It took me one and a quarter hours to get to my destination, nursing my engine all the way. When I arrived there I took note of all important defences and knowing that Edmonds who had gone there about three quarters of an hour earlier would have warmed them up, I came down from 4,200 feet to 3,000 and dropped my two bombs. One hit the railway near the bridge at the junction; the other went on the riverbank about twelve yards right. Very heavy machine-gun fire opened up, and I afterwards discovered one bullet went through my tail float and thence through the tail. The place was well defended with guns and trenches. A train moved off as I approached.

The return journey was made in one hour over territory and ten minutes over the sea, during which I watched the rev counter and engine gauges with an eagle eye. I sang to myself and ate chocolates. Halfway back the engine coughed, and I thought – here goes – but the beast must have only done it too annoy me. I could see the *Ben-my-Chree* from thirty miles inland. Up at the bridge, Adrianople was just in the distance and the Black Sea beyond.

Near the sea I saw Wright, who with Childers and wireless were looking out for us, if I came down near the mouth of the river, to wireless the ship to send an armed motorboat in to our rescue. However, all went splendidly and after two hours twenty minutes I once more got aboard *Ben-my-Chree*. Edmonds had returned safely too, but I had not seen him on his return journey. He got two bullets through the planes. Commander Samson also went up to bomb the bridge in a land machine from Kephalo. Neither of us hit the thing, but we must have stirred them up and made them use piles of ammunition anyhow.

9th: Left Kephalo in morning for Gulf of Saros, where Wright and Childers spotted for a monitor on a road bridge at the northern shore and Edmonds and Childers spotted on a Turkish camp. I went out in a 100hp Monosoupape Schneider for the first time and found it very controllable after the big shoots. I dropped bombs on a village. (It is untrue that I strafed a baby farm.) After a busy day's flying we return to Kephalo.

11th: Went to get a tooth filled at the field dentist. In afternoon coaled ship. Kitchener arrived at Mudros.

12th: Kitchener went to the Helles front. We did nothing, as a very strong wind blew all day

December

1st: Intended to go up and get a trial wireless communication with the ships in the harbour, but my engine refused to start so Wright went instead. Coaled ship all afternoon. Admiral Freemantle came on board.

2nd: Went up with Childers and did the W/T communication with HMS *Russell*, *Zealand* and *M-18*. Flew around Milos harbour close over the village up on the hill where Childers took a photo and stood on the control wires, which is a habit of his. I finished by stunting round the ships and a banked turn around the flagship.

3rd: Wright went up to do some new bomb experiment.

4th: One of the Snotties discovered in the *Times* of 20 November that I have got the DSO. Won't Ma be pleased! Of course, I'm awfully bucked about it. It's such a surprise and a very good Xmas present, but the papers do write hot air. Went ashore with a navigator in the afternoon to shoot. Only shot one crow and a snipe, but we put up plenty of the latter, and one large duck. I got a turtle as well, but when I put it down to shoot a snipe, it hopped off. We are having flowing wine for dinner tonight, so I writing this before in case of the consequences.

5th: Woke up with a fearful head, and found I was duty pilot, which means getting up in the early hours. Everybody, including the lower deck, has been awfully good to me in their congratulations and after all, they are all part of the little effort; only I happened to be the key one.

6th: Went ashore with the fishing party in the afternoon and took the seine nets and the dinghy over the beach onto a salt lake, where we got about 300 good fish.

7th: Stayed in bed with a heavy head and general weariness, including toothache.

Flight Sub Lieutenant R. S. W. Dickinson

7th: Had rather a bad night what with the visions of Fokkers and watching hundreds of destroyers go by without taking any notice only a few yards off! North wind still blowing. Woke up with a thickish head, sore eyes, fairly stiff all over and right knee hurting; otherwise unexpectedly fit. Many visitors and kind enquiries. Stayed in bed till 10, and then made some tea and cooked two eggs. Walked to K Beach with Fitzherbert, Jacob and Blandy after tea. Both my watches are done in now and I'm lost without the time. Also lost my little pocket lamp, which is annoying.

8th: Slept like a top this time. Strong north wind still, sunny and warm. Went on board the *Savage* with Davey to return thanks and the clothes we had borrowed. Met the Sub who attended to me, Archdale by name; also the skipper and the skipper of the *Scourge*. Learned that the men were quite unwilling to pick us up thinking we were Huns! Also that it was an AB who had sighted us. I didn't get his name, I am sorry to say. Went on to FAU and told the whole tale to Bloggs. Had tea there and walked back with him and Williams.

9th: Cloudy, gusty, colder. Early service at 07.30 held by Padre of the *Russell*. Then a parade service in C Flight Bessoneau. Excellent sermon and the band helped the hymns more than a little. In the evening, Simpson and Bush returned, the former bringing five waistcoats and a letter from mother.

10th: Strong wind and cold during morning, but wind dropped after tea and I expect we shall have a south wind tomorrow and flies. In the evening Nicholson called me in to consult about a bomb- and pamphlet-dropping trip to Constantinople at night. Both Barney and Bush failed to appear very keen about it; but of course it is just what I have wanted to do all along. So we are going to draw for it. Of course, I was a fearfully excited at the news and lived through the whole trip (successful or unsuccessful) several times during a most disturbed night.

11th: Heard this morning that I'm out of the running for Constant as the other three are to have prior choice and there's no chance of them not taking it, though none of them is as keen to as I am, for once. Anyway, I suppose it's all for the best which is a consolation. CO went up in the new streamlined BE 8881 during morning and rudder jammed as he started swinging to the right round A Shed and then evidently trying to make a steep turn to get back into the aerodrome he must have over banked, spun round and nosed-dive into the ground at the foot of the hill by the old hospital. The whole machine was completely wrecked and by a miracle the CO seems to have escaped with only a fairly severe cut across his cheek. I hope he will be all right. The wind has gone round the south and, as there is only a very little of it, is very hot and animalcules of various species have reappeared. Undoubtedly a north wind is the best and we shall be crying for a strong gale from the north when it gets a bit hotter. In the afternoon it went around again and was blowing hard by the evening. Savory, Hooper, Brisley and I went to dine on board the *Russell*. Got very wet going out as a big sea was running. Excellent time; got back about 11.30pm when Brisley came and drank whiskey in my cabin and we had a tremendous talk until nearly 2.00am.

12th: Missed breakfast. Woken at 10 by Barnato and Nicholson coming to say that they had tossed and Barnato had won and now Nick and I had a toss – and he drew the wrong one. I'm afraid he was very disappointed and I hope I haven't been very selfish. Well, it seems that 3914 and 3902 and a BE with Savory are going the first good night. The sooner the better, I think, as I am so excited about it, but I fear I shall have restless nights until it is all over. Pray God that he looks after me once more. But whatever happens, it will be something worth doing and something to have attempted, and I am certain that none of those at home would have had to hold back and say nothing and let another go when the chance was offered me.

Went and examined 3914 and got things ready. Went down to K Beach after tea and looked over *E-11*, Naismith's boat, as *M-2* and Bennett had not come in yet. They came alongside at 6.00pm, all looking very strange and unwashed and dressed in sweaters and duffle coats etc., most unlike the smart naval officer that Bennett looked when I saw him last. Taken to the *Russell* on the *Cornwallis* boat and while the Padre changed was shown the ship by Wetherall. Excellent dinner. Came off at 10.00pm fully determined that if I come back tomorrow night I shall try to get leave to go with them at least to Malta.

13th: Fine, but north wind blowing vigorously. Made all arrangements and looked over machine. At HA during morning receiving instructions. Pamphlets to be dropped broadcast over Constantinople, Stamboul, Galata and Skutari. Savory and S.P. doing western corner, I am to do eastern bit of Stamboul on both sides of the Golden Horn, while Barnato does Skutari. Then we are to drop bombs on return journey on powder factories. Wish we had gone last night as I fear this wind is not going down. At 5.30 it was decided not to go and as a result the wind dropped completely. Now there's scarcely a breath and everything is gloriously bright and clear in the moonlight.

14th: Today has been lovely, much hotter, with a little wind, but what there was went round to the south at lunch. It clouded up in the morning, but now (6.30 pm) the clouds have blown off and we are going. I have filled my Thermos with very hot black coffee in case he tries to catch me out. Pray God that he brings me back safe, but if by ill fortune that is not to be, don't be anxious darling ones at home, as I shall be perfectly safe and well and He will look after me.

And so He did, as what follows will show.

With considerable difficulty I write two days after, because all night were such a rushing series of violent emotions that it is almost impossible to recount what happened quite impassively. Smyth Piggott started just before 8.00pm for Adrianople. Savory went off a few minutes later, I left at 8.07 and Barnato left last. At this time it was perfectly clear and cloudless; but before we had left half an hour it was overcast and stormy, as we learnt on return. I had taken a lot of food, some brandy and some coffee, but I was never able to get anything the whole time except one sip of coffee, for a reason which will appear. After crossing the Salt Lake I turned left and almost immediately my rev counter broke so that I could not know whether I was running her full out or not. I climbed to about 3,000 feet by the time I crossed Anzac, and up to now there was scarcely a movement in the air; but a little later I began to be bumped rather severely and for a long time I thought I must be getting Savory's backwash. All the time I was very keen to reach Constant first and so travelled very fast. The wind was abaft the beam and before I got to Gallipoli the sky was covered with clouds; but the moon was visible through them, and though I knew I ought really to turn back, this fact and the knowledge that Savory would go on made me determined to get there.

Marmara I reached in just the hour and soon after I passed through two small showers of rain, which seemed to make me somewhat apprehensive of the return journey. I saw also a largish steamer below and his lights were very pretty on the water. The wind drifted me rather too far north and I had to run out from the coast in order to approach the St Sophia district of Stamboul from the south. The town presented a very lovely sight, though there were not as many lights as I expected. But the pontoon bridge was ablaze with lights and when the ships began firing green rockets the whole scene was one never to be forgotten. I reached the town at 10.05pm – just five minutes before Savory – and flew along the north side of Golden Horn across to Kyoub and part of the way back to St Sophia, dropping pamphlets for all I was worth for nearly twenty minutes; but I ran out of my munitions and so turned off inland to the west intending to approach the Zeitunlik factories from the north. This I did, and dropped my eight incendiary bombs; but it was now very dark and I could only judge where my mark was for what I remembered of his position on the coast and I doubt whether I hit anything. The pamphlets were the chief object of the expedition and so, that accomplished, my next object was to get home. I steered along the coast, being fired at from half a dozen places round St Stefano; but after nearly an hour's flying I ran through a rainstorm in which I lost my course and got drifted to the south-east of Marmara. That island I re-passed to the north soon after midnight. Up till now it had been very rough, so rough that I could not take a hand off the wheel to get any food or drink and I was never for a second level either way. But worse was to follow and I shall, I hope, never again spend two and a half such terrific hours, hours of unadulterated terror, as the hours between midnight and 2.30am of the morning of the 15th.

15th: Before me I saw coming up between me and home two terrible thunderstorms, one over Europe, the other over Asia. The wind had backed a few degrees and was dead ahead of me and now at last I realised why it was so terribly rough. On one occasion my machine turned quite suddenly right around and continually I was travelling at right angles to my real course. Also she was rising and falling so violently that I was continually out of my seat and the force of meeting it again has left my backside one big bruise. I can give no account of my journey between Marmara and Saros. I scarcely know what did happen, but that fifty miles took over two hours and I was frightfully sick before I saw safety beneath me in the shape of the Gulf of Saros, where I knew ships were looking out for me. All I will say is that I passed through the fringes of two terrific thunderstorms, being blinded every few minutes by the flashes of lightning on both sides of me. I also encountered two severe rainstorms. What with the awful knocking about that I was getting, what with physical exhaustion and sickness, and what with the living terror that I must confess I endured, I almost despaired of ever reaching the Gulf of Saros. It was only the remembrance of those at home that kept me from giving in and going down and trusting to old man Turk to treat me well. I had reached that stage when I really didn't care a damn what happened from my own point of view. However, the knowledge of how much anxiety it would cause, kept me going and at last I saw the Gulf. I had now been out six and a quarter hours and, at the rate I was going, I would never reach Suvla before my petrol ran out. So I came down towards the island of Saros looking for a destroyer, but failed to see one. So I fired a Very light to attract attention and opened up again. Providence was undoubtedly looking after me, for a minute later I saw in the middle of a patch of moonlight which happened to get through a hole in the clouds a little black speck – and I should never forget the relief of that moment.

I spiralled down and swished past quite close so that she should not fail to see me and then took the water at a terrific speed – 60mph I should say. For a moment I did not know what had happened for I was right under water and much entangled in wires and it took a considerable time – it seemed ages – and the swallowing of much salt water before I extricated myself and came up between the planes, to find the tail perpendicular above me and the trawler turning about 100 yards off. I shouted for help and a boat took me off in a very few minutes. I had come into the water so fast that my nose had gone straight under and the noise of my immersion had wakened men sleeping below. However, I had got back to safety; but I was almost prostrated with exhaustion, physical, mental and moral, and it was only the shock of my sudden immersion in cold water that saved me from a collapse. Now the extraordinary thing is – and this would account for the speed with which I hit the water – that whereas above 5,000 feet the wind was undoubtedly over 50mph, when I landed there was not a ripple on the water and the winds did not get up until later. I was given a thick pair of drawers and a hot drink of brandy, and then retired hurriedly to the Commander's bunk where I dozed fitfully till daylight, though I couldn't sleep soundly owing to a bad headache. However, this passed off and about 7.00am I went on deck for some fresh air to find that the Commander had, against my advice, taken the Henri in tow and that she was broken and sinking owing to the waves, the sea having got up considerably. With great difficulty we got her up on deck in a strange condition, being now a smashed nacelle and engine, a warped propeller and a tangle of wires, broken spars and sodden fabric. It was obviously no good but this I hadn't the heart to tell the Commander as he was so keen to bring it back. I retired to bed again but couldn't sleep and was sick again after a little. We entered Kephalo about 11.00 and I got up and dressed and ate a couple of eggs and some tea for which I was most grateful as I was now very hungry. The *Russell*'s boat took me off and I was greeted by Halliwell on the pier almost with tears in his eyes. I went to HQ and wrote my report and then, nearly 2.00pm, came to the aerodrome. The signal from the trawler didn't come through until 4.30am and for three hours they've given me up for lost.

AM1 Stammers

Arrive Taranto rest camp after about six stops at 9.00pm. The authorities here have been expecting us since 1.30. This camp is built with a recently erected block of houses right on the shore of the inner harbour. A newly-built railway leads from the main line. Nissen huts by the score. Took our hammocks with us and after a while allowed to have our kit bags as well. All the huts are provided with mosquito nets. Did not use our own bedding, plenty of blankets about. Piped down, two of us under a net. I do not know why we use the nets unless it was to keep away the flies which came in swarms about us as we use this hut to mess in as well as sleep. Tea and food served out 9.30pm, piped down at 10.00pm.

19th: Awoke 6.00am. No signs of mosquitoes. Had a stroll around the camp before breakfast, very large place but not complete, things not so far advanced as at Faenza. Flying boats and an SS airship out on patrol duty. Standing on the shore we can just see the seaplane station to the left and the main harbour beyond. Mussel beds in water near the camp. All the buildings are built of the same kind of stone here; wood appears to be very scarce as there are no large trees, even those there are, are only used for burning on the railways. The people themselves all burn this wood. Truckloads on railways.

Plenty of bully for everyone. Here they are very generous with the rations. The climate is just ideal at present and no inclination to eat meat at all. Sun helmets are used when working outside the huts. At 8.00am we fetch our kitbags. Much delving and diving and changing things from kitbags. Nothing more lost. The Otranto draft leaves us at 11.00am, only twenty-eight of our crowd left now, much quieter. Might catch the boat for Malta tomorrow. The Italians have a swinging bridge as an entrance of the harbour and will only lift it at certain times. Our petty officer's number is 2831, mine is 2830, a coincidence which may turn into something. News at last, at 2.45 we have orders to muster our kit and gear on the pier to sail at 4.30 for the *Queen* in the outer harbour, our depot ship. No boat to fetch us arrives so we lounge in the sun till teatime, then we bring our stuff back to the huts. Cigarettes and tobacco served out. Piped down at 7.30pm. Orders to fall in at 7.00am tomorrow. Food during day very satisfactory.

20th: Awoke 5.30am. Breakfast 6.30. Our gear and goods down to pier and on to the tender waiting. By 7.30 push off for harbour and HMS *Queen* at 8.00am. Lying beside the *Queen* is our transport HMS *Isonsa*, a 22-knot two funneller that runs between Malta and Taranto twice a week. Some Italian cruisers, *Vittoria Emanuelle* and *Andrea Doria*, and the British TB *Rattlesnake* and several Italian destroyers. Rum allowance dished out at 11.00am; 'good'. Dinner an improvement on army rations. Settle down on pile of kitbags for a cosy afternoon. Sun very hot. Leave HMS *Queen* at 4.00pm after loading up with stores and the mails. I was asleep till we just got off. Passed out through the swinging bridge and harbour booms at 4.30pm. The outer boom consists of several large buoys chained together about twenty feet apart and at intervals are large barges with 3-inch guns mounted and a crew standing by. Very cloudy. Have some tea and piped down on deck, I am afraid there will be no chance of sleeping tonight as it is too crowded to be comfortable. Lifebelts served out to sailors and us. We are told to put them on and in case anything happens not to go near the boats as they are for the military. The belts are our boats.

21st: At 1.30am, lying on deck covered in smuts half asleep, down comes the rain, everybody rushes under the boat deck, scuppers all blocked, deck two inches deep in half a minute. No chance to see or move, all lights out and very cold. Sailors to port and military to starboard side of ship, starboard side getting all the sea, military people come round on port side, overcrowded still more now. I think it quite time to find new quarters, so leaving my gear to look after itself I climbed up onto the boat deck in the dark, get down under a tarpaulin behind engine room skylight, nice and warm and dry, no more rain, sleep here all very comfortable until 4.30am. Just catch Sicily on the starboard. Sleep again until 7.00am. No arrangements made or to be had for washing. We are all coal black by this time, being aft of the funnels. Breakfast corned beef and tea. Nearly everybody asleep now, having had no sleep last night. Sun coming out now, 9.30am; hope to arrive Malta at 12 midday. Do not sight Malta till 3.30, arrive Grand Harbour at four. Moor up to buoy below the Valletta Gardens at 4.30. Maltese boats flock round to take people ashore. Two lighters come alongside and we get on board with our gear. Taken in tow to the Egmont, one of the forts, a naval barracks facing Valetta at 6.30pm. Hargreaves loses his kit somehow. Cart all gear etc. up to fort. Detailed to Mess 45 with seamen. No tea or supper. Draw hammocks and pipe down at 10 o'clock.

22nd: Awoke 6.00am. Returned hammocks lent at Fort. Breakfast bread and jam and tea. Detailed for provision party, see nothing of chief of charge of party. March to bakery and carry 60lb of bread back to fort. Halfway along someone says RNAS fall in, fetch your gear to eastern gate, lorry waits for you. Down bread, rush for gear and in RN tender like lightning. All aboard – leave for a station at Kalafrana eight miles around the coast at 9.00am. Hairpin bends, up hills, more corners and into what is called the country. The fields are bare plots of reddish earth walled in four-feet high by stones piled on one another, no hedges to be seen. Arrive at Seaplane Station at 10.20. Report to CPO Hughes and get detailed to Number 1 Mess, port watch part two. Have dinner, more corned beef, 'groans'. Get into ducks and parade at 1.45pm; detailed to working party. We are here at last. For how long I wonder. I will now write as if it takes me or its events occur.

November

5th: Our staple food consists of stewed meat and onions so far; no sign of potatoes. We have several journeys to Valetta, the liberty boat leaves at 5.00pm every day. There are two watches, port and starboard. Liberty every other night until 10 o'clock. Another draft of our boys has arrived here, on draft for Mudros under canvas at Fort Ricasoli on the harbour entrance. Spent several evenings with them in town. Very sad place, nothing to do but plenty of things to spend money on. It is the same thing here; we had to buy anything choice we want. Butter is not supplied, so buy! buy! buy! Cakes are very dear and sweets practically unobtainable. The station is large and very well situated. Chiefly mine and submarine patrols by Shorts. The first lieutenant is leaving soon, Lieutenant Tait, a very sound fellow but anxious for active service.

December

24th: Christmas Eve. Decorated our hut to represent an orange grove, oranges and all complete.

25th: Christmas Day. Everyone very pleased with themselves. Make and mend today. Get busy around mess decorating etc. Church parade at 10.30; short service by CO. Officers rounds 11.45. CO and officers visit all messes, toasting same and making a present of 200 cigarettes. He remarks on my 'Kaiser Bill' drawing. Fine dinner, roast pork, potatoes and cabbage, Christmas pudding and custard. Coffee and nuts and figs and cigarettes and cigars following. Cards and talk all afternoon. Concert in evening very good. Pipe down 12.15.

Flight Lieutenant George Bentley Dacre

December 1915

8th: Up again. The *Scotia* came in with thirty RFC officers who were on their way to Alexandria. Several came aboard and we had quite an interesting few hours with them.

16th: Left Mudros at 8.30am for Kephalo. Very little activity is taking place here. The battleships here now include HM Ships *Lord Nelson*, *Euryalus* and *Talbot*. We started our rehearsals for the Christmas theatricals.

17th: Went ashore in afternoon and at the landing place saw the wreckage of the last gale: heaps of broken up picket boats, etc. At No. 2 Wing RNAS we learnt that only Suvla and Anzac are being evacuated, not Helles. The Hun comes out every other day and drops bombs. They have as many machines as we have now and fights in the air are daily occurrences. Also they have now got the new revolver anti-aircraft gun and one of our machines has been hit at

10,000 feet. Rose and his observer were killed here a fortnight ago by a nose dive after engine failure. Flight Commander Robinson RM is missing after a bomb attack. Nothing has been heard of him. They have lost three machines in the sea. They use the Bristol Scout for a strafing machine, being faster than the Hun.

18th: Wright went up in a hurry to look for a submarine reported near Suvla. Lots of horses, troops, equipment arrived at dawn from Suvla and Anzac. Today and tomorrow nights have been fixed for finally evacuating Suvla and Anzac. There are 47,000 to get off. At sunset tonight hundreds of picket boats, cutters towed by trawlers and the destroyers started out for Suvla. The weather is calm and foggy, which is in our favour. We may be going over also as we are one of the reserve ships in case any get sunk or the men have to be taken off in a hurry.

19th: Last night the whole embarkation was a complete success. Only three shells were fired during the night and all but 18,000 were taken off. We had a rapid anti-aircraft stations in the afternoon as a Hun showed his nose in our direction, but pushed off when our Bristol Scouts went up. At 2.15 a heavy bombardment was heard at Cape Helles. We could see the shells bursting thick like the day of the Suvla landing, with 14-inch monitors helping. It turned out afterwards that we had blown up several mines and had captured the craters; this is a bluff to keep attention off the evacuation.

20th: We woke up to see all the ships returning from Suvla and Anzac. The whole evacuation has been a wonderful surprise and success. Not a single casualty. The Turks were hoodwinked. We got off every man, 200 and all but twelve guns and ammunition – the twelve guns being blown up before leaving – all animals and a great quantity of stores and signal stations. The men left gramophones in the front-line trenches before leaving. Hours after every man was aboard, the Turks were seen shelling our empty trenches and fixing up some barbed wire in front of their own.

At daylight several ships went close inshore and heavily bombarded the remaining stores which had previously been soaked in petrol and the whole lot were destroyed. It is funny that one of our own aeroplanes should be spotting the ships onto our own stores. The Turks will be sick. At 1.00pm we left Kephalo from Mudros with 127 men of the beach parties. At sunset it started to blow up to a gale. What wonderful luck to have completed the evacuation in calm weather. Large mail arrived in evening, mostly Christmas parcels which caused more than usual excitement on board.

21st: Still blowing a gale. We went alongside a store ship and took in three months' stores. In afternoon we started to leave Mudros in company with three or four ships full of troops, but we were stopped at the entrance and sent back.

Twelve out of fourteen motor lighters which had taken troops off the peninsula have been missing on the way here from Kephalo. They must have been caught in a sudden storm yesterday, which today is blowing from the opposite direction.

22nd: Went aboard the hospital ship *Oxfordshire* to lunch with Edmonds. Saw a dozen nurses on board, but none very beautiful. We were given a Christmas hamper and cigars and returned to *Ben-my-Chree* with the *Oxfordshire* captain and a Captain Joy RAMC. Have a grand rehearsal of our 'Revue' in the hangar this evening.

23rd: Heard in afternoon we are to go to Mitylene once more, but this was put off until tomorrow. We went round some of the ships to see what we could cadge for Xmas. We visited the *Princess Mary* Christmas ship which contains, amongst many things, forty-five pianos and 1,150 gramophones for the troops. They could not give us anything, so we went off to a hospital ship full of nice nurses and saw the skipper who was a very decent sort of fellow. He gave us a fine fat turkey from cold storage so now we are all right. Legg from the *Roberts* came aboard with much news. The *Aquitania* arrived here in the afternoon so some of us have pushed off to see what we can get out of her for Christmas.

24th: The skipper, Hull, and Steen, who came back from the *Aquitania* last night reported that they had had a splendid time as they arrived when their Christmas dinner was on. They brought turkey and some real butter back. The butter does taste good after our grease aboard. Left Mudros at 7.30am for Mitylene where we arrived after a rough passage. All RNAS offices stuck it out without being sick, but the RN flight commander was sick. Splendid victory. *Canopus* and two destroyers were the only ships now in Mitylene. We decorated the wardroom and made things as cheerful as possible in the circumstances.

Christmas Day: started at 4.00am having the morning decoding watch. Church party went to *Canopus* at 9.00am. I didn't. Went ashore with Wright in the afternoon and walked into Mitylene town. Very hot walking in spite of no waistcoats and white cap covers. Had an excellent lunch at the Cafe Grande Bretagne, which felt quite civilised. We found all the shops open, so did a lot of shopping and discovered the town kept almost everything we wanted. Most surprisingly civilised. We then sat in the gardens and walked up to the hill and had a squash at the cafe. Although it was Christmas Day we were glad to be in the shade out of the sun. We then paid a visit to the English family, the Whittalls, whom we got to know last June and had a very homely tea in their company at home. We got back to the ship via a two-horse *gidoria* (cab) fast and furious over awful roads and hills. Half of our men on leave ashore were adrift and one or two turned up in paralytic state.

We decorated the mess with chains and crackers which lent a Yuletide air to the place. The flight officers then visited the Air Mechanics' Mess and entertained them for an hour or so, after which we were carried shoulder high back to the water with 'he's a Jolly good fellow', etc.

We dressed up for dinner in odds and ends and masks; had turkey, plum pudding and fizz and wound up the evening with a very lively singsong in which old men over forty played touch with each other like young boys.

January 1916

6th: Went ashore with Hall to Mitylene. Did some shopping, but we were done by everybody had to pay 1/3 [6p] for a 3d [1p] tin of glow polish. We had tea at the Whittalls which we found full of NOs, and walked back.

7th: Last night *Canopus* marines landed and bagged sixteen German, Austrian and Turkish agents in Mitylene, including the German Consul. Several resisted with arms and one of *Canopus*'s lieutenants got wounded in the scrap. They seem to have had a fine evening's sport. We played a pick-up team at hockey ashore, and got a watch, two waistcoats and a scarf stolen by the Greeks. The Greeks are the worst race on earth. They are taught from childhood to beg and steal. We hunted around for them without result and eventually by means of an interpreter, informed the Chief of Police who, half an hour later, came aboard with the missing goods. He asked if we wanted to give the thief a year or two years' imprisonment and got 10 shillings [50p] for his trouble. The truth was the whole business was arranged by the police to go halves with the thief out of the reward.

8th: Played *Canopus* at hockey and lost 10-3, but had a splendid game. Tonight the evacuation of Hellas takes place. Let's hope with the same success as Suvla.

9th: News has come through that the evacuation has been a complete success – only one casualty is recorded – wonderful! So now there is no land war on out here and we wonder what we shall do next. I went to the *Canopus* with the church party today. In the afternoon we went ashore and walked to the village of Lutra, which was horribly dirty and dilapidated. The Main Street is a river and drain combined and all the houses are built on the mountainside. All the children as usual follow you and cling on to you shouting all the time 'un pen'. We then climbed up the mountain to over 2,000 feet and, being tired, plodded our way back to the ship through miles of olive groves.

10th: Coaled ship and received orders to proceed to sea at 4.00pm for Port Said. So we are about to start in a new theatre of war. We haven't got much money but we do see life.

Flight Sub Lieutenant R. S. W. Dickinson

It turned out that Barney had obeyed orders and turned back, reaching home about 11.30pm. S.P. had then returned utterly exhausted just before midnight and Savory and I were expected any moment. But they soon realised that we must have gone on and no one ever dreamt that either of us would get back. Nevertheless, they stayed on the aerodrome, most of them at least, until Savory landed before anyone knew he was there. Still they waited hopelessly for me, and long before it was light Blair, Reid and Kinkhead were going out to try and find me in the Gulf of Saros when the signal from the trawler arrived and told them that there was no need for it. Everybody was awfully nice about it all, but poor Barney was so upset at having turned back, though really he was the only one to do the right thing. In the evening the CO, S.P., Savory and I went on board the *Russell*. We had a short and quite pleasant interview with Rear Admiral Sidney Freemantle and then an excellent dinner in the wardroom. Left early as the *Russell* was off to Mudros. Very tired when we finally got back. Turned in, but still rather restless. What a week I have had!

16th: Southerly wind, fine. Woke and had a late breakfast, feeling very stiff and rather heavy in the head went over to HA to see Jones about leave. Down to K Beach with Reid to meet Fitz and Portal, but neither arrived.

17th: Unsettled. Reid and Blair in the Gunbus and Kinkhead in the Scout, gave us a bad time by landing on Tenedos and we heard nothing of them till they had been gone over four hours. The first two returned during the afternoon. Severe rain during evening. Duty Officer.

18th: Kincaid returned from Tenedos.

19th: South wind, fine and hot. Over to FAU to see Bloggs and have tea. Came back to find Savory and CO going to England tomorrow. Opened cellar in his honour and everyone was fearfully drunk. Alas, I drank too much, though not to the extent that I was actually 'bottled'. In fairly late.

20th: Up in EP tent from 6.30 to breakfast. Saw CO and asked for leave. He was very nice but I shall have to wait till next week, and then only to Malta I fear, and I do so long for a few days at home.

21st: Very hot. Jacob, Barnato and Nicholson all came back safely from attacking old seaplane shed and no one hit it. CO and Savory left in *Empress* last night for England. Lucky dogs, though of course they both have far more right to go then I have. Went over to RND and saw the padre and had tea with him. In early.

22nd: Very hot in the morning. Went and had tea on board the *Grafton* with Oxley. Submarine scare just before we came back. Barney had gone up to Goo

Goo and left a Lieutenant Bellairs, Naismith's Number 1, to look after himself. Very interesting talk with him. In early; not feeling well.

23rd: Easter Sunday. Strong south wind; cooler with a peculiar mist about. S.P. refused me leave to go to Panaghia. Seems to have his knife well into me for some reason or another. Feeling better. I do dislike all these crawling creatures which are beginning to appear. Especially big tarantulas and centipedes quite six inches long and of a nasty scarlet colour. Wondering whether S.P. will give me the leave that CO promised me. Down to meet the ferry which brought Portal back, still unaware that he had a DSC. Small mail but very excellent, including a bill for £1-13-6 [[£1.67.5p] from Emmanuel for my drill suit.

24th: Very hot. South wind letters most the day. Bathe in Alski with Oxley. In early.

25th: Still very hot. Last night a most curious fog rolled up from the south and enveloped everything. This morning it returned, but only as far as the harbour where it hung about all day near nearly. Bathe before tea with Kincaid. Had my hair cut for the first time since Malta! Spent the evening in Jacob's cabin. I grow to like Jacob more and more every day. I wish I could set down my impressions of these moments when we are all together listening to the gramophone. Jacob stands at the door with his Cheltenham blazer and his glorious smile; old Barney sitting in the middle strokes his beard unceasingly; on the settee to the left are Reid, Portal and Belton, Portal being very busy dealing with the Primus and making cocoa. I sit reading diligently some very light literature in the old Caudron seat in the corner. Bremner and Kinkhead sit silently at the other end, one on the bed and the other on a broken-down chair, while Blandy fidgets with his Sam Browne waiting to hear the Master at Arms inform him that he is 'Ready for rounds, Sir'. I wonder how often these scenes will recur in the years to come. The wind is getting up.

26th: A terrific wind blowing from the north. Measured out tennis court with Nicholson. Asked Smyth Piggott if I could have leave. He looked very ill tempered, asked what I wanted to do and then said he would see about me when Hooper got back. Later in the evening he told me that there was a big raid coming next week and put it in such a way that I had to agree to stay and go on with it, much as I want a few days away. In fairly late. The wind was so strong that the cabin swayed about all over the place and it rained vigorously at times.

27th: Wind and rain early so that I escaped having to stand by from dawn. Severe headache, so went to bed feeling very sick before dinner.

28th: Still bad headache. Terrible thunderstorm last night. Doctor came in and gave me some calomel. Up at 12.Stayed in all the afternoon.

29th: More rain last night. Up several times between 4 and 7 owing perhaps to aforementioned calomel? Up finally about 11.00am. Fine and warm. Excellent game of rounders versus Petty Officers; not finished. Shirked dinner; boiled myself two eggs; had a bath; began *Wilhelm Tell* and went early to bed.

30th: A most exciting day. Practice for a big raid at 11.00am. Long and most interesting talk with Mitchell during afternoon and had tea with him and Halliwell. Continued game of rounders after tea. Got a signal saying that Smyth Pigott, Savory and self had been given the Croix de Guerre. Most exciting, although S.P. says we have got to go and be kissed by Sarrail at Salonika!

May 1916

1st: Woken just before six by a lots of people talking in front of my cabin and went out to find a Hun flying towards the aerodrome. He turned over harbour and dropped his bombs at Kephalo Point, but I think it was a reconnaissance. After a bit Fitzherbert went off in his pyjamas and Bremner followed. Both very cold, saw Hun land at Galata.

Duty officer. Not feeling very well with a bad head. Simpson accused me of pot hunting and other things, but Kinkhead, as always, proved a splendid comforter and confidant. I have been so full of my own news that I have quite forgotten to mention two occurrences of this week. Of course the most important is the news of the fall of Kut-al-Amara, which is very terrible. I can only hope that it may urge the Turks to seize the opportunity to make peace with good terms. The other, and to me personally the sad incident, is the loss of the *Russell* with a number of officers and men.[3] This is my first real sight of war, and that 900 miles away – but I see those lads in the gun-room and those delightful hospitable men in the wardroom and it is very terrible to think that probably half their number have crossed the last river. I wish we could hear the casualties soon. Altogether it has been a bad week although, thank God, the rumour that Verdun has fallen is untrue. And to think that I nearly went to Malta in the *Russell*! In late.

2nd: Very hot, went over to HA to get map for tomorrow's raid. Bathed in Aliki with Fitzherbert. Very warm and pleasant. Wind changed about four times in the evening while Jacob and Fitzherbert and Blandy were up after a seaplane

---

3. HMS Russell, *a Duncan-class battleship, struck two mines laid by a German submarine off Malta on 27 April 1916; 125 officers and men were lost.*

reported from Mudros, so that the first two both landed with the wind, though from opposite directions. Jacob had four attempts, making a fine landing in the last, but old Fitz did a glorious landing at about 70mph running right the length of the aerodrome. Very perturbed because Blandy did not turn up and it was a great relief when at last the signal came through that he had landed at Tenedos. Looks rather like dirty weather tomorrow.

3rd: Up early to test my machine for the combined raid. Rain. Waited all the morning in tremendous thundery heat which gave me a headache. In EP tent during afternoon. Raid cancelled. Wind got up during the afternoon.

4th: Standing by for general attack, which was cancelled. Strong northerly wind, very nice and cooling. Vice Admiral de Robeck came round with Commodore Keyes, Colonel Wilson and two others. Of course at the moment I was at HA with the commander of the *Triad*! Had to race back full tilt and arrived a very hot and breathless. The VA shook hands, congratulated me and said some very nice things; then we walked round the place while I talked to Keyes and Wilson, both of whom were very nice. S.P. looked at me with eyes of fury. He hates anyone else getting any of the limelight. Scarlett arrived after lunch. Asked S.P. for the leave of which he cheated me last week. He refused and was very curt and rude, saying that I would not go except on sick leave. How I hate that man, as almost everyone here does. Mail in during morning. Two parcels from Harrods, also nine letters, all of congratulations.

6th: Strong north wind. Called over to HQ by Doctor. Discussion as to what he could put me down for sick leave. Promised to send a note to S.P. which he did later. Some excellent sets of tennis in the evening. Courts far better than I expected. Down to sleep in EP tent.

7th: Fitzherbert, Bremner and Blandy off before dawn to bomb a big ship which is reported in Ach Bashi Liman. Slept better. Much cooler, north wind. S.P. Told me that he had sent to the Wing Captain for his approval for my leave and that I could go next week.

Part Six

My Time as a Prisoner of War

By Flight Lieutenant G. B. Dacre

A prison is a house of care,
A place where none can thrive;
A Touchstone True to try a friend,
A Grave for man alive.
Sometimes a place of right,
Sometimes a place of wrong;
Sometimes a place of rogues and thieves,
And honest men among.
Old inscription

It was over a cocktail before dinner in HMS *Ben-my-Chree* at Port Said, where I was a guest for the evening, that Commander Samson said to me, 'Let's see, you haven't been put down for coming on this next stunt of ours, you'd better come in this ship and see the fun.'

So it was settled that I should go in the *Ben-my-Chree* for the first day's stunts and then transfer to HMS *Raven* in place of Squadron Commander Malone, who was to be an observer on the second day's stunt with the Commander. Accordingly, having left Meade in charge of the Seaplane Depot where I had two busy days filling up the *Ben-my-Chree*, *Raven* and *Anne* with machines, stores and personnel, I went aboard the *Ben-my-Chree,* my old ship of five months previous. T.H. England was then Flight Commander, so I had a more or less visitor's existence, very different to my overworked existence as a flight lieutenant.

Ben-my-Chree left Port Said about 4.00pm on 24 August, *Raven* and *Anne* having gone out during the morning. The ship's band, consisting mostly of string instruments, was mustered on the foc'sle to play us out of harbour, much to the amusement of the Port Said populace and the HM Ships in port. Past SS *Jupiter* the band played 'And the green grass grew all around'. This ship having been berthed for some considerable time, it was reported she had grown to the bottom. Past the Casino, the usual waves of fair visions left behind, and a final wave from two sisters in a sailing felucca brought us to sea once more.

I was rudely awakened before dawn by my camp bed giving way and discovered that the cause was that the ship had run into Syria in the dark and we were hard aground. Much shouting, of course. Machine guns were mounted in the bows while the screws going full astern churned up plenty of sand and the siren called up our little TB escort. Some of us were rather pleased at the chance of something novel: the cause of this running aground I can hardly write as carelessness, but it was certainly rather comic. After an hour's going astern with the Chief Engineer's help – he always had steam up his sleeve for special occasions – we came clear, went on our way and arrived at Haifa Bay, our rendezvous. Here the *Raven* and *Anne* had already arrived. Seaplanes were at once hoisted out and the Commander, with his machine having a red tail fin, got away, followed by nine others. Away in the distance one could see a long line of machines disappearing to El Feulie on their errand of destruction. All returned safely about fifty minutes later, some having shot holes in, but all were enthusiastic about the damage done to the railway junction.

A second flight was to be made to this junction by three machines, myself with Wedgwood Benn MP as observer. Benn had arrayed his tunic with many false medal ribbons, thinking that if he were taken prisoner he would be treated as a general. I had the commander's machine, but after hoisting out I found the engine was too bad to get off the water, so I was told to go away in another. Again luck was against me, the engine was bad and I could only get about 800 feet, dropping overland where there were bumps. From my point of view I was fed up as the other two machines returned and said the junction was then a sight worth seeing, while I had not been able to get there.

We left Haifa Bay and went south, meeting on our way two hostile dhows in sail. We stopped these with our 12-pounders across their bows. One ran ashore with sails up and the crew legged it. The other we captured as a prize and took the crew of five prisoners. They didn't seem displeased as they only had bread and water to live on and aboard they got a square meal. We hoisted the dhow aboard and went on to a place off the shore between Askelon and Gaza where various raids were to be started, each ship having a different objective. Orders were a bit vague until the last moment, so there wasn't much time to look over one's allotted machine.

I was allotted one of the new Clerget Schneider machines which had only recently arrived at Port Said, the fastest thing in boots. I left the *Ben-my-Chree* about 4.30 after some difficulty in starting up. Once away I climbed rapidly and made off rapidly inland to my objective, a camp. My engine was going well and the weather was good. I watched other seaplanes on their return journey with a careful look out for the Hun. I followed inland over a wadi, or dried-up water course, over the sand dunes thinking what a nice machine this was, when at about 3,000 feet up and twelve miles inland, my engine spluttered and died out. I waited a few seconds to see if it was going to continue, but no.

Now I'm for it, I thought. I gazed at the petrol gauge as the nature of the stoppage was like a petrol failure. No petrol in the fore tank. Perhaps the fore tank had a bullet through it. I changed over the taps to the back tank and pumped up the pressure. No result. Taps were alright. Switch was on. The only explanation I could, on the spur of the moment, think of was that the tanks had never been filled. By this time I found myself 100 feet up, faced with landing this rapid machine on *terra firma* on its floats. I used this last height to turn head to wind and to square up, wondering if a few seconds later would see me alive. I got to within a few feet, pulling her back and back to do a pancake landing. I seemed to be actually travelling very slowly just before I touched, but when I did hit Turkey she went over on to her nose like a flash.

I obeyed Newton's laws and carried straight on, landing mostly on my right shoulder and head and did two somersaults. I got up dazed with a pain in my shoulder; nothing broken, thank God! I returned to the machine and having no matches or petrol to destroy the machine, which was not badly smashed, I was looking inside for any possible cause of the failure and breaking the instruments with the butt of my revolver. I tore up the chart and tried to get the machine gun out of its fittings without success. Arabs from all around were then running up and, while I was fishing out my revolver and ammunition pouch, I was seized by the Arabs and held.

At first I shouted 'Allemagne' hoping to bluff them that I was German and saying by signs I wanted to go to Gaza. This they took and my hopes of reaching the coast near the ships ran high, but alas!, one blighter on a horse knew the Allied marks on my machine and shouted 'Inglese' (English) and then they fairly went for me, in spite of my arm which was hurting badly. They tore my clothes off me leaving me only in a vest and trousers. They drew their nasty looking knives, threatening me and intimating they would cut my throat with a horrid grin on their faces. They took my watch, cigarette case, money, slitting my pocket down with a knife to get it, cap, water bottle and all.

By this time a whole Arab village was around me. The women, being most anxious to have my blood, took the opportunity to hit me over the head with sticks and throw clods of mud in my face. They tried to get my shoes, but I kicked out and kept them. What a crowd of savages I had fallen into. Some were pitch black, others copper, dirty, evil-looking brutes with hair matted like sheep's wool. There were about eight holding onto me, squabbling like jackdaws for my possessions, and in the squabble they distracted their attention for a while and I broke away and ran like a hare followed by a howling mob of savages with swords waving. My arm pained fearfully to run, but I could have got out of their clutches and away had not a horseman ridden up and hit me over the head with his sword. The crowd rushed at me and I thought my finish had really come but they just pulled me to bits every way. One man made a dash at me with his dagger, a horrible glint in his eye, but the others kept him off. They sat me down and tied my arms behind my hack. I knew then they were going to do me in by their manner and I sincerely hoped they would finish me off quickly. But no, a Turkish NCO rode up and drove them off with a whip saving me by a few minutes from the unpleasant operation of having my throat cut.

This treatment in the hands of the Arabs is very nice for a cinema show, but very different if you happen to be the unfortunate victim. The Turkish NCO, who could speak French a little, gave me water and a cigarette and attended to my arm. I complained to him about my belongings and he led me to understand they would mostly be recovered for me. I was very grateful to him for his kindness and for saving my life. A soldier was placed over me while the NCO went and looked over my machine. Later, more soldiers arrived, bringing me black bread and dates and, by the light of a lantern, they requested me to take the bombs off my machine. This I couldn't do even with two hands, but I explained how they came off, requesting one man to each of the four bombs, while another pulled the lever. Volunteers were not forthcoming and, with much strafing and fright, four were pressed into service and to the others' amusement the bombs came away. They got in another funk when I went near them to explain that the fans when unwound made the bombs dangerous, but I was kept away.

About 12 midnight I was lifted on to a donkey, but this proving uncomfortable they put me on a horse with a leash. Thus I went in the night accompanied by six camels and five other cavalry to Gaza. I longed to break loose and gallop in the night seaward, but my arm gave me gyp, especially when the horse stumbled over the uneven track. Three and a half hours riding saw us at Gaza, one of the first towns mentioned in the Bible, which I knew well from above but now from the floor. I rolled somehow off my horse and was taken immediately to the Commandant's HQ, an old domed room up stone steps used by Napoleon in his attempted conquests of Syria. The Commandant and all his staff were there although it was 4.00am; the reason I gathered later when they questioned me. They gave me a decent supper and cognac; the latter was pressed freely and so were cigarettes. Their manner was most polite and they told me to make myself feel at home as I was no longer an enemy now. I was on my guard about all this as I knew they were going to question me.

Via an interpreter they asked me many questions to which I told as many lies and, in all seriousness, the Turk having little sense of humour, everything was put down in writing. They wanted to know how many troops were in the ships and where they would be landed. It was then that I saw they feared a landing was going to take place with the presence of large ships off the coast, bombarding by the ships of the dhows, and exceptional aerial activity. They promised to recover my clothes and, even after my questioning, were quite cheery to me, thanks to the cognac I hadn't drunk. A doctor fellow was exceptionally decent, rubbing my shoulder with embrocation and doing it up in a sling and providing me with a coat. At dawn I went, accompanied by the Commandant and his staff, through the town to the other end and it occurred to me this was rather odd. Were they after all going to shoot me at dawn after considering me no use for information? Somehow things looked that way. However, my fears were only short lived, for at the end of the town we met an Arabian wagonette in which they told me I was to go to Beer-Sheba. So with a loaf of bread and handful of Red Cross chocolates in my pocket, I started with many a salute and adieu for a long journey across the desert of forty miles.

My guard was a sub of about forty-five years – silent, but with an inexhaustible supply of cigarettes. The journey was at first cold and later very hot. A Bedouin on a camel trotted in front as a guide with a trooper as escort. There was no road, only tracks in places. We went over many wadis and the jolts fairly gave my arm hell. The tracks were littered here and there with skeletons of fallen camels and horses. After eight hours we drove through much heat and sand storm into Beer-Sheba, a desert town on a rise 600 foot high, consisting mostly of modernised buildings. Beer-Sheba was (up till the war) the terminus of railway to Egypt from Damascus, but it now runs on some twenty miles to El Auja, and might be extended further except for the lack of rails and labour. I recognised the place well from photos taken by us. The aerodrome to the north and the square of scrubs and flowers laid out in the form of a carpet pattern were particularly noticeable.

I was taken to HQ and from there without seeing anyone to the local hotel the Eschelle Abraham, run by a Jew with a beard two feet long. I was given food and was glad of it after eleven hours without. The son of the proprietor, aged about fourteen, spoke a little English and attended to my wants. A doctor speaking English, having spent most of his life in the States, came and chatted to me and then took me to the hospital to have my arm attended to. Here I was surprised to see the place so clean and well organised. There wasn't much work for the doctors, so they all came and looked at me. First one would lift my arm up and watch my face screw up with the pain and then another, until about six had done it making me pretty fed up. After a consultation they said it wasn't broken, bound it up and said if I liked I could stay in hospital a few days. So I stayed, knowing this would be cleaner than the hotel. I was rudely awakened at dawn on the following day to go to the station in a cab in the cold hours, only to wait again. This time I was taken to a carriage, second class, with wooden seats, but a vast improvement to a van. My guard picked up two pals, one a motor van driver, the other a soldier NCO. The latter had a mandolin on which he played appalling Turkish music and sang a continual drawl. I had to tolerate this as they gave me bread and water melon, my guard having only produced flat bread, some cheese or rather 'soap' and grapes.

The journey to Islahiah was uninteresting and uneventful, but rather quicker. We arrived there at noon – a place composed mostly of wooden huts and the railway terminus where one starts for a journey across the Tarsus mountains. The usual journey is done in two days by caravan, but by an excellent German system of motor lorries in six to eight hours. There was a scramble to get the few available motor lorries for passengers. Of course, as usual, my guard went buzzing off to find someone to ask what to do, so, as spaces were filling up in the lorry and I didn't wish to wait here a night or to take a caravan, I got in and we started without the guard, the latter having to run a mile to catch us up. His pride was somewhat lowered as I laughed at his breathlessness.

The lorry, owing to a lack of rubber, was steel-tyred. Inside we were packed ten of us with baggage. Leaving Islahiah we traversed much worn tracks, with an appalling surface; in fact the surface was only projecting rocks. Over this we bumped at about 8mph. The vibrations were indescribable. We were chucked about like ninepins, holding on with both hands, sitting on available baggage, a thick dust pouring in at the back. I didn't like the prospects of six to eight hours of this as it was not only very fatiguing and sore, but shook one's inside up badly. The man with his mandolin was amusing as he had to hold it up with one hand to prevent it being broken. Occasionally a shout would come from someone whose foot was being squashed by baggage. After enduring this for an hour the road got better until eventually it came to a newly made proper road.

Here we started to climb and did so for two and a half hours, winding up in continual zig-zags up the mountainside, passing much traffic. Slowly winding up at 4mph we could see the road winding below, with many other wagons also climbing. We passed a stopped car, the German driver amusing himself shooting at buzzards with his rifle and, further on, some Hindu prisoners from Kut working on the roads. At last we started to descend and then stopped at a rest camp to change over to another lorry. Here I met a German naval officer aviator on his way to the Caucasus front. He gave me some news and showed me a Fokker aeroplane packed in a lorry nearby. Our descending journey was over unmade roads again, quite pretty through villages, and would have been enjoyable except for the appalling bumps and lack of food. Eventually, at sunset, we bumped over level ground again and fetched up at the railhead of Marmura.

This place is a small village at the present head of the railway. The railway is being constructed rapidly to join up at Islahiah across the mountains by means of tunnels and mountain railways. This place is very bad for fever and I was warned before by Hungarians against drinking the water. I was mighty thankful to end this bumpy journey and being very dusty indeed I got clean under a pump and looked for the promised supper, only to find bread and water melon. I went along to a bungalow in the midst of a small German colony of motor drivers. Here a German medical officer spoke to me in French and said he was sorry his dinner was over but would I like a glass of wine. This I eagerly accepted and sat down to my bread and water melon. Later a German NCO came to have his supper. He had been a fellow sufferer in the lorry and as he spoke English he got in conversation with me, giving me more wine and half a tin of sausages and cabbage. The German officer said he was sorry the accommodation for officers was absolutely full but he would have a place screened off in the barracks for me. This treatment was somewhat different to my previous treatment on the journey.

I wasted the evening looking at the papers in the small library in a log hut and listening to a concertina being played in the still and misty dusk. Next morning I had a good wash early and got some coffee and bread and jam from the Germans, leaving Marmura about noon in a rather better carriage than the previous ones.

Amongst my fellow passengers were two Germans; one had fever badly and the other, a student who had been on the peninsula, spoke French. He was sorry for me in the food line and having no money, so he offered me a 50 piaster note if I would like to take it and repay it after the war. I took it and thanked him for it, exchanging addresses. We stopped at Adana some hours. Here I came across about twelve British Tommies who I got in conversation with. They looked very ill and said they were Kut prisoners just out from hospital on their way up the line to work. The American Consul had kept most of them alive at Adana by good food and clothes, but many had died in Turkish hands in hospitals. They told me the story of their most awful treatment after Kut fell and how hundreds died by the wayside for lack of food and care.

Bazanti village, consisting of mostly wooden huts and shelters, was a busy centre, full of war material. It is very prettily situated in the mountains with a fast-running stream running through it. My first idea was food, now that I had a little money, so I told my guard so and he told me to wait. I was tired of this objectionable fellow, so I approached a German officer about it which had the desired effect. I then went immediately to the cafe shelter, my guard bringing a pal with him, and there had a meal for which I was obliged to pay both for the guard and his pal. I came across a few British Tommies and some of our submarines' crews in the village and had a chat with them. They said they were under the Germans there and got paid for their work on the line. If they kept fit and out of the hospital they were fairly well off.

Later in the day I went down to a Turkish cavalry camp alongside the river where a tent was cleared out for me. After dark the Turks made a camp fire and sat round it on blankets for camp-fire songs. To this I was invited and listened to weird drawls on mandolins. Some sang, others did comic dances. I offered to sing also as I wished to get on the right side of them, so as to get some supper out of them if possible. I sang three songs starting with 'Because', which they applauded. Next 'Here we are again', which wasn't so popular and finally 'The Rosary' which they liked well. It was all very comic round a camp fire on a still September evening with a running stream alongside, in a circle of squatting Turks, but my singing had the desired effect. They produced food and also in the morning washed my, now filthy, whites for me. I slept well, but was very much bitten by bugs. In the morning, as I was lousy by this time, I bathed in the river. The Turks thought I was mad, but really it was most refreshing, after living in one's clothes so long. My arm still hurt me when I tried to swim.

With much persuasion and threats I got my guard to take me to the Hungarian hotel on the hill where I met a charming Hungarian lady doing war work there. She spoke English well, having lived a lot in India. She was sorry she had run out of food, but I was able to buy a cup of coffee and a slice of bread and jam. She also sold me two apples, which were really her own, and a box of cigarettes. I had now nearly run out of my 50 piasters and food seemed very scarce here.

I later came across 240 Tommies of the Kut garrison in the most miserable state imaginable, hardly a stitch of clothes, absolute skeletons, ninety per cent sick, all bivouacking beside the river. I had a long chat with them, but couldn't do anything for them. Their stories of misery would turn the hardest man. They were dying like flies from lack of food, treatment and care. Two died while I was there and no one seemed to care. They were too weak to help each other. These men who had survived the trek from Kut were, without rest and treatment, put on to work on the railway where they died in hundreds of fever, dysentery and neglect. The Germans had intervened and had had them sent to the prisoners' camp at Afion Kara Hissar. The sight of these poor fellows was a terrible one. Hardly a single one of this 240 lived through the winter.

I left Bazanti in a third-class compartment full of soldiers along with 240 Tommies who were put into vans. I learnt here that by my ticket I could have travelled second class, but was unable to find another German officer to protest about it; also I learnt that I was going to the prisoners' camp at Afion, instead of to Constantinople. I was disappointed about this at first as I had heard so much about the good times officer prisoners had at the latter place, but I found out later this was all a myth and that Afion was better both in treatment and cheaper living.

Winding through rocky gorges it gradually got dark and I went to sleep, feeling very cold and wondering how the poor Tommies who were so badly off for clothing were faring. At every long stop, more Britishers were taken out dead and carted off on stretchers without any inquiries as to names. They would probably be buried like dogs. By midday we arrived at Konia where I had a few minutes' talk with the Tommies and tried to cheer them up a bit. I then was taken into the town by a broken-down horse tram. My guard and a few others went to the mosque while I wandered about in the courtyard and examined the exterior. Later we spent an hour or so in a cafe where I was given a glass of tea, then a day's food in the shape of a meat meal was actually given to me at a filthy restaurant. I then went round the town and with my remaining money bought some biscuits and a small bottle of Greek brandy. This I thought would be useful to revive some of the Tommies in their deplorable condition. I went back to the station, where I found a Turkish officer superintending carting four dead Britishers off in an *araba*. Two more almost dead went off in another. One more fellow almost dead, unconscious, and a mere skeleton, was left lying on the platform in the hot sun. I got him moved into the shade and found, by a mark on his braces, that he belonged to the Norfolk Regiment. I protested to the Turkish officer about the care of these men, but got no satisfaction.

After much travel, Dacre was imprisoned in the PoW camp at Afion.

The room had three windows facing south. The unpapered walls had many photos sent from home arranged upon them. These photos of familiar faces or places were an envy for us to look at. Big cupboards formed the end of the room, one being a washing stand with charcoal stove below and the other for storage of provisions and bottles. Nails on the door, cupboards and walls provided pegs for hanging up things. The furniture consisted of three beds, a folding table (bought) and plank-made table with one leg mended by the addition of another piece of plank, two highly-coloured tin-covered boxes, one chest cupboard and another table cupboard, one stool and one deckchair. A carpet bought locally gave the room a less attic appearance.

At night a candle placed on the table would cover it with grease, or a sputtering of olive oil wick would flicker out its illumination. A plank-made bookshelf hung on the wall and a wooden box just nailed to the wall held odd papers. You could not say it was a tidy room; having no wastepaper basket, all cigarette ends, matches, paper etc. went on the floor. The numerous bottles of all shapes, in various parts, of the room looked very bad, but were really an accumulation of non-returnable alcohol being purchasable by cheque at very high price from the 'Economic' at Constant. 'Raki', the local grape spirit, could be bought at 3/- [15p] a bottle. This gave cheer to us on days when hopes were black and the weather miserable. Under the circumstances in which we lived it is a wonder we were not driven to drink. Maps used to adorn the walls, but these were forbidden. On the table at the present moment are the following articles: a hand mirror, bottle of water, empty Raki bottle formerly gin bottle, five or six glasses, a corkscrew, dog collar and string, Huntley and Palmer cake tin full of letters, a box of cigarettes, a Turkish lesson book, a lamp burner, two mess account books, an empty Abdulla cigarette box full of odd buttons etc., a bottle of ink, a tin of camphorated ice and a pair of gloves. A good deal of candle grease and cigarette-end burns deface the table.

On one particular day Paul took it into his head to do some pastry making. So, using the above table for carrying out his schemes, he opened a tin of oatmeal for oatmeal cakes and mixed this up with flour and milk, covering everything, including the floor and my bed, with flour. Then, kneading and rolling it on the table, he managed to successfully clear this and baked the result in the kitchen oven. We ate it (brave fellows) and, in our pain which followed, we had the horrible thought that the oat meal would swell inside us. However, we live to tell the tale. Our servant was one of the survivors of the Kut garrison men. He came to us thin and suffering from fever and ague, but with good feeding he visibly grew fat. He was very slow moving and untidy, but willing.

The Mess was really the landing at the top of the stairs. In it was a pantry rigged up with a long table and forms, all being made by the officers. I found myself appointed Honorary Mess Secretary in November and it would be interesting, especially to housekeepers, to know what we lived on and the price of various items. The difficulties of catering with ever-rising prices meant much work. Mess members always shouted for living as they found it at home, but without money this wasn't possible. Everything had to be cut down to a minimum. Variety was hard to get, but we always had four meals a day and a good dinner. After December 1916 messing went up to 690 Piasters (£5.15.0 or £5.15p) a month each in a mess of ten officers with four servants and one private servant. Our pay was 700 Piasters a month plus, Embassy money nearly £2.10.0 [£2.50p] a month.

Clothes were difficult to obtain, especially when one was captured and had no money. Most of one's clothes were taken off one, as mine were. The American Embassy used to send down things every now and again; in the meanwhile I borrowed things, local cloth and tailoring being too expensive. The first Embassy suit I got was a rough brown frockcoat thrown together; this and trousers to match were a really comic sight on me, together with a black felt hat I bought locally and a month's beard on my face. However, later I got a better double-breasted tweed which had to have all the seams re-sewn, otherwise they fell to bits. The men were always badly off for clothes and we had to part with everything we possibly could for them. The daily dress of the officers was very mixed. Some who were fortunate enough to get clothes through in parcels walked about immaculately dressed; others like myself wore no collar and tie. The summer garb was shirt, shorts, socks and shoes. Some wore woolly hats made out of scarves in winter. When once settled down we weren't badly off for clothes as far as warmth was concerned.

All the naval officers and a good share of the soldiers started growing beards in the autumn of 1916. It saved a lot of trouble and kept one's face warm. Great was the competition for size and quality. Everyone had theirs trimmed on Xmas day. Later the soldiers shaved theirs off while the NOs except one carried on. Soon after I arrived in the lower houses a search was organised. We were all called out into the yard while the Commandant and other officers went through everyone's gear, taking all diaries, books, letters, maps etc. Great was the indignation from everyone when they found in some cases a year's work gone and all sorts of private affairs removed. Scarfe, the senior officer of No. 3 house, refused to give up certain books and told the Turks what he thought of them, so for his trouble he got taken off to jail for ten days. The jail was a filthy stone cell full of vermin, ill lit and ill ventilated. This punishment had been meted out to other officers for similar offences. The men got beaten for small offences, even the sergeants. Personally I only lost my diary in the search, not having had time to accumulate other stuff. The 'bag' was put into sacks and locked up in a hut in the yard and later sent to Constant. Some time after, we got the books back censored and our diaries with the written part torn out. After the search we weren't allowed to keep diaries, uncensored books, maps or more than two sheets of writing paper a month. Notebooks for languages etc. had to be censored before and after use. Paul did a smart piece of work in recovering some of the more important diaries and data. The hut in which the sacks were stored had a tiny window about a foot square. While some of us engaged the *posta* on guard in conversation he squeezed in through this window, ransacked the sacks and passed out all the important stuff. The interpreter also made a faux pas by mixing up the sacks of censorable stuff with the uncensorable, so we got back one sack of stuff which was to be sent to Constant for inspection containing valuable diaries.

The two days of Christmas 1916 and New Year 1917 are voted the best we had in Turkey. Apart from the entertainments got up, we had hope of new conditions in the present state of affairs in 1917. Two days before Xmas a pantomime took place. The rehearsals were very amusing and the show itself perhaps gave most enjoyment to the players. I officiated as a scene shifter with Elliot. We rigged up a stage in No. 3 mess, scenery being mostly an arrangement of blankets. The panto being 'Jack the Giant Killer' had as a cast the widow, the widow's son, the King and Princess, the giant, the villain or the pirate chief and his crew. The costumes were a marvel, being made out of nothing, face paint being water colours. The widow was splendidly done by MacDonald while the Princess, who made up as pretty as any girl, was done by Davenport. The songs were mostly parodies of old well-known songs put to new words by our playwright Scarfe. The whole show was full of take-offs and amusing side shows, especially during the scene aboard the pirate's ship when periscopes and anti-aircraft guns were introduced. The show wound up with an excellent supper in No. 2 house including tinned lobster.

Delegates of the Prisoners' International Commission from Geneva visited us in November 1916 and learnt our moans. They didn't like the journey a bit. We put before them all our grievances. They gave us a little news and said we were the most cheerful prisoners they had seen. God help the other countries' prisoners. We were photographed and questioned. They said the men's conditions were very bad and when they left our treatment was certainly better. The death toll amongst the men had shown what their treatment had been. Hardly a day went by in the later part of 1916 when we were not to see dead Britishers being taken to the cemetery on stretchers, with a small sheet hardly covering them. They were buried without clothes only two feet down with no service, until the commission arranged otherwise. A wooden cross with no name marked the spot where one or more were buried. Most of the poor fellows died through neglect, especially in outlandish places when they got sick. At Afion once they got strong they went along alright, and when later their treatment was much better and more cheerful they had brighter prospects.

Those who arrived from outlandish parts weak with fever and dysentery were so weakened by the tiring journey that they went to hospital and seldom came out. The men always dreaded going to hospital on this account. Guest Nights by houses used to be given, but as living got higher these became fewer. They were very amusing, always finishing up in the early hours after a sing–song or dancing. On Sunday nights a service was held in one of the houses.

Twice a week during the winter dances were held in each house in rotation. They started dancing classes, but (these) developed into popular entertainments with great keenness. Programmes were booked up a week in advance. You couldn't quite compare it with ordinary dancing. It generally got acrobatic, but whatever it was it kept one warm in the cold weather and was most amusing to see old majors being young.

On Christmas Day 1916 we started by early morning greetings, followed by decorations of mistletoe given to us as a present and Chinese lanterns, which we made out of wire and tissue paper all painted up. A service was held in the morning, while later the men were allowed a walk past our houses. They were full of cheer which pleased us very much. They sang 'It's a long way to Tipperary' and cheered as they passed. We threw from our windows boxes of cigarettes and tinned stuff which was eagerly scrambled for. I saw Adcock during this procession and was able to have a few words with him. The afternoon we had an enthusiastic football match vs the upper houses which we won.

We had Dinner in No. 3 house ensemble and very good it was too. A splendid blow out, including turkey, plum pudding, drinks, etc. After dinner we all adjourned to our house for dancing, one room being made into a bar from which hot punch was served. Next day I felt very heavy headed and declared that the sun was rising over the hills in the west – but a football match against the servants put my liver right again.

On New Year's Eve, Dinner was in our house with No. 3 house as guests. We decorated our Mess with coloured paper in Empire style with a wall notice having a light behind it showing 'A Happy New Year'. Candlesticks and pink shades were on the table. Nearly all were in fancy dress, some making excellent girls. I went as a tramp. Menus, hand painted and suitably worded, added to the table decoration. We had cocktails in rooms before dinner and as guests arrived it was hard to tell who they were through their disguises, some having removed their beards for the occasion. The dinner was a marvel in eight courses, including coffee, taking into consideration the local produce. After our port and cigars we drifted to No. 4 House where we spent a most enjoyable evening at a fancy dress ball with an attendant bar in one room. Cards and games also figured amongst the entertainments for non-dancers. At 12 midnight we sang 'Auld Lang Syne' and then ate a large supper mostly of tinned delicacies and trifles. One game I introduced was drawing a two-minute picture on a panel of paper on the wall. These varied from truly artistic to scribbles. By the way, on Xmas day we gave a tea to the upper houses. A large iced cake made by our cook couldn't have been obtained better in London itself.

One evening in February 1917 we were aroused after dinner by a great deal of excitement and band playing. A procession passed the house twice headed by a band

and the schoolboys singing. As they passed us they cheered and we replied. Those of us who could speak Turkish declared that they said 'Long Live the English'. There was no doubt about the cheering, but we couldn't get any information as to what it was all about. We were naturally very excited about it as it was such an extraordinary affair and it would be in this way that we should first hear of peace. We asked the *postas* if it was peace, but they didn't know. A few days later we found after many false rumours in between that a Pasha had visited the town to make a speech and he said to the people that the war would soon be over.

About 9.30pm one winter's evening we were aroused by rifle shots close at hand, followed by others all around the houses and excitement amongst the *postas*. A hurried roll call was made and all found to be present. Apparently the *posta* on guard in front of the houses saw someone flash a light near the house and a black dog go by. So, shooting in the air with a challenge and receiving no reply but shouts from other *postas*, he aimed at the position of the dog, or whatever it was, followed by much firing from other *postas*. One bullet went through a tree in front of the house and another hit the house. We all had a good laugh at the comic Turkish display and carried on with our occupations.

Rumours used to come from all sorts of sources to us, some good, some bad, on good authority or otherwise, but only about one in twenty were true. We got most of our news via these rumours, especially when the paper stopped, and whether authentic or not, good rumours brought optimism. When a good rumour came we thought the war would very soon be over, but when a bad one came we looked as if we never would get out of this place. Rumours came from prisoners arriving from other places, the dustmen, the tradesmen and the *postas*, or elaborated stories from our letters. Whenever we met the other houses, the French or Russians or got a mail, everyone asked for news. False rumours were often got up to pull people's legs, but the individuals got such a bad time when they were found out that this wasn't often practised afterwards.

A gold Lire in Dec 1917 can be sold for six paper Lires, showing the state of Turkey's finance. The internal conditions of the country are deplorable. When the hard winter set in in December, firewood and charcoal became unobtainable. The houses who hadn't a winter stock in were obliged to burn up doors, cupboards and furniture for cooking purposes. When wood could be bought it cost 6d [2.5p] a pound and charcoal 1/1d [5.5p] a pound.

Christmas 1917. Once more a Christmas came upon us adding a slight relaxation to the monotony. We were allowed certain privileges, including visits to the other camp each day for a week, late hours and more walks for the week. A Red Crescent representative arrived before Xmas with a good many parcels, clothes from the Dutch Embassy and some of the goods ordered by us from the stores in Constant including 'Alk'. We had some amusement getting this down to our camp in a cart on the ice-covered roads. Several of us had to hold the back of the cart in the middle of the road to prevent it going down into the ditch. On Xmas day we had guests for lunch with sliding on the ice in the yard afterwards. For dinner we had No. 4 House in as guests, a very good dinner with a sing-song afterwards.

During the week we 'tea-ed' out several days at the other camp and, on the 29th, dinner in Paul's house, going to another house afterwards to see a play. The play was exceeding clever, the music composed by the orchestra's master was wonderful and the girl most real. A rowdy supper followed in another house. Fifty officers all doing scrums in a small jerry-built room. New Year's Eve we had a Fancy Dress dance as we have done in past years in No. 2 House. A games room and a bar was also set up. The dresses were marvels of something out of nothing, most effective. I went as Sir Walter Raleigh. Five very well-dressed girls were present, whose wigs continually came off. A real funny evening and much enjoyed. The guards thought we were mad. New Year's Day we had a return dinner in No. 4 House, a good fill and well served up. Each house had decorated in their own style. A sing-song and a small dance wound up the 'Biram'. After these festivities were over, money was scarce and remorse took its place.

A lot of rumours have gone around lately about exchange and we are optimistic. Wallace my room companion went off before Xmas for exchange for appendicitis. We have heard that he and others who went before had not left Constant at the end of January. Other unfit officers are recommended for exchange. Four French have also left here and the doctors may go. We pin our hope on exchange.

Lieutenant Philpots RFC was captured in Mesopotamia in October 1917. He got dysentery on his way here, as so many others have done, and after being put in quarantine here for several days was carted off to Turkish hospital and by now most people know what these places are like. Our doctors say that if they had him in their hands they could have easily cured him but, as our doctors are not allowed to attend patients, he went to hospital where he got worse and, after a month's suffering, died on 14 January 1918. He is the fifth of the Afion officers who have now died out of at present seventy-five. The percentage of men is very much higher.

Those who craved for some excitement got what they wanted when the earthquake gave us a visit on 16 January. The first shock was felt about 9.00am, followed by small ones and then two large shocks at 6.00pm – other smaller ones throughout the night and following days. Fortunately our houses are made of wood and mud and take a lot of shaking down. The feeling is altogether uncanny. Pictures swing about, everything creaks, a low rumbling is heard, crockery rattles. It feels rather like being in a ship in a rough sea, shaking in the waves. Some houses made a bolt for the yard as the shocks came. At nightfall it is a debatable question whether to remain in the house until it falls over your ears or go into the cold yard and be shot by the guard. It is not at all amusing. Poor prisoners!

On 2 November, preceded by many false rumours, an official telegram came to the town to say the Armistice was signed. The townsfolk showed no signs of excitement or mouldiness. They just went slowly on as before, except that prices dropped. In the afternoon we were set at liberty to wander out anywhere without *postas* except for long walks where an armed *posta* was necessary against attacks by brigands. We leaped out like unleashed hounds, went down to the station buffet in the evening and sang 'Rule Britannia' with a hearty voice. It felt quite funny to be free again and not to have a *posta* always following one's footsteps. The country is absolutely done. We gave food to the starving wounded that came through in trains without attention, food or money. The general inhabitants are very pleased to think the British will take over the country; nowhere is there hostility towards us and they, like all beaten Orientals, bow submissively to our will. It is great to be a Britisher in a conquered country. Those at home do not realise what British Power and Prestige means until they have been in foreign countries.

The long-waited-for day has arrived. We never thought of such a complete debacle in our enemies' camps as has happened. The next question is when we shall leave Afion. We know it is only a matter of a day or two before the great homecoming.

On 4 November we received official news that our camp and sixteen from the top camp with orderlies would proceed to Smyrna on the 5th, making half the Afion officers. Great was the excitement thereof; 5 November, of all days, was a day for a bonfire. We burnt furniture, trees, everything that the locals would not give us a decent price for. It was a fine flare-up and nearly did down the houses. Most of Afion were outside the front of our houses, just like a pack of hungry wolves, scrambling and fighting for the odds and ends we threw out the window. They fought like cats for the smallest article, women included. Several casualties occurred which our MO attended to. Later on, the crowd got rather pressing and began swarming in at the windows, so we were obliged to keep them out with water squirts and buckets of water and stick. They were a howling mob of savages, not hostile but howling for 'Backshish', with a continual howl of 'Inglis, Backshish'. We sold, smashed, burnt or gave away all our gear except what was necessary and evacuated our houses with great joy about 4.00pm.

We waited until 9.00pm before we pushed off. Each house had a horse truck, so we had one for nine officers and gear. These trucks are much the best method of travelling in Turkey when you clean them out and disinfect them. Ordinary carriages are full of vermin and too cramped to sleep in. We had with us lashings of grub and most of our Xmas wines. We cleared out the truck and disinfected it, then arranged our mattresses and gear. We had a cheery supper and a cheer to be at last rid of Afion and, after a somewhat bumpy journey, more for the rest than for myself as I had a hammock, we arrived at Ouchak at 3.00am, where we spent twelve hours.

At Ouchak we met several officers who had some time ago weakly given their parole to be free and are somewhat looked down on by us. They were concentrating on the railway from their camp at Gedes. One party on the truck got held up by brigands and robbed of their money and gear. One officer who made a bolt for it got shot and lightly wounded. Even on the Smyrna line these brigands have on occasions held up the trains and robbed the passengers, and even torn up the rails. What a country.

Our journey was the usual Turkish one – very slow and tedious. We have to take our own drinking water from Afion as the water down the line is not fit for drinking purposes. On arrival at the outskirts of Smyrna all the inhabitants gave us a huge welcome as we passed. We arrived about 3.00pm and went off into the town. No officials were there to take us over so we were at perfect liberty to do what we liked and stay where we liked. The Turks had completely washed their hands in any matter of looking after us or handing us over. We got our gear on carts and took a carriage to the best quarter. All the inhabitants came out to greet us with waves and cheers. It was difficult to gather the new situation with all the welcome given to us, and although the town is Turkish we no longer regarded ourselves as prisoners. We fixed ourselves up at the Egypt Hotel and then I went aboard HM Monitor *M-29* alongside the quay to report myself. Here it gave me great joy to see our own people again who gave me so much news and real whiskey and soda, State Express cigarettes and the latest wireless communiqués to read. The skipper, Commander Dixon, said he could send me to Mudros the day following, but strongly advised me not to go as the ship for our transport would arrive in a few days and we would get back to our jobs quicker by that way.

It was all very interesting to see Smyrna from the ground after my acquaintance with it three years ago. I am afraid all the demonstrations in our honour are only because we are top dogs. If we had lost the war, the same population would probably spit at us. However, being top dogs, we accept the situation as it is with good cheer. The Greek citizens say they hope that Smyrna will become Greek, while the English colony say give it to any European control but the Greek or they will have to clear out. By the invitation of Pass, our old house party had dinner with him at the Kraeme Palace Hotel. We were surprised to find we could so easily accommodate ourselves to civilisation again – table manners, speech and habits. Later we went and saw a play in Greek at the theatre but, as the acting appeared to us so coarse, we roared with laughter and left before the end. When we went to bed we were reminded that we were not yet out of Turkey by being eaten alive by bugs. So the next morning we shifted our gear to the Smyrna Palace Hotel which was quite clean. We were free to do just what we liked under no one's orders. We watched with interest the weird and animated crowd of Levantines who swarm by on the Esplanade all day. The Esplanade is bounded by hotels and cafes, all Greek. We went sailing and did anything there was to do.

On Saturday night, 10 November, a Special Ball was held at the Kraeme. The ballroom was splendid and the music good. It started at 6.00pm and went on until 1.00am. Most of the English Levantine colony turned up and introductions were flung round. These people, who mostly have been born in Smyrna, fared pretty well during the war. They have been perfectly free to do what they like. They were all extremely well dressed, in spite of shortage of material, and picked up our new dance quickly. It was somewhat of a shock to us to speak and dance with pretty girls again, but we found no difficulty in getting on with them and having a most enjoyable evening. Although it was November, the temperature was frightfully hot. Funnily enough, none of these people who have lived all their lives in Smyrna have been to or know anything about the interior of Turkey. It is hard to realise Smyrna is in Turkey. We have forgotten our captivity already. The cafe bands play 'Tipperary', 'Rule Britannia', 'God Save the King' and the 'Marsaillaise' every evening. Everyone is all over us, but only the English Levantines' appreciation is genuine.

Smyrna has a reputation for pretty girls and it is certainly correct. They are pretty vivacious and dress well. In fact some of the officers have gone off their heads and want to settle down here. The pastries are the best I have seen anywhere. I have spent hours eating them and drinking 'Mastik'. We thoroughly made the best of our stay, with dancing, sailing, lunches, dinner parties. I went out by train to Bournabak to the English colony and there had two teas, first at the older Whittalls and then at the younger. Their houses and gardens are magnificent and most homely. They have shown us the greatest hospitality in spite of their privations and hardships and insults during the war. This English colony is 200 years old and the present generation has been born in Smyrna.

On 18 November the great and longed for day arrived. At 9.00am we went with our gear on board two ferry steamers. A large crowd of British residents and other *Ententists* gathered to give us a cheery send off. As we left the stage they cheered us heartily while we replied more so. It was noticed that several pretty maidens had tears in their eyes, which shows what ten days will do. Probably they enjoyed the ten days as well as we captives did. After a three-and-a-half-hour trip to the outside of the Smyrna Gulf we arrived alongside the Indian Native Hospital Ship *Empire* where we embarked and found they were only prepared for Indians. However, on a homeward journey one does not get too particular. Two hundred officers were accommodated in one hold and we lived on bully and biscuits, tea, jam and onions. It was a very uncomfortable two-and-a-half-day trip, as we got it rough and a great many of the passengers were seasick. The hold where we slept was frightfully foul. A concert was given on the last evening and a ration of gin and vermouth was wacked out. As I close this little book of my experiences as a prisoner of war in Turkey, the buildings of Alexandria show up in the distance. Patience is at last rewarded. It has been a long two and a quarter years, but what a glorious ending to the war with all its appalling sufferings.

21 November 1918. 'Der Tag' at last '
Three cheers for England!
GOD SAVE THE KING! GOD STRAFE THE TURKS!

Part Seven

Armoured Cars in Gallipoli and Russia

PETTY OFFICER A. L. WATSON

9 SQUADRON, ROYAL NAVAL ARMOURED CAR DIVISION

July 1915

11th: Landed [at Alexandria] and went to [Mustafa Pasha] Camp. Here we lived under canvas. The heat was terrible; we could do very little during daytime. If we paraded fellows would drop in a faint from standing in the heat. Here we were served out with webbing gear and rifles.

21st: Left camp and went aboard the *Seang Bee* of Rangoon which was bound for the Dardanelles. She was a very poor ship, in a filthy state, in fact most insanitary. Stood by in harbour until the next day.

22nd: Set sail at6.30pm.

25th: Arrived at Mudros on the island of Lemnos at 6.00am.

26th: Left Lemnos for Cape Hellas at 12 o'clock midnight on HMS *Whitby Abbey* of Hull. We arrived in the early hours of morning and could hear the boom of the artillery guns.

27th: Anchored off Cape Hellas at 10.45am. We received our christening of shellfire when the Turks began shelling the shipping. One shell dropped within a few yards of our stern, so we weighed anchor and moved farther out. We took on board some wounded and left after midday for Lemnos again, where we arrived about 5 o'clock and trans-shipped the wounded on to a hospital ship. We then trans-shipped to the *Seang Bee* until 28 July.

28th: at 4.00pm, landed on Lemnos and pitched camp.

31st: Details from 3, 4 and 10 Squadrons joined us.

7th: Slight attack of gastric catarrh.

8th: Getting worse but on guard all night.

9th: Much worse, sick several times during the night, carried on until 11 then visited doctor and was put on milk diet. Feeling very ill, but hope to pick up before leaving.

15th: When we left for Gallipoli at 7.30pm on board the *Osmanieh* of the Khedival Mail Line, we had on the board some of the 54th (East Anglian) Division Cyclist Corps. Stopped alongside HMS *Royal Edward* from which we managed to get a good feed, which we needed. We had boiled ham, pressed tongue and new bread. This proved to be our last decent meal for several months. We slept anywhere on deck this night as we only had about the night to stay on the boat. During the night I was picked up by drunken Irishman who stood about six feet. I was half asleep and wondered what was happening and found he was going to throw me overboard but we managed to quieten him in the finish.

16th: At 6.15am, landed at Suvla Bay. We could hear the firing in the firing line quite easily. At about 6.30, Turks started shelling. We were drawing some tea from a dixie when the second shell dropped about ten yards from us, burst in the earth, smothering us with earth, causing us to fall over each other in our eagerness to take cover. At 9.00pm we started for the firing line, carrying our packs, rifles, ammunition, Maxim guns and tripods. What a march, we got lost and did not reach the firing line base until 2.30am.

17th: took up positions under cover of darkness. Water is very scarce and we have already found out the value of it. When taking up our positions we soon began to learn what we are up against and take advantage of cover. The most surprising thing was the number of dead strewn about in different attitudes; one, the poor fellow, had his back to a bush and his sightless eyes were staring at us. Others were in all sorts of attitudes as they had been struck down, and floating on through the night would come the wounded men's cry of 'stretcher bearer' and 'water' and then the awful groans. When we reached our positions, the order came to lie flat or we would get sniped. I dropped beside a man already lying down and began talking to him. After a minute or two questioning I found I could get no reply and was kindly informed by his mate that he had been dead several hours.

18th: A fellow was shot through the neck about six yards from Sid and me and, before he could be removed, the doctor was also sniped while attending him. This happened through a breach in the parapet and altogether we had about sixteen fellows shot here in two days.

19th: Began to realise that we never knew where the next drop of water was coming, so we began to go without – except when absolutely necessary. Sid and I had a pint of water each, two tins of bully and about twelve biscuits to last us three days. Men are continually being sniped when trying to get a drop of water. Fellows were continually coming up and offering us a dollar for a mouthful of water, but it was too precious to us then to sell it for even for pounds. In fact, it got so bad that some of the poor fellows even drank their own urine and seawater; the consequence was that several went mad and were taken away. The regiments with us at first were the 4th Norfolk and 8th Hampshires. We were relieved after a few days and our rest consisted of digging a dug-out and fetching water, carrying ammunition and stakes, etc. to the firing line. We were often called out during the night, so we would much rather be in the firing line. When we came out of the line for a rest, our resting place consisted of a dug-out about twenty or thirty yards behind the firing line, so it made very little difference whether we were in it or not.

September

1st: About 7.30pm Turks began shelling the firing line and rest camp. Sid had just taken provisions into the trenches so was on the spot; we were taken in as support, there was simply a hail of shells. A shell struck the dug-out wall just as I was coming out and a piece of earth struck me on the back of the head knocking me flat, breaking my teeth (false) and splitting my lips and I still have a bruise which is very sore. Sid was blown several yards, the concussion of a shell bursting close to him. Sid and I were looking for each other all night and were greatly relieved next morning to find each other with a whole skin. During the bombardment, Bartlett and Williams were wounded in camp and Hurst and Bennett were wounded in the firing line. Whitehead sustained a rupture on the firing line.

2nd: Turks dropped coal boxes on the rest camp. Had a slight attack of dysentery.

3rd: Dysentery much worse but still carrying on.

4th: Shelled by Turks practically all day. A. Clark killed. Sid and I just missed by a piece of one of the coal boxes [large-calibre shell].

5th: By some miracle or other we had an egg each.

6th: We had a very severe shelling by the Turks. Two poor fellows were blown to pieces by a shell only about ten or twelve yards from us. We were nearly choked by the dust and fumes from it.

9th Turks strafed us again all morning, one shell came slick through the wall of gun emplacement only missing us by inches.

12th: Sid and I were both taken ill, so we were relieved from the trenches for a day or two, although we were only stationed twenty yards at the back. I was suffering from a severe cold, pains in the stomach and head. Sid was very queer too.

BRITISH NAVAL ARMOURED CARS IN RUSSIA

A Report by Commander Locker Lampson RNVR

Vladikavkaz
July 3rd, 1916

The Director of Air Services,
Admiralty,
London

Sir,

I have the honour to continue my last report. I left London and returned to Alexandrovsk with Major Mairis on 15 April. I found the British Naval armoured car force at Alexandrovsk in the best of spirits and health. The sun first rose on 22 January and conditions improved immediately perpetual darkness went. Captain Nugent of HMS *Albemarle* had inspected the force on 29 January and also had inspected *Umona* by special request. All billets are very comfortable and had electric light installed in most of them by means of a plant which we had landed, and Staff Surgeon Scott had fitted out an admirable hospital. It was here that they undertook successful operations upon the survivors of the SS *Sappho*, as well as an extensive stomach operation upon a merchant seaman from one of the ships in the harbour.

The weather during the month of February improved considerably and the light hours of the day were spent in careful training. A proper rifle range, complete with pit, revolving targets and field telephone was installed. A Maxim range was also established and at both these ranges portable wooden huts on sledge runners were constructed, also structures in wood representing exactly the turret of an armoured car in which training was conducted. These huts and the pit were heated with braziers, so that the men could work Maxims in comparative comfort. It is worth noting that in the intense cold, so hard was the ground that it took nine men three weeks to dig the markers' pit alone. The most useful work was perhaps done with Maxims, which had to be adjusted to meet the changing atmosphere from France and Belgium where they were last used. General drill, three-pounder firing, revolver practice, company drill, signalling, field training continued during the day with lessons for Morse, Russian, cooking, topography, first aid, etc. during the evening. The fatigue work was considerable, involving sometimes 100 men a day. A large number of sledges had to be made by the carpenters to carry wood, which was the usual fuel, and our water supply was obtained in barrels on sleighs which were filled at a lake half a mile away, by buckets dropped through a hole in the ice.

Considerable assistance was given to the Russian authorities in the working of ships in the harbour and the credit of saving the SS *Belgravia* (badly damaged in the ice and with a cargo worth at least a quarter of a million) is in no small measure due to the efforts of our men in pumping and salvage work. In no single case did we refuse assistance when asked for it by the Russian authorities.

As regards recreation, a football league was organised as well as tobogganing competitions and skiing. Throughout the whole stay at Alexandrovsk both officers and men were absolutely teetotal. No alcohol of any kind has been permitted and not even rum has been taken into Russia. We are probably the only non–alcoholic force now fighting in this war. As for rations, we lived at first on less than the naval ration, which was supplemented later on by the issue three times weekly of frozen reindeer meat. Vegetables were not obtainable and the lack of them was felt.

On 21 February, the force was inspected by Captain Kemp. Previously on 5 February, a party of two CPOs and 11 POs under the command of Lieutenant Commander Wells Wood and Lieutenant Lucas Shadwell (at the request of the Russians) left for Kandalaksha to assist in guarding German prisoners and helping in the transport of ammunition from Kola to Petrograd overland by sleigh. One party was away for seven weeks and received the congratulations of the Russian authorities on the work they had performed. They have since received the following medals for the work they have done:

Lieutenant Commander Wells Wood: Order of St Anne

Lieutenant Lucas Shadwell: Order of Stanislas

Two chief petty officers: Medal of St Anne

11 petty officers: Medal of Stanislas.

On 22 February another party of eight drivers in charge of acting CPO Petrie at the request of the Russian authorities were employed for eight weeks in driving cars laden with munitions across some frozen lakes in order to complete an unfinished link in the railway from Kola to Kandalaksha. Altogether 4,000 rifles a day were handled.

During the month of March the weather was exceptional and brilliant sunshine accompanied by intense and crisp cold prevailed. Field training became much easier and three more Maxim gun ranges were laid out. Route marching and extended field exercises took place daily. For the first time a small money advance was made to the men on account.

On 15 March the force was inspected by Admiral Phillimore, CB, MVO,

RN and he also inspected the establishment. On 17 March we received orders from Admiral Phillimore to mount guard over the Peterhead-Alexandrovsk cable. The cable comes ashore in a bay in the Kola peninsula a mile from Alexandrovsk and was separated from our force by very bad country. A three-pounder was towed across country on a sleigh and the regular force of twelve men, one CPO and one officer, two Maxims and a three-pounder constituted the guard. A double-skinned house had to be built for the men by our men as the temperature was very low. It took four days to complete owing to lack of material, wood having to be drawn by reindeer overland. Blizzards hampered his work considerably.

On 24 March the SS *Theseus* arrived with stores and the first mail for four months. Throughout the month considerable assistance was given by us to the Russians in unloading ships. We also re-arranged and re-organised the wharf and overhauled and repacked all their lathes, aeroplane engines and other machinery awaiting transportation to the front, for which we received the grateful thanks of Captain Krotkoff, the Russian Senior Naval Officer. Towards the end we ran out of bread and had to subsist on black bread and biscuits.

As a case of smallpox occurred amongst the Russians in the neighbourhood, the whole force was re-vaccinated and all the officers and men also received two inoculations against typhoid, two against para-typhoid and two against cholera. During the month of April the weather became milder with intermittent thaw, which increased the difficulties of training the force. The men's kit also became very bad and we were unable to renew it owing to the non-arrival of our supplies. On 15 April I rejoined the force from England with Major Mairis RMLI.

The month of May proved a difficult month, alternating between blizzards and heavy frosts. On 7 May I sent back to England a few men whose services we could dispense with, having arranged with General Beliaeff in Petrograd to reduce the force slightly. On Thursday, 11 May I left Alexandrovsk in order to get quickly to Petrograd in advance of our force. My object was to try and secure the approval of the Russian authorities in Petrograd for our force to proceed to the Caucasus. I felt that this was probably the best theatre of war for armoured car operations and that the difference in economic conditions between our men and the Russian soldiers would be less noticeable there than elsewhere on the Russian front.

I took a small boat from Alexandrovsk to Vardo, whence I proceeded down the Norwegian coast. An attempt was made to stop me but, being in plain clothes, I succeeded in getting through and reached Stockholm where I received my mail from the under Secretary of State for War, General Beliaeff, who received me with great courtesy and after sundry other visits it was arranged that force should proceed to Tiflis.

Meanwhile, our force at Alexandrovsk was in great difficulty as to whether it should proceed to Archangel in English or Russian ships. Captain Kemp was in direct touch with the Admiralty, but being 700 miles away, communication from him to Captain Nugent took over a week to reach the latter. The result was that while arrangements were being made by him, different arrangements were being put forward by the Russian authorities at Alexandrovsk which could only be communicated to him seven days later. We did not like to refuse the Russian offer to help, especially as Captain Krotkoff went out of his way to show us every kindness and courtesy.

BRITISH ARMOURED CARS, RUSSIA

By Petty Officer N. E. Martin 2779

1916

March 11th: changed over from the Russian to Roumanian train in the morning. Have to get the cars over yet. We are taking an ambulance up with us. Lost one of our trucks last night. Hunted for about two hours, but could not find it. According to the railway officials it has gone on to Galetz. No room to pipe down tonight.

12th: Was up all night. After a lot of messing about, started to get going about 5.00am and arrived at Galetz at 6.30am. Had another hunt for the lost wagon and found it after about an hour's search. Get off the train and arrive at billet about 3.00pm and have orders to be ready for the trenches at 5.30pm.

13th: Left the billet about 9.00pm for the train to take is to Triane via Darbosh. The train left about 12.30am and arrived at Triane about 3.00am. Got into rear billet, but no sleep again. Have to go into the front-line trenches this morning. Leave about 8.00am. It is a walk of about three and a half miles. Full gear and bedding, some walk. Arrive here and start making a new gun emplacement. Have to bring the gun and place it, etc. after dark tonight. No sleep again by the look of it.

14th: Got the gun ready in position last night. Started firing at 9.00am but had to give it up on account of trees in the line of fire. Cleared these away and started firing again at 2.00pm and did well. Got rid of 124 shells and am deaf for the rest of the day. On guard at 10.45pm.

15th: Went on guard but coming back afterwards, got out of the trenches at wrong place and lost my way. Walked for about two hours, and was finally brought to our dug-out by a Russian soldier. No firing today as it is very misty. Work on our dug-out all day. The guard is done away with now and [I] am jolly glad.

22nd: Still raining. Kept on all day to about 4.00pm after twenty hours of hard rain. Slept in with the officer last night as much sleep as could be caught. Both of us had a rotten time. The trenches and everything washed down with about a foot of water in the bottom of them. Was relieved about 8.30pm.

23rd: Had a bath in the morning and feel fine. Nothing much doing. Rifle inspection at 6.00pm. Should not be surprised to go to the outpost again tomorrow, as we are so short of men. I'm going on leave in the evening. Weather today is fine. Received a letter from Alf when I got back last night.

24th: Had a decent little evening dinner and a nice glass of lager. Am going out again in charge of party to the outpost tonight. Think I have struck perpetual motion. The weather looks very bad too. I expect it will rain like blazes. Just my luck. Arrived at the post about 8.30pm. Some very bad news, see 25th inst.

25th: Our-three pounder fired from the new position, and the enemy replied with 6-inch high explosive. Killed two of our chaps, both pals of mine. J. Graham was blown absolutely away and P. Smith was terribly smashed, decapitated, disembowelled etc. All that could be found of J.G. was two bits of legs. One Russian officer with both legs blown off and three soldiers severely wounded. Was shelled heavily during the afternoon. One Russian soldier wounded here. At this place and our gun they sent 160 shells.

26th: Very nice and calm last night. Made a new gun emplacement, as our left-hand position was blown down yesterday. It was here that the Russian was wounded. Got the gun mounted on new place by about 11.00pm last night. The weather this morning is grand, sun shining nice and warm. Another day's shelling in the afternoon, sent over about another sixty. This place is nearly levelled to the ground. Was relieved about 8.30pm.

April 13th: Weather fine this morning, but a gusty wind blowing the dust about and making it rather uncomfortable. We're going up this post tonight, as the Nos. 2 and 3 Squadron men are going back. The Russians relieved us about 9.30pm with one Maxim and one Colt machine gun. Took everything of ours away and had some job taking it right back to the car. Everyone eventually got home about 2.00am, had supper and went to bed, feeling rather tired.

14th: Got up about 10 o'clock this morning. Doing nothing today. The weather is cold and rather depressing. The soldiers have numerous meetings and demonstrations about keeping in the war and otherwise. The average Russian soldier is quite the most ignorant piece of nature's handiwork that I have ever seen, looking on with a vacant expression on his face (or natural, as it is to them) and eating the eternal 'parrot's food'.

15th: Weather still cold and threatening. Heard this morning from a good source that we are going home in October, one squadron at a time, on destroyers. Hope it is true. At any rate I am going to look forward to it. Also I heard that the Russians start their push on this front and the Jassy and other fronts on the 18th of this month. Hope it is so. The position of the Russians is still in the balance. A large portion of the soldiers want to withdraw from the war, the officers and artillery try to keep on fighting.

16th: Raining during the morning. Doing nothing today. Writing letters as a mail is going in a day or two.

17th: Tense excitement here today. Apparently Russia is withdrawing from the war. We are in an awkward position if this is true. I understand we're going to the Roumanian Army near Jassy if we have to leave this country, but I don't believe it, as we should be worse off than ever! I think the Admiralty will recall us. Feel like having a good fight with Russian soldiers for giving up. Feel jolly sorry for our lads on the Western front.

1st July: At about one this morning the enemy anticipated an attack and counter-attacked. It lasted until 2.30 and I cannot describe what it was like. How anything lived through it is a marvel. Hell let loose. It quieted down but we were shelled all the early morning. The Russian attack was timed for 10.00am and about half an hour before, the soldiers started entering the trench from the second and third lines. At about 9.55am the German artillery started up and shelled us to blazes. [Ten o'clock] came and the soldiers on our sector would not go over the parapet, only a very few getting over. Really I could not blame them, as it was perfectly devilish (the fire) in its intensity. If they had advanced, I would have had to take the gun over the top myself. The enemy bombarded heavily from 10.00am till 4.00pm, the fire then slackening down. I had to fire over their heads of the advancing infantry but did not fire much, as the Russian soldiers did not understand and would not go over.

Petty Officer A. L. WATSON

October

9th: A very big improvement in my health.

10th: Received a parcel – cake bad but another fellow had a cake so we had a little tea party in the dug-out.

11th: Rained again. Piarsall, B Section, killed at Hill 10.

13th: Suffering from pains in my head and very feverish, must have caught a chill!

14th: Everyone getting fed up, we are being treated like navvies, supposed to be resting and digging dug-outs from 6.00am. Until 7.00pm, I in one shift; this has been going on for some time.

16th: Turkish aeroplane came over base flying very low, we had a bit of excitement watching gunfire – it was so low that rifles were also fired at it, but it escaped without injury.

17th: As a result of this visit one of our batteries received a heavy shelling. Sid and I went to Hill 10.

19th: Had best meal since leaving Alexandria. We managed to get a decent piece of meat, roasted it in an oven made from a petrol tin, boiled some desiccated potatoes and with the stuff we had bought for the canteen we had a good feed.

22nd: Received orders to rebuild our gun position and dig a trench eight feet from it. This meant digging with a pick and shovel in the solid sandstone.

24th: Been in digging for three days and only got down about a foot in six yards in length. We are proper navvies now, we work from 6.00am to 8 or 10.00pm. And then mount guard at night.

28th: Turks sent over 7-inch shrapnel shells.

December

2nd: Turks shelled Hill 10 very heavily. Shells are coming over six to ten every minute. Shrapnel and HE Shells are bursting all around our dug-out.

3rd: Turks again shelled Hill 10. Two shells hit the back of our dug-out. I went out to see what damage was done and saw a fellow lying there with his head and shoulders buried in the earth. I jumped into the trench to see whether he was dead and as I pulled out I found the shell had taken the top of his head off and his brains lay in the trench. He turned out to be one of the Dublin Fusiliers.

5th: Sid went to base with influenza and asthma. I still managed to stick it although some days I feel dead beat.

12th: Turks sent over 7-inch HE shells which shook the earth when they burst.

13th: Heard of the expected evacuation of Suvla.

15th: Battery on Hill 10 moved two guns. We began digging new gun position.

16th: Sid came to see me before leaving for Imbros. We did not like parting, especially at a time like this.

17th: Finished new gun position and crew took over. We stayed where we were. Battery at Hill 10 cleared altogether and dummies set up.

18th: Suspense of waiting to evacuate getting somewhat trying. There are only ten men to a mile in the firing line and the troops with us in the second line of defence are very few and are leaving us tomorrow; they are the Hampshires.

19th: All troops left Hill 10 leaving only ourselves with machine guns. Two of our guns were taken to Hill 28 to command the Chanak Road. About 5.00pm the Turks started sending over 7-inch shells and we thought they had 'twigged' our little game, but it was not so and at nine o'clock we received our orders to evacuate. So we left and arrived at the beach without a shot being fired. We took all tripods, guns and spare ammunition with us and went aboard a lighter and then trans-shipped aboard HMS *Magnificent,* which took us to Imbros where we arrived about dawn.

20th: Landed at Imbros and was stationed at RNAS Headquarters camp. Met Sid but he was stationed at another camp. Thought I recognised Uncle Tom.

24th: Christmas Eve. Had a jolly good concert.

25th: Christmas Day. I am on guard today and tonight. Had roast beef and Christmas pudding for dinner.

29th: Met Alf Brennan of Mowbray Street, he is in the Royal Marine Light Infantry. Also met Len Hobbins from Paynes Lane.

31st: Our party on fatigue in the harbour all day from 8.00am until 6.00pm. Unloaded the *Baron Ardrossan*, a store ship. Saw an aeroplane dive into the water.

January

1st: Helping to erect anti-aircraft gun. Worked on this till completed; beside having other fatigues nothing else particular happened until 24th.

24th: I went into hospital with stomach poisoning. They put me to bed and put a plaster over my heart.

27th: Came out of hospital at 5.30am and set sail from Imbros on HMT *Ermine*, bound for Mudros. Arrived at Mudros at night – trans-shipped to the paddle steamer *Hendon* and from this trans-shipped on to HMT *Hestor* of the Blue Funnel line, a boat of 15,000 tons supposed to be the largest single-funnel boat afloat.

Commander Locker Lampson RNVR

Provisional arrangements were made for the force to embark on the Russian Volunteer Transport *Dvinsk* at Simeonova. This transport was to carry 400 sick prisoners whom we agreed to guard and medically supervise. On 12 May Commander Gregory and Staff Surgeon Scott preceded by motorboat to Simeonova to inspect the ship. On 17 May orders were issued to the squadrons to pack and the small collier *Graf Schuvalov* was put at our disposal to assist in the embarkation of our force, and an advance party of one of the squadrons and part of headquarters and the sick bay proceeded to the *Dvinsk* under the command of Lieutenant Commander Wells Wood.

On the 16th for the *Graf Schuvalov* arrived at Simeonova and the advance party transferred stores to the *Dvinsk*. The *Graf Schuvalov* was intended to return to Alexandrovsk to embark the remainder of our force on 24 May. But all the arrangements had to be cancelled as the Russian authorities increased the number of the sick prisoners from 400 to 1,300. [Ninety per cent] of these sick prisoners were a terrible condition, suffering from advanced scurvy, lice, sores and dirt. Some were so bad that they could not speak; their mouths were festered and matter trickled from their lips. Staff Surgeon Scott urgently requested that the remainder of our force might not be embarked on the *Dvinsk* under these circumstances. I attach an extract from Staff Surgeon Scott's report upon the conditions on the *Dvinsk* and cannot too warmly praise his work on this occasion.

Commander Gregory returned on the motorboat in order to make arrangements for this, but a blizzard, which had been blowing for some time, increased in strength and became so furious that he could not make the port of Alexandrovsk. He decided to return and run before the gale to Simeonova. But at 4.00am on the morning of the 19th his engines broke down and after two hours drifting in a helpless condition the motorboat struck the cliffs on the east side of Kola Gulf. The boat began breaking up and had to be abandoned and the party, consisting of Commander Gregory, two petty officers and four Russians scaled the cliffs and made a bivouac in the snow. Two other Russians managed to reach a village in the neighbourhood and the remainder of the party were rescued by British trawler after being on the cliffs twenty-four hours.

On 22 May, the remainder of the force embarked on the Russian transport the *Czar* and the Russian icebreaker *Bruce* and on 23 May the *Czar* and the *Dvinsk* left for Archangel. Ice was encountered on the 24th and on the 25th both ships stuck on the ice for over twenty-four hours. The mail bags were transferred from the *Dvinsk* to the *Czar* by being carried over the ice. The *Dvinsk* being a stouter boat got free of the ice on the 26th but the *Czar* being unable to punch through the ice drifted into a position that caused much anxiety. However, by letting anchors through holes cut in the ice and by going ahead and astern and then charging the ice (which must have been six feet in thickness) she was extricated with difficulty from a treacherous position on Saturday evening, the 27th. Her bows were damaged in this manoeuvring and fifty tons of water was shipped in the forepeak. On 27 May the *Czar* got free of the ice at midnight and reached Archangel on the 28th to find the *Dvinsk* and the *Bruce* already arrived.

The weather prevailing during the embarkation at Alexandrovsk is considered to be the worst known in these regions at this time of the year for the last forty years. At Archangel the force met with the greatest kindness and hospitality. As the special request of the Governor, the force marched with arms through the streets of Archangel and was presented with a valuable Ikon many years old, representing St Michael, the patron saint of Archangel. This Ikon was specially taken from the Cathedral and was presented to the force, *firstly*, as it was the first British force land in Russia and *secondly*, out of gratitude for the return of the church bell taken by the British from Archangel during the Crimean War, and sent back by them in 1911. Men and officers were feted and entertained and speeches of the greatest cordiality were made. The officers were entertained to dinner by Captain Kemp, and the Governor of Archangel inspected the force before leaving Archangel on June 1st.

A train consisting of forty-seven carriages, with first- and second-class accommodation for the officers and third-class for the men, was provided for the force and the comfort during the long voyage to Vladikavkaz cannot be too warmly acknowledged. From Archangel right down to Vladikavkaz the reception accorded to the force has been unprecedented. At all stations passed, the population of the town in question would be ready waiting on the platform whatever the hour of day or night in order to welcome us; and wherever we stopped, bands headed by the military and civil authorities and accompanied by great crowds had collected, and an enthusiasm prevailed to which people in England are quite unaccustomed. Food, chocolate and cigarettes were always ready for men and officers. On 3 June the force arrived at Vologda where a stop was made for the officers to be entertained by the Governor, and for the men to be given a dinner by the municipal authorities.

On 5 June the force arrived in Moscow at 3.00am. Special arrangements had been made for them to remain there three days to rest and see the city. Guards and bands received us in the city and men and officers were given two days' leave, the first leave they have had for over six months. On 7 June at the special request and with the approval of the military authorities the whole force marched through Moscow with arms to a divine service in the English Church. The British chaplain conducted the service, which was attended by the whole British community. The streets were covered with flags, mottos and garlands and an immense crowd followed the force through the streets. A special dinner was given to the officers by the Automobile School and other functionaries and Princess Marie Feodorovna graciously received me and a few officers and presented each man with tobacco and the officers with testaments.

Similar cordiality and hospitality were encountered upon the journey at Rostov and the various towns on the way to Vladikavkaz. I regret to report that Petty Officer Donnelly while bathing in the River Don on 11 June was drowned. His body was recovered from the river and he was buried in the Brothers Cemetery at Rostov on Don with military honours.

Accompanied by Commander Gregory and Staff Surgeon Scott I went ahead to Tiflis expecting our base to be there. On arriving there on 11 June late at night I found that our base was to be the other side of the Caucasus at Vladikavkaz, two days' journey from Tiflis by rail. A distance of 200 *versts* over the mountains separates Tiflis from Vladikavkaz by road and on the 12th I motored to Vladikavkaz. The scenery is rugged and mountainous. During the space of one hour the traveller passes from intense heat in the valley to intense cold and snow on the mountains. The road is very winding with steep gradients and hairpin bends and sheer three-verst drops. There is now no motor traffic along it, only cart traffic and the horses are very frightened of our car.

I arrived at Vladikavkaz early on the morning of 13 June and the force arrived the same day at 10 o'clock. The Governor with the military and civil authorities of the town and Colonel Marsh (our representative at Tiflis) were present when the force de-trained and we marched through decorated streets and cheering crowds to the Cadet barracks. These barracks are now given over to us and we are, all of us, very comfortable. We have been entertained by the municipal authorities, by the civil authorities, by the Governor and other functionaries, and the greatest kindness and hospitality has been shown to both officers and men.

The enclosed telegram (No. 1) has been received from the Grand Duke and enclosed telegram (No. 2) has been sent by the General in command here.

I regret to report that an outbreak of dysentery has occurred involving many officers and men. I have lost one petty officer, who died from dysentery and was buried with full military honours on 25 June. The General in command and Staff attended the funeral. Orders have been given to the men not to eat fruit and to drink only boiled water and we have now got the epidemic well in hand and no new cases have since occurred. The force awaits here the arrival of the cars and once our cars arrive it will proceed by road with them over the mountains in an attempt to traverse this route in a given time. This car trek across the mountains has been decided upon as a test of efficiency by the Grand Duke in order to see the capabilities of the cars.

Meanwhile, time is being spent in getting the men acclimatised to the change from intense cold to considerable heat and route marches of fifteen miles per day are taken by the squadron regularly. Orders have had to be given for officers to carry revolvers as brigandage in the neighbourhood is very bad. The chief of the brigands, who has terrorised the district for over ten years and killed over 108 people, has only recently been captured. No officer or man is allowed off the roadside after dark alone as brigands take arms, horses and money from anybody who strays from the road. Last night one of the cadets was shot by a brigand on the road opposite the quarters and his rifle taken from him.

I would like to single out the following officers for praise:

Staff Surgeon Scott for his work throughout the difficult time with the prisoners on the *Dvinsk*.

Lieutenant Commander Bolt for its conduct of affairs ashore during my absence for Alexandrovsk.

Lieutenant Hannah for his consistent good work as Assistant Adjutant.

I would venture to urge that this expedition has assumed a character which should not be ignored. As the first and only British force to fight for Russia in Russia, we have received a welcome which even in this country is rare and the force now holds a position which must be maintained. Hitherto, Russians have had but little evidence of Englishmen in khaki; the photographs of them daily and weekly in the Russian papers; the cinematograph films appearing throughout the towns and villages in Russia have assisted a complete change of public opinion. The Consul at Moscow and other judges consider the progress of British troops to the heart of Russia as perhaps the greatest factor in removing the prevalent and false idea as to England's contribution to the common cause. The ability of the force to continue playing its part adequately henceforward depends in no small degree on the support given from England.

I have the honour to be,

Sir,
Your obedient Servant,
(signed)
Commander RNVR.

Telegram No. 1.

From: The Grand Duke Nicholas
To: Gen Fleisher.

With my whole heart I welcome the arrival of the armoured car detachment from England, the great ally of our glorious armies. As the Hetman in command of the Cossack armies on the Caucasus I greet them. Wishing health and prosperity to the brave British Army and Navy. I warmly thank Gen

Fleisher for his message of greeting and goodwill and I hope soon to see and welcome personally the British armoured division.

General Commander-in-Chief Nicholas.

Telegram No. 2

From: Gen Trotsky, director of the Vladikaukasian Cadet Corps and the Officers of the Corps.

To: His Excellency the British Ambassador, Petrograd.

Celebrating as we do the arrival of the British force, with Commander Locker Lampson at its head, to the home of the Vladikaukasian Cadet Corps and the company of Polotsks officers, we, British and Russians, stand now united by a common feeling and purpose, which I, for my part, may perhaps the allowed to translate into a message of goodwill from us to your Excellency as the representative in Russia of our great ally Britain. We desire to send you and yours our heartfelt wishes for health and prosperity

From: Sir George Buchanan, British Embassy, Petrograd.

To: The Director of the Corps of Cadets General Staff, Gen Trotsky, Vladkavlaz.

Deeply touched by your Excellency's telegram. I thank you sincerely for the goodwill and kind messages sent to me and my family and I am very grateful to you for the cordial reception given Commander Locker Lampson and his detachment.

Petty Officer N. E. MARTIN 2779

2nd: The Russians advanced on the right and left flank, but on the centre sector where I was, no advance was made. The Maxims were taken out last night. I regret to say that the other gun crew suffered heavily, the Chief Petty Officer killed, two of the crew killed, and with one wounded badly, only one man being free from injury. One other CPO was killed and one chap wounded who were repairing the bridge for the cars to go over the trench. A CPO was killed and one man wounded from No. 3 Squadron position away to the right, so yesterday's list of casualties was heavy for our small corps. Got into bed about 4.00am and did not get up until 5.00pm when I had to go into the trenches again to where our fellows were killed and dig out the ammunition. Got it and returned about 11.00pm. Got up about 9.00am.

3rd: Nothing doing for me today. Our cars are in and out of action nearly every day. The Russians have lost heavily but we hear good news from the flanks today, large numbers of prisoners being taken. I hear the Russians are nearing Lemberg. I am going on the heavy armoured 3-pounder tomorrow.

4th: I am on the 3-pounder today, standing by on the road at the third line, waiting for orders to go into action. It is interesting to say that a large number of the prisoners we have taken are Germans, and our chaps have been speaking to some of them and they say they are Prussians and have come from Arras in France, to withstand and repel this attack.

21st: Left the camp at Teleachi at dawn this morning and stopped at the aerodrome between Podgiatza and Monastirysr. The Russian transport retreating is miles long, the heavy artillery all shifting back and everything looks like a serious retreat. The cars were all in action today and we lost a lot. We lost three light armoured, one heavy and one Ford armoured. My car was amongst the lost. All the crews escaped. Two chaps are missing but were discovered two days later. They had made their way towards Tarnapol.

22nd: Slept at the Aero camp last night. Shifting the staff all back to Buczacz as the Russian infantry are all running away and God knows when they will stop. A panic started in the afternoon that the German cavalry were a couple of versts away. I am on the Ford armoured car today. Had to scout with the Ford on the right, but saw no enemy cavalry. See end for desertion of Russian infantry. I am afraid that the Russian soldier is about done.

23rd: Left Buczacz about 8.00am as the Ford is out of action. After a hell of a ride we arrived at Proscurov about 9.00pm. At last I received the parcel mail. Got two parcels and was jolly pleased. Here we are billeted in a Cossack barracks and are very comfortable. I had a decent night's sleep, the first for several days. The Cossacks in this town are rounding up Russians and sending them back to the front. They are drastic in their methods, any refusing to go get decapitated with the Cossacks' swords, with which there is no argument.

24th: Doing nothing yesterday. Heard our other cars do well on the Tarnopol Road. Another light armoured was lost today and all the crew of another car wounded. Our casualties during this retreat up to the present are one officer and eight men wounded, four cases rather serious. Got another mail today and got a number of letters up to the end of June so am jolly pleased.

3rd August: Saw the Russian officer who speaks English and he told us that the attack was successful, the Russians gaining their object. Left Yusiffovka after dinner and reached our old camp on the road about 4.00pm. Went to the stream and had a bath and feel tons better after it. The name of this camp is Dabrovka.

4th: I am going back to Proscurov with my pal for a bath and clean-up, etc. and leave Dabrovka about 10.00am. Arrived in Proscurov and had a bath, haircut and shave and a decent meal, so I'm feeling rather satisfied with myself. All our squadron came back in the afternoon. I think we are about finished on this front, as the Russians seem to be holding the frontier all right.

5th: Doing nothing today. Hear good news from the Western Front but the Russians are doing very bad; they are retreating on the right flank, evacuating three or four large towns. They are absolutely useless as a fighting army. Shall be glad when we leave this country for good.

6th: Raining this morning. I'm in charge of guard mounting at noon today. Nothing much to do. Went out on the grounds in the evening and arrived back about 2.00am. This barracks is a very large place, having dozens of big blocks of buildings, married quarters, etc.

7th: Nothing during the morning. Came off the guard at 12 noon today. I think the Russians will retreat again on this front soon as the enemy are expected to break the line north of Jassy, making a retreat on this front inevitable.

24th: Travelling all night. The train is a fairly good one, not stopping long at any other stations. Expected to get to Moscow tonight, but shall not get there until midday tomorrow. We have to be on the boat at Archangel by the 27th, as the boat is due to sail by then.

25th: Still going but not so fast today. Pass through Nara and reach Moscow about 1.30pm. Messing about till dark. Have to go to the other Moscow station and expect to leave about midnight. Piped down 11.00pm.

26th: Woke up this morning still at Moscow. Messed about all day being shunted up and down. Finally left Moscow about 5.30pm, travel very well, reaching Alexandorof about 10.00pm. Strolled about the station for about an hour or so and piped down. We are to leave here about 2.00am, I think. Fell asleep about midnight, raining heavily.

27th: Woke up this morning in Rostova Yarostavl, stayed here the rest of the day and are supposed to be moving at 11.00pm. Went out in the afternoon, but nothing much doing. Moved off during the night, but I was asleep.

28th: Woke up this morning in Vologda, not much of a place. We are joining up a fast train here for Archangel and reckoned to do the journey in about fifteen hours. Left Vologda about 2.00pm. Travelling fairly well until I fell asleep, weather fine but a bit chilly.

29th: Arrived in Archangel about 9.20 this morning to learn that the boat left for England at 6.30. Messed about all day. We are going on board the *Ormiston* tomorrow morning and expect to sail about Sunday, so that isn't too bad. Played a game of football in the evening.

30th: Left the train this morning and came on board later. We are in a very decent place just below the bridge, and shall have a good time if the weather is calm and submarines are polite. There is leave to Archangel but I'm not going. Slept in a hammock again last night, the first time since on the *Umona* coming out.Was very comfortable though.

31st: Went across the ferry and into the town this morning. The town is not very nice and the Russian money is practically worthless. Cannot get English money for it at all, so spent most of mine on some three-course dinners.

1st September: Sailed from the quay this morning about 4.00am and went down the river to the south. Heard three subs were reported inside Ukanski Bay. Anchored in the river until about 4.00pm when the convoy of four trawlers took us down into the White Sea. Very calm and the boat goes well. The speed is rather slow, as we had to keep behind the convoy, who are sweeping for mines.

2nd: Travelling through the night until we ran into a thick fog and anchored. Did not get going again properly until about 8.30pm when the captain, seeing the fog lift a bit, up anchored and set off leaving the convoy behind.

3rd: Going during the day, still with the fog about, sometimes running into a bank of it, but generally in the thin fog. Reckoned to reach Lerwick about Friday night or during Saturday. Still calm but cold.

4th: Still cold and calm. Fired the gun at her practice wooden target this morning. It is a 4–inch Vickers gun and Pfizer 34lb shell. It is mounted on the poop deck, right aft. Cannot say whereabouts we are as they will not tell you.

EPILOGUE

This book has quoted from a wide range of experience, mostly of war. Some of the authors could be speaking today, such as the young men, fresh from home, donning uniform and experiencing military discipline for the first time; or the novice pilots with their frequent descriptions of exhilarating flight above the clouds. Other voices are startlingly antique, such as the ex-public schoolboy R. S. W. Dickinson in his flimsy biplane, agonising over the effects of dropping three 65lb bombs on a Turkish town at a time when many believed that bombing from the air was an atrocity. His aircraft could only barely be described as a weapon of war, although the quality and military effectiveness of RNAS aircraft improved rapidly as the war progressed. We tend to forget, in these days of high technology and the consistent reliability of modern aircraft, the extraordinary fragility and unruly flying characteristics of those early machines. What seems today to be the sheer recklessness of those aviators was, perhaps, inevitable under the pressure of war, but their attitudes reveal the gulf in time that separates us from them. A few quotes illustrate the prevailing atmosphere:

> Engine failures were still numerous, 10 to 15 minutes was an average sort of flight. Of course, the knowledge that something was likely to happen every few minutes kept you all alive. (Eugene L. Gerrard, writing after the war about the early days of flying.)
>
> The actual dangers of war in the air are small compared with the aviation accidents. (George Bentley Dacre, in the Dardanelles, 1915.)
>
> I had not, perhaps strange to say, a good map with me, but only a very small scale atlas map which I had torn out of some book and which showed up on one small page the whole of the Dutch coast from the German border to Belgium. (Culley, on the day in 1918 when he destroyed Zeppelin L53.)

It is beyond the scope of this book to examine the reasons for the absorption of the RNAS into the nascent Royal Air Force in April 1918. With a few notable exceptions, most RNAS aircrew opted to join the new service rather than continue with careers in the Royal Navy, so that the peculiar ethos of purely *naval* aviation, which emerges so clearly from these memoirs, was lost for a generation. The Royal Navy certainly showed that it could specify and procure outstanding fighting aircraft during the

First World War, such as the Sopwith Triplane and Camel. The same, sadly, could not be said of the aircraft with which the RN was equipped at the outbreak of the next war; this has often been attributed to the lack of direct aviation experience among senior Naval Staff Officers.

The broad range of warlike activities experienced by the RNAS will, perhaps, come as a surprise to some readers. Winston Churchill's ill-directed enthusiasm for war-making led many poorly-trained men, recruited as sailors, into employment in armoured cars (essentially as infantry) on several fronts. By contrast, the rapid development of embarked aviation – the deployment and support of aircraft from warships and specialist aircraft carriers – was a peculiarly British achievement, attributable to the enthusiasm and openness to innovation of RNAS people.

Whether in aircraft, armoured cars or balloons, on the Western Front, off the Dardanelles or in the depths of the Russian winter, the men of the RNAS (many of them from what today we call the Commonwealth) made a valiant contribution to the war effort. They *were* all men, incidentally; there are no female voices in this book. Almost invariably, they were young men, with an often adolescent sense of humour. Perhaps we should leave the last word to a twenty-year-old pilot, after many months of stressful flying against a determined enemy:

> A French General came and presented Norton and self with a Croix de Guerre avec Gold Star, not too bad. A most amusing show with kisses. Norton kept on making funny remarks under his breath, and it was all that I could do to keep a straight face. (Guy Leather, on the Western Front in November 1916.)

GLOSSARY

ABBREVIATIONS

AA	Anti-Aircraft
AB	Able Seaman
AM	Air Mechanic
ASC	Army Service Corps
CB	Companion of the Bath
CFS	Central Flying School
CMB	Coastal Motor Boat
CO	Commanding Officer
CPO	Chief Petty Officer
DFC	Distinguished Flying Cross
DSO	Distinguished Service Order
FAU	First Aid Unit
HE	High Explosive
HMS	His Majesty's Ship
HMT	Hired Military Transport
HQ	Headquarters
MAA	Master-at-Arms
MO	Medical Officer
MVO	Member of the Victorian Order
NCO	Non-commissioned Officer
NO	Naval Officer
PO	Petty Officer
PoW	Prisoner of War
RAF	Royal Air Force
RFA	Royal Field Artillery
RFC	Royal Flying Corps
RM	Royal Marines
RMA	Royal Marine Artillery
RMLI	Royal Marine Light Infantry
RN	Royal Navy

RNACD	Royal Naval Armoured Car Division
RNAS	Royal Naval Air Service
RNR	Royal Naval Reserve
RNVR	Royal Naval Volunteer Reserve
SMS	*Seiner Majestät Schiff* (His Majesty's Ship)
SOFFAAM	Society of Friends of the Fleet Air Arm Museum
SS	a) Steam Ship.
	b) Submarine Scout
TB	Torpedo Boat
VA	Vice Admiral
VC	Victoria Cross
W/T	Wireless Transmissions (or Transmitter)
WRNS	Women's Royal Naval Service

DEFINITIONS

Archie	Anti-aircraft fire
Bessoneau	A type of temporary canvas-covered aircraft hangar
Blimp	Dirigible airship without a rigid skeleton, whose shape depends on the pressure of gas within. Supposedly of American derivation, since the US Army was said to classify airships as Type A- Rigid, and Type B – Limp, hence blimp. Alternatively, said to mimic the sound made by flicking the inflated envelope of the balloon with the finger.
Bully	Tinned corned beef, widely issued as rations. Originally from the French boeuf boilli or boiled beef, which was prepared as a ration meat and stored in glass jars.
Crusher	Regulating Petty Officer, a naval rating responsible for discipline.
Immelman Turn	An aerial manoeuvre, supposedly named after Max Immelman, a German air ace. It consisted of diving to pick up speed, then pulling up to near stalling and applying rudder. Difficult to carry out without stalling or spinning, if executed correctly would re-position the aircraft into an attacking position above an enemy aircraft.
Jaunty	Master at Arms, the senior non-commissioned officer responsible for discipline.
Kite balloon	A type of stabilised balloon, with rudimentary inflated fins, capable of being towed behind a warship and carrying an observer aloft for gunnery spotting and general surveillance. Known as the 'Cacquot type' after its designer, this design survived into the Second World War for use as barrage balloons.
Lewis	A .303-inch calibre machine gun, of American design, widely used by British land forces and a popular airborne weapon,

	usually fired by observers and air gunners. Ammunition was provided in a 97-round drum-shaped magazine.
Liberty Boat	A boat taking sailors ashore on 'liberty' i.e. leave. In the custom of the RN, also used in shore establishments for buses filling the same purpose.
Make and Mend	An afternoon when no work is scheduled, deriving from sailing-ship days when sailors were given time off to make and mend their uniforms.
Maxim	A .303-inch calibre heavy machine gun, designed in the late nineteenth century by Sir Hiram Maxim. A bulky weapon, usually mounted on a tripod and served by a crew of three.
Monitor	A shallow-draft naval vessel, usually mounting a single large-calibre gun and used for shore bombardment.
Pipe Down	Routine activities on board RN vessels are governed by 'pipes', so named because signalled on the Bo'sun's call, a type of whistle. In major vessels with a Royal Marine detachment, activities are signalled by bugle calls. The day's routine starts with Reveille at 7.00am (07.00) and proceeds with calls including those for meal times, Secure (cease work) and ending at 10.30pm (22.30) with 'Pipe Down', i.e. turn in. 'Pipe down' is often used as a peremptory order to sailors to stop chattering.
Quirk	A First World War term used to describe trainee pilots.
Rotary engine	Probably the most widely-used aircraft engine for scout and fighter aircraft because of its favourable power-to-weight ratio, the rotary engine was of the radial type, usually with a single row of an odd number of cylinders. In this engine, the crankshaft is fixed and the entire engine and attached propeller rotate around it.
Submarine Scout	The designation for smaller dirigibles in RN service.
Uhlan	German light cavalry
Vickers	Somewhat heavier than the Lewis gun, the Vickers .303-inch calibre machine gun became the standard forward-firing armament for British fighters, e.g. in the Camel, which had a twin mounting. The closed-bolt design enabled the gun to be synchronised with the propeller, enabling forward fire in the pilot's eye-line.

INDEX

Establishments, Squadrons and Organisations